LEGAL AND ETHICAL DIMENSIONS FOR MENTAL HEALTH PROFESSIONALS

LEGAL AND ETHICAL DIMENSIONS FOR MENTAL HEALTH PROFESSIONALS

Patrick Brendan Malley, Ph.D.
Associate Chair
Department of Psychology in Education
University of Pittsburgh

Eileen Petty Reilly, M.Ed.
School Counselor

USA	Publishing Office:	ACCELERATED DEVELOPMENT
		A member of the Taylor & Francis Group
		325 Chestnut Street
		Philadelphia, PA 19106
		Tel: (215) 625-8900
		Fax: (215) 625-2940
	Distribution Center:	ACCELERATED DEVELOPMENT
		A member of the Taylor & Francis Group
		47 Runway Road, Suite G
		Levittown, PA 19057-4700
		Tel: (215) 269-0400
		Fax: (215) 269-0363
UK		ACCELERATED DEVELOPMENT
		A member of the Taylor & Francis Group
		1 Gunpowder Square
		London EC4A 3DE
		Tel: +44 171 583 0490
		Fax: +44 171 583 0581

LEGAL AND ETHICAL DIMENSIONS FOR MENTAL HEALTH PROFESSIONALS

1 2 3 4 5 6 7 8 9 0

Printed by George H. Buchanan Co., Philadelphia, PA, 1999.

A CIP catalog record for this book is available from the British Library.

∞The paper in this publication meets the requirements of the ANSI Standard Z39.48-1984 (Permanence of Paper).

Library of Congress Cataloging-in-Publication Data
Malley, Patrick B.
    Legal and ethical dimensions for mental health professionals / Patrick Brendan Malley, Eileen Petty Reilly
        p. cm.
    Includes bibliographical references and index.
    ISBN 1-56032-687-5 (alk. paper)
    1. Mental health personnel—Professional ethics. 2. Mental health personnel—Legal status, laws, etc. 3. Psychotherapists—Professional ethics. 4. Psychiatric ethics.
    I. Reilly, Eileen Petty. II. Title.
    RC455.2.E8M34   1999
    174'.2—dc21   98-31545
                                                CIP

ISBN: 1-56032-687-5

TABLE OF CONTENTS

PREFACE ix

PART A
HISTORICAL AND HELPING PERSPECTIVES 1

CHAPTER 1
THE MENTAL HEALTH PROFESSIONAL IN A
HISTORICAL CONTEXT 3

Early Historical Roots 3
The Somatogenic Hypothesis 5
The Psychogenic Hypothesis 6
Summary 10
Learning Facilitation and Focus 10

CHAPTER 2
IN A HELPING CONTEXT 13

The Helping Relationship 13
Summary 19
Learning Facilitation and Focus 19

PART B
ETHICAL AND LEGAL DIMENSIONS 23

CHAPTER 3
IN AN ETHICAL CONTEXT **25**

Ethical Codes 25
Ethical Principles 26
Ethical Theory 27
Learning Facilitation and Focus 30
Ethical Virtues 44
Learning Facilitation and Focus 47

CHAPTER 4
IN A LEGAL CONTEXT **63**

Legal Terminology and Laws 63
The Special Relationship 66
Elements of Malpractice 68
Preparing for the Special Relationship 70
Implementing the Special Relationship 80
Summary 85
Learning Facilitation and Focus 86

PART C
MULTICULTURAL CONTEXT **93**

CHAPTER 5
THE MENTAL HEALTH PROFESSIONAL IN A
MULTICULTURAL CONTEXT **95**

Changing Demographics 95
Multicultural Terminology 96
Definitions of Multicultural Counseling 96
Values and Multiculturalism 98
The Culturally Skilled Counselor 101
Summary 107
Learning Facilitation and Focus 108

PART D
RELATIONSHIPS WITH SPECIAL POPULATIONS **111**

CHAPTER 6
CLIENTS WHO ARE DANGEROUS TO THEMSELVES
OR OTHERS **113**

The Client Who Is Potentially Harmful to Self 113
Learning Facilitation and Focus 129

The Potentially Dangerous Client 133
Learning Facilitation and Focus 139
The Client with AIDS 146
Learning Facilitation and Focus 152

CHAPTER 7
SEXUAL ABUSE AND HOMOSEXUALITY **155**

The Abused Child 155
Learning Facilitation and Focus 164
Adult Survivors of Child Sexual Abuse 165
Learning Facilitation and Focus 168
The Therapist-Abused Client 168
Learning Facilitation and Focus 177
The Homosexual Client 178
Learning Facilitation and Focus 184

CHAPTER 8
OTHER SPECIAL RELATIONSHIPS **187**

The Spiritual Client 187
Learning Facilitation and Focus 193
The Client Who Is a Consultee 193
Learning Facilitation and Focus 201
The Client Who Is a Minor 202
Learning Facilitation and Focus 206
The Client in Managed Care 207
Learning Facilitation and Focus 212
The Substance-Abusing Client 213
Learning Facilitation and Focus 219

PART E
CONSIDERATIONS IN SCHOOLS, GROUPS, MARRIAGES,
AND FAMILIES **223**

CHAPTER 9
THE MENTAL HEALTH PROFESSIONAL IN THE SCHOOL **225**

The School Counselor 225
Special Issues 228
Student Referral 232
Summary 233
Learning Facilitation and Focus 233

CHAPTER 10
IN A GROUP CONTEXT 237

Group Counseling 237
Group Theories 239
Characteristics of Group Leaders 242
Competency and the Group Leader 243
Confidentiality 246
Privileged Communication 247
Ethical Guidelines for Group Counselors 247
Summary 259
Learning Facilitation and Focus 259

CHAPTER 11
IN A MARRIAGE AND FAMILY CONTEXT 261

Marriage and Family Therapy 261
Determining Who the Client Is 262
Biases 263
Confidentiality 264
Privileged Communication and Informed Consent 265
Therapists and the Law 266
Training Issues 266
Summary 271
Learning Facilitation and Focus 272

PART F
CONSIDERATIONS IN TRAINING 275

CHAPTER 12
IN A TRAINING CONTEXT 277

Training and Ethics 277
Supervision 278
Dismissal Processes in Training 281
Credentials of the Mental Health Professional 282
Research with Human Subjects 283
Summary 285
Learning Facilitation and Focus 286

REFERENCES 289

INDEX 325

ABOUT THE AUTHORS 339

PREFACE

Mental health professionals are expected to understand the legal and ethical mandates germane to their profession. In today's legal climate, counselors, social workers, and psychologists cannot plead ignorance of their professional, legal, and ethical obligations; they are held to the standards of responsibility for their professions. Therefore, practicing mental health professionals must understand the legal and ethical standards by which they will be judged while fulfilling their obligations to their clients.

This book was written to help readers understand the legal and ethical obligations of mental health professionals. The values and rules that guide such professionals are myriad and sometimes conflicting. For example, the concepts of confidentiality, informed consent, and privileged communication apply differently to a school counselor than to a private practitioner, because the context of the counseling and the nature of the clients are different. In this book, we discuss the ethical and legal issues facing mental health professionals working with several different populations in several specific contexts, including these:

- historical
- ethical
- multicultural
- school
- family

- helping
- legal
- special relationships with special populations
- groups
- training

At the end of each section we have provided exercises to facilitate and focus the reader's learning.

We will begin with an historical perspective of the mental health movement, then look at the temperament and character of the helping professional in the counseling relationship. We will demonstrate how to use ethical principles to solve dilemmas and discuss the current controversy over training of ethical principles versus ethical virtues. Another heated argument we will examine is how much emphasis should be given to the teaching of multicultural counseling.

Next, we will look at the legal system and how it functions, how and why laws are enacted, and which laws are most relevant to mental health professionals. We will pay special attention to the counseling relationship that is legally defined as *a special relationship*. We will discuss the implications of transgressions such as negligent behavior or breach of contract. Other relevant concepts we will examine include informed consent, confidentiality, privileged communication, dual relationships, client records, advertising, therapist burnout, client referral, and court appearances. Students are advised on what to do if they receive a subpoena or are named in a lawsuit.

Within the context of the special counseling relationship we will highlight potential ethical and legal problems as they pertain to special populations. We will consider counseling clients who are:

- harmful to self or others

- HIV-positive

- abused children

- adults abused as children

- therapist-abused

- spiritual

- homosexual

- consultees

- minors

- in managed care programs

- substance abusers

Finally, we will review issues related to marriage and family counseling, group counseling, school counseling, and counselor training. Along with the specific ethical and legal issues associated with these issues, we will discuss philosophical and contemporary professional issues such as the marginalization of marriage and family therapy, the importance of disclosure statements in group counseling, peer sexual harassment programs in schools, and current studies of supervision in training programs for mental health professionals.

The guiding force in this text has been to provide an introduction to the many legal and ethical issues mental health professionals must face. We have also tried to present an overview of contemporary philosophical concerns and research findings regarding therapist training.

> The question is not whether mental health professionals will interact with laws and legal professionals; it is *how* they will act both now and in a future in which intercessions by legal professionals into mental health professional practice become even more intrusive. (Swenson, 1997, p. 32)

Part A

HISTORICAL AND HELPING PERSPECTIVES

Chapter 1

THE MENTAL HEALTH PROFESSIONAL IN A HISTORICAL CONTEXT

EARLY HISTORICAL ROOTS

The search for methods to ensure mental and physical well-being can be traced to ancient times. Some of the earliest writings in medical history are found in the Assyrian Tablets, dating back to 2500 B.C. Passages in these tablets speak of the formulas magicians chanted to tribal gods. Some reveal challenges to demons or diseases to yield to the magicians' superior powers and exit their victims' bodies (Ehrenwald, 1976).

In the non-Western world, Buddhist and Taoist doctrines were not focused on healthy adjustment to the demands of life. Instead, they devised methods of escape from life's pressures. Measured by Western standards, Buddhists seemed to escape human suffering by withdrawing from the world in ways comparable to the defenses found in psychosis (Ehrenwald, 1976).

In the Western world, people relied for thousands of years on the super-natural to explain psychologically different behavior. From primitive times the explanation for mentally disturbed behavior was spiritual intrusion by demons, werewolves, vampires, or devils. Without exception, the most feared super-natural source was the devil—also known as Satan, Lucifer, or Belphegar. The devil remained the major instigator of abnormal behavior for thousands of years. People "possessed" were considered evil, nefarious, sinful, or cursed by God (Mears & Gatchel, 1979). Typical methods used to cure those possessed by the devil were bodily contact between patient and healer (e.g., laying on of hands), the power of sympathy, and the analysis of dreams to discover an appropriate treatment (Ehrenwald, 1976). Ellenberger (1970) described these other methods used to expel intrusive spirits:

1. Expelling the spirit or demon by physical means—beating, bleeding, exposing the possessed to foul odors or loud noises, or having the possessed drink horrendous concoctions.

2. Transferring the spirit into the body of another creature—either the shaman or an animal.

3. Exorcising the spirit through "psychic means," including incantations, tricks, magic, or prayer.

The *shaman*—a special priest, witch doctor, or medicine man—played a key role in treating spiritual intrusions. Typically, the shaman would excite himself into a wild frenzy and pass into a trance, at which time he would acquire supernatural power and perform unearthly feats of healing (Wilson, 1991). Belief in demonic possession flourished in the Greek and Roman Eras, until the Greek physician Hippocrates (460–377 B.C.) suggested that mental disorders might have their origin in some physically caused brain dysfunction.

> Hippocrates was a contemporary of Plato—which means that he lived at a time of unprecedented concentration of genius in ancient Greek civilization, or for that matter, in any other period of history. Hippocrates' contribution to this civilization was that of the medical man, drawing on a vast store of clinical experience based on methodical clinical observation.
>
> Born in the fifth century B.C., the son of a Greek physician, he is called the "Father of Medicine." But more important than this widely acclaimed paternity is the fact that Hippocrates was the first medical man to make a deliberate attempt to separate his art—or his science—from philosophy and from magico-religious beliefs. Although his approach was mainly concerned with the physical and environmental aspects of illness, he achieved a degree of psychological understanding of mental disease that few had before him.

> This is best illustrated by his essay "On the Sacred Disease," with
> its emphasis on the natural origin of epileptic disorders and, by im-
> plication, of many other disturbances usually attributed to demo-
> niacal possession (Ehrenwald, 1976, p. 171).

The decline of Greece and Rome signaled the demise of the rationalism espoused by Hippocrates and his contemporaries. Humane treatments of the mentally impaired disappeared—replaced by lunatic asylums—and demonology was resurrected. In the 1800s, Spenger and Kraemer (cited in Robbins, 1959) noted the prevalence of witchcraft and related how God was opposed to witches and sanctioned their extermination. They also gave specific directions for extracting confessions from suspected witches. Proposed methods included thumb screwing, whipping, binding, tearing the flesh with red-hot pincers, and pushing the accused into a spiked chair. It is estimated that, between 1603 and 1628, 70,000 people were burned as witches in England alone, 100,000 in Germany, and 200,000 in all of Europe (Robbins, 1959). At the same time, those believed to be possessed by demons (usually through witchcraft) were thrown into lunatic asylums, where they were chained, beaten, forced to go naked, and subjected to pubic ridicule and mockery (Bromberg, 1975).

In the nineteenth century, the care of those afflicted with mental illness became more humane. The French physician Philippe Pinel (1745–1826) is credited with initiating moral management techniques with patients in Paris. Instead of chaining up those who were institutionalized, he treated them with kindness. Dorothea Lynde Dix (1802–1887) championed the humanitarian movement to improve treatment conditions in the United States. The American Psychological Association (APA) declared her the greatest social reformer in American history.

THE SOMATOGENIC HYPOTHESIS

Ultimately, by the middle of the nineteenth century, the theory of Hippocrates had been resurrected: Mental disorders were considered diseases of the brain. Medical scientists attempted to establish that tissue changes were responsible for illnesses. Scientists looked toward abnormalities in the body to establish a *somatogenic hypothesis* for a particular illness.

> The confidence in somatogenesis was based more on faith than facts.
> … Notwithstanding these difficulties, the somatogenic hypothesis
> was a great advance in the understanding of mental disorders. It
> demanded a search for essential causes rather than a preoccupation
> with surface phenomena. (White, 1964, p. 15)

The culmination of the thinking that mental disorders were physical diseases appeared in the works of Emil Kraepelin. His first work, *Lehrbuch der Psychiatrie* (*Textbook of Psychiatry*), was written in 1883; the ninth edition was published in 1923. Kraepelin painstakingly integrated his clinical data to isolate the symptoms associated with specific mental disorders. On the basis of his classification system, two major forms of severe mental illness (or psychoses) were identified: *Dementia praecox*—which today we call schizophrenia—and *manic-depressive psychosis*. Kraepelin believed that these two diseases were organic in origin. He did not take into account the importance of psychological factors. Kraepelin's position eventually was modified, forming the basis for the classification system ultimately used in *The Diagnostic and Statistical Manual of Mental Disorders* (*DSM*), which was adopted by the American Psychiatric Association in 1952 as the official classification schema of mental disorders.

THE PSYCHOGENIC HYPOTHESIS

In contrast to the somatogenic hypothesis, which holds that disordered personal reactions have their genesis in somatic or bodily disturbances, the psychogenic hypothesis attributes causative significance to psychological processes. We can give it a crude first statement ... by saying that disordered personal reactions occur because the patient's thoughts, feelings, and strivings are disturbed. His somatic processes, even his brain and central nervous system, may be working in an entirely normal fashion; it is the content of what he feels and imagines that throws his personal reactions into disorder. We can begin to speak of psychopathology at the point where ideas or some other psychological processes are held responsible for disordered behavior. Pathology means the science of disease processes; psychopathology deals with those disorders which have their origins in psychological processes rather than tissue or chemical dysfunction. (White, 1964, p. 20)

Psychology began as an outgrowth of physiology (the part of biology that deals with living organisms) and medicine. It was in the nineteenth century that physiologists began studying the brain and other psychologically relevant structures. During this time, Wilhelm Wundt (1832–1920) founded the first laboratory dedicated to the scientific study of the mind. The first psychologists were graduates of this laboratory. One of them, G. Stanley Hall, founded the American Psychiatric Association in 1892. It was composed of 26 members. In the United States, the field of psychology was best represented by William James (1842–1910), a medical school graduate.

In sharp contrast to Wundt and James, who studied conscious experience, Sigmund Freud argued that behavior was a result of unconscious forces. He likened the human mind to an iceberg: The small tip we can see above water is the conscious part; the vast part beneath the surface of the water is the unconscious part of the mind. Wundt, James, and Freud were ranked by 29 historians as the first, second, and third most important psychologists of all time (Korn, Davis, & Davis, 1991). Freud's theory of psychopathology can be summarized as follows:

1. There is an inner conflict between drives and fear that prevents drive discharge.

2. Sexual drives are involved in these conflicts.

3. Conflict has not been worked through to a realistic solution. Instead, the drives that seek discharge have been expelled from consciousness through repression or another defense mechanism.

4. Repression merely succeeds in rendering the drives unconscious; it does not deprive them of their power and make them innocuous. Consequently, the repressed tendencies/drives fight their way back to consciousness, disguised as neurotic symptoms.

5. An inner conflict leads to neurosis in adolescence or adulthood only if a neurosis or a rudimentary neurosis based on the same type of conflict existed in early childhood. (Meissner, Mack, & Semrad, 1975, p. 542)

Freud quickly acquired a number of devoted followers, but before long another group of professionals—dubbed neo-Freudians—began to question his theories. Scholars such as Alfred Adler, Erik Erikson, and Eric Fromm placed more importance on interpersonal experiences as the precursors of psychopathology.

Before long, theories on the etiology of maladaptive behavior and methods of intervention were myriad. Eric Berne believed that the primary needs of individuals should be noted and recognized. He developed Transactional Analysis (TA) as a mode of intervention. Carl Rogers—who developed client-centered therapy—believed the primary need of individuals was an innate drive to express their potentialities. French sociologist Emile Durkheim related depression and suicide to acts of individuals within a social context; he suggested a sociological approach to treatment. These theories and their resultant intervention strategies are but a few examples of the evolving theoretical orientations since Freud. Smith (1982) reported the following theoretical orientations of more recent clinical and counseling psychologists:

	Theoretical orientation	Percentage of psychologists adhering to the theory
1.	Transactional analysis therapy	.96%
2.	Reality therapy	.96%
3.	Rational-emotive therapy	1.69%
4.	Gestalt therapy	1.69%
5.	Existential therapy	2.17%
6.	Family therapy	2.65%
7.	Adlerian therapy	2.89%
8.	Behavioral therapy	6.75%
9.	Person-centered therapy	8.67%
10.	Other therapy	9.16%
11.	Cognitive behavioral therapy	10.36%
12.	Psychoanalytic therapy	10.84%
13.	Eclectic therapy	41.20%

At the same time, new categories within the mental health professions became commonplace and specialties within existing categories were created. Often the creation of these specialties was (and still is) the cause of confusion and competition among mental health professionals.

> I see one counselor saying to the other, you know your professional parentage? Nope. Me neither, let's write some bylaws and apply for divisional status in APA. We'll call ourselves counseling psychologists; whenever we're with counselors, we'll talk psychology; whenever we're with psychologists, we'll talk counseling. If ever we're with a group of counselors and psychologists, we'll talk about the weather. (Kagan, 1977, p. 1)

* * * *

Unlicensed employees of accredited educational institutions and governmental agencies usually may perform psychological services as part of their employment responsibilities. Unlicensed professors and teachers may work for salaries but they may not perform most services other than giving lectures and disseminating research results for fees. They may earn fees as a consultant or expert—which is a form of lecturing instead of *doing* something—in addition to their regular salaries. All types of professionals and trainees must communicate their true professional status to clients. ... In California the rule is that none except licensed psychologists may present himself or herself to the public as a "psychologist." However, unlicensed employees of educational institutions or government agencies may use official titles containing the word *psychologist*. Persons with master's degrees hired as "school psychologists" may be called that, but they may not call themselves psychologist. In most states it is legal for professors of psychology to refer to themselves by that title or as "psychology professor." They cannot legally call themselves psychologist. (Swenson, 1997, p. 131)

* * * *

When we move to the helping professions themselves, we find the same diversity within the field. Employee assistance counselors, marriage and family therapists, preretirement counselors, rehabilitation therapists, drug and alcohol counselors, psychiatrists, high school counselors, clinical psychologists, vocational and employment counselors, counseling psychologists, elementary school counselors, student personnel workers in higher education, gerontological counselors, crisis interventionists, mental health agency therapists, social workers, educational psychologists, pastoral counselors, psychiatric nurses, teachers and corrections counselors ... The list of occupations that are indirectly and directly allied with counseling and psychotherapy is staggering and continues to grow. (Gilliland, James, & Bowman, 1989, p. viii)

Thus, today's mental health professional is represented by a myriad of titles and may use many theoretical orientations when he or she implements the helping relationship, or represents himself or herself to the general public. This diversity of professional orientation and representation has created many ethical and legal implications for present-day mental health professionals. The subsequent chapters in this text address many of these issues and implications.

SUMMARY

Psychological maladaptions originally were thought to be the work of evil spirits. Belief in the power of demonic possession was prevalent until the time of Hippocrates. The decline of the Greek and Roman Empires signaled the fall of rationalism. For centuries, people who were considered abnormal were subjected to ridicule and abuse. Eventually the inhuman treatment in insane asylums was replaced by a more moral management, and many of the problems people had were found to be psychological in nature rather than physiological.

Freud focused on unconscious psychic energy forces. Through the years scholars broke with Freud and replaced his psychological theories with theories of their own. Presently, most mental health professionals use some combination of many of these theories in their treatment interventions.

LEARNING FACILITATION AND FOCUS

Exercise 1.1

The psychological adjustment one makes in life is probably determined by several things. Some believe a child's rearing and unconscious repressed material are important. Others believe adjustment to life is correlated with social forces such as discrimination. Still others believe interpersonal relationships, humanity's search for meaning, behavioral reinforcement, conscious cognitive processes, and family interactions are of paramount importance. List below some of the variables you think are important for psychological well-being. Also note why you think they are important.

Variables   **Why they are important**

_____   _____

_____   _____

_____   _____

_____   _____

_____   _____

_____   _____

Exercise 1.2

After you have listed your most important variables for psychological adjustment, explain what your intervention strategy would be:

_____

_____

_____

_____

_____

_____

_____

_____

Chapter 2

IN A HELPING CONTEXT

THE HELPING RELATIONSHIP

One of the major jobs of mental health professionals is providing counseling or therapy. The counseling or therapy pairing often is referred to as the *helping relationship*. This relationship has been described in many ways:

> Helping professionals engage in activities designed to enable others to understand, to modify, or to enrich their behavior so that positive change takes place. They are interested in the behavior of people ... and their attitudes, motives, ideas, responses, and needs. (Shertzer & Stone, 1980, p. 5)

****

> My interest in psychotherapy has brought about in me an interest in every kind of helping relationship. By this term I mean a relationship in which at least one of the parties has the intent of promoting the growth, development, maturity, improved functioning, improved coping with life of the other. The other, in this sense, may be one individual or a group. To put it in another way, a helping relationship might be defined as one in which one of the participants intends that there should come about, in one or both parties, more appreciation of, more expression of, more functional use of the latent inner resources of the individual. (Rogers, 1961, pp. 31–40)

****

1. Counseling involves responding to the feelings, thoughts, and actions of the client ... some approaches (person-centered, existential) favor an emphasis on feelings; others (rational-emotive, reality therapy, behavioral) emphasize the importance of behaviors and actions; an eclectic approach would acknowledge the importance of being able to identify and respond appropriately to feeling states, behaviors, and relationship patterns.

2. Counseling involves a basic acceptance of the client's perceptions and feelings, irrespective of outside evaluative standards. In other words, you must first accept who the client is before you can begin to consider who the client could be.

3. Confidentiality and privacy constitute essential ingredients in the counseling setting.

4. Counseling is voluntary.

5. Although there are times when counselor self-disclosure is appropriate, counselors generally do not complicate the interview by focusing attention on their personal life.

6. One skill underlying all systems of counseling is that of communication. Counselors and clients alike continually transmit and receive verbal and nonverbal messages during the interview process. Therefore, awareness of and sensitivity to the kinds of messages being communicated is an important prerequisite for counselor effectiveness. (Cormier & Hackney, 1993, pp. 6–7)

****

Helping another human being is basically a process of enabling that person to grow in the directions the person chooses, to solve problems, and to face crises ... to avoid feeling patronized, helpers define desired help on their own terms and fulfill their own needs ... some helpers, for example, *need* "victims," meaning that the helpers may maintain relationships to satisfy their own affiliation and dominance needs. ... Doing anything for other people without their initiative and consent frequently is manipulative and often destructive ... we have stressed the significance of helpee *responsibility* for such goals and self determined growth ... we, as helpers, also must assume some responsibility for creating conditions of trust whereby helpees can respond in a trusting manner and help themselves. Helpers do this through the *process*, a term that refers largely to their methods for reaching helpee goals. These outcomes are realized through managing the environment, providing conditions for understanding and comfort, and modeling trusting behaviors. A trusting approach means that helpers view their task as facilitating and supporting rather than teaching or persuading. Helpers who are open and honest about their own ideas and feelings tend to be perceived as trustworthy by their helpees. Consistent behaviors that show caring and are clearly in the helpees' best interest also inspire trust. (Brammer & MacDonald, 1996, pp. 4–7)

Corey, Corey, and Callanan (1988) believed that the personal attributes of the mental health professional are the most important variables in the helping relationship. In their view, the mental health professional should possess the following attributes in order to achieve successful therapy:

1. *Good will.* Effective counselors must have a sincere interest in the welfare of others.

2. *The ability to be present for others.* This ability stems from the counselor's openness to his or her own struggles and feelings.

3. *A recognition and acceptance of one's personal power.* Effective counselors recognize their personal power, not in the sense that they dominate or exploit their clients but that they are in contact with their own strength and vitality.

4. *A personal counseling style.* Effective practitioners strive to develop counseling styles that are expressions of their own personalities.

5. *A willingness to be vulnerable and open.* Ideally, counselors exemplify in their own lives the courage and openness they hope to promote in their clients.

6. *Self-respect and self-appreciation.*

7. *A willingness to serve as models for clients.*

8. *A willingness to risk making mistakes and to admit having made them.*

9. *A growth orientation.* The most effective counselors remain open to the possibility of broadening their horizons instead of telling themselves they have "arrived."

10. *A sense of humor.* (Corey, Corey, & Callanan, 1988, pp. 28–29)

The effects of cross-cultural differences on the helping relationship now assume paramount importance in the literature. The mental health professional must realize that prior assumptions regarding rapport and understanding with clients may change because of differences in meaning inherent in behaviors.

> One of the critical issues in interviewing is the fact that the same skills may have different effects with different individual and cultural backgrounds. Eye contacts differ, for example. In our culture, middle-class patterns call for rather direct eye contact, but in some cultural groups, direct eye contact is considered rude and intrusive. Some groups find the rapid-fire questioning techniques of many North Americans offensive. Many Spanish-speaking groups have more varying vocal tones and sometimes a more rapid speech rate than do English-speaking people. It is also important to remember that the work culture can be defined in many ways. Religion, ethnic background (for example Irish-American and Black-American), sex, and lifestyle differences as well as the degree of a client's developmental or physical handicap also represent cultural differences. There is also a youth culture, a culture of those facing imminent death through AIDS or cancer, and a culture of the aging. In effect, any group that differs from the mainstream of society can be considered a subculture. All of us at times are thus part of many cultures that require a unique awareness of the group experience. (Ivey, 1988, pp. 49–50)

In this chapter, we will present our thoughts on the helping relationship. We will use the word *therapist* or *counselor* in our definition to represent the helper.

The heart of helping is communication: a transmitting of the thoughts, feelings, and attitudes that shape our lives. The counselor has an active role in this process and, as such, is responsible for understanding the personal qualities (thoughts, feelings, and attitudes) he or she brings to the relationship. Counselors speak from a context of personal experience and leaning. Therefore, they must be aware of who they are as helpers, of how personal experiences influence their image, and of how that image is communicated to their clients.

For any substantial communication to occur between two people, a common humanity must be recognized. Although relationships between people may be unequally weighted in power of one sort or another, one must strive to grow beyond this. If one identifies only with the roles one plays in one's relationships with others, one's communication is limited, literally, to role-playing. No one grows. One must develop trust and accept vulnerability enough to reach beyond role-to-role relating so growth can occur. This is especially true in the relationship between counselor and client. Counselors must remember that their clients may see the world very differently and may give significance to events in life in ways that do not immediately make sense. Although we cannot have direct experience of how a client sees the world, we can try to make sense of the client's explanations. This process is the beginning of honest communication.

Honest communication requires not only understanding where the client is but also responding in a genuine, person-to-person manner. To create such an environment, counselors must strive not only to be transparent to themselves about their values and prejudices, but also to be transparent to their clients. Clients should be able to see and feel that the counselor is present in the session and responding in a genuine manner. To accomplish this, a counselor should suspend judgment, at least temporarily, and just listen. Certainly, this is easier said than done; most therapists periodically find themselves making premature judgments about their clients. But if we are conscious of the reason for our responses, and if we try to understand the client's world as it is presented, we can go a long way toward creating a genuine environment.

It is important for therapists to see the world through the eyes of their clients for two reasons:

1. because the potential for discrepancy between what is real for the client and what is real for the counselor is always present, and

2. because understanding the world as the client sees it is the backbone of communication. Not having such an understanding is a threat to the helping relationship.

Understanding why someone behaves or feels as he or she does is an important component in the helping relationship. For beneficial communication to exist, we understand the world as our clients perceive it.

However irrational people's behavior may appear, they are making choices that make sense to them in the world as they experience it; and if we as therapists can understand these choices, we will begin to understand the world in which our clients live. And, if we can then use our understanding to help our clients see how their experience has shaped their perception of their world, we can help them see they have other possibilities. As we become more aware of our reasons for making choices, we become aware that we have the freedom to make other choices, however frightening those choices may be.

So just as counselors must be conscious of the reasons for their responses, clients must be helped to see the reasons for their responses to their own situations. No matter how difficult the situation, clients always have some choice of response; it is the job of the counselor to help clients see this for themselves. Evasion, denial, avoidance, and self-affirmation are all choices. What is comfortable may be unauthentic. What is authentic may be painful and evoke a hostile response. Developing self-awareness and actively choosing are central to living responsibly; helping clients understand this is an important part of the counseling relationship.

One of the goals of therapy is to help clients see that, whatever situation they find themselves in, they can always assert themselves in self-affirmation. This assertion is a condition of our freedom. We can assert ourselves or we can deny that we have this possibility. To recognize this freedom is to accept the responsibility it brings. As Sartre noted, "We are our choices." In Sartre's terms, choice can be in good faith—accepting personal responsibility for one's decisions—or in bad faith—avoiding personal responsibility and making excuses.

In a counseling situation, we can see how our clients have responded to the challenge of their own freedom by being sensitive to how they describe their world and how they react to the choices available. We don't mean to imply that freedom is without limitation. All people have limitations, whether physical, intellectual, societal, or financial. How clients respond to these limitations is the important focus. If they believe the future is determined by forces entirely beyond their control, they deny their freedom and their responsibility for making an authentic life. They deny they have the potential for change and growth; they accept that they are objects controlled by others. If, on the other hand, they see their limitations as challenges, then they see themselves as autonomous beings. They may be making difficult or unpleasant choices, but in doing so they participate in making their own future.

Not all clients are capable of or interested in developing personal freedom and responsibility; this is a fact all counselors must face. But even when a client does not participate at the start, the counselor can view his or her interventions as an invitation to participate in the future.

At the other end of the spectrum are clients who see themselves as entirely free of limitations. They are living in a state of disembodied fantasy: The world will constantly frustrate their choices; their physical being will only be a burden; and, in the end, the limitations of human existence will be forced upon them.

In making authentic choices one creates the values of life. Authentic choices recognize both poles of being human—the infinite and the finite. When someone sees the possibility for authentic choice, he or she feels the necessity for a personal decision and develops a new orientation toward the world and the future.

One central issue that must be resolved before we begin relating to clients is whether we will analyze them as objects or understand them as human beings. We believe a relationship with clients must respect the dignity of their humanity; our function is to help our clients experience themselves more fully, become aware of their potentialities, and become able to act on those potentialities. Developing self-awareness is central to growth. In order to help foster this self-awareness, we must "be there" in our relationships with our clients. Our relationships must be real ones. We do not want to simply provide a reflection of the client's concerns or problems or to make a diagnosis of them, but to be a real person concerned with understanding and experiencing the client's world. Remember: One is first a person, then a counselor.

SUMMARY

Mental health professionals are known by many roles (school counselor, psychiatrist, psychologist, etc.). However, no matter what occupational role the mental health professional fills, he or she aspires to develop a helping relationship with clients. The essence of helping is the quality of communication between the counselor and the client. This communication is affected by the personal qualities and skills the counselor brings to the helping relationship. It is imperative that mental health professionals are aware of their personal qualities and attributes, and of how they determine the quality of their communications.

LEARNING FACILITATION AND FOCUS

Exercise 2.1

List all the personal attributes a mental health professional should have to be effective:

_____

_____

_____

_____

_____

Now rank order the five attributes you think are most important:

1. _____

2. _____

3. _____

4. _____

5. _____

Exercise 2.2

What does it mean to give help? What does it mean to receive help? How are these two things similar, and how are they different?

Giving help:_____

_____

_____

_____

Receiving help:_____

_____

_____

_____

Similarities and differences between the two:_____

_____

_____

_____

_____

Exercise 2.3

Self-disclosure happens when a counselor discloses to a client his or her feelings about the process. An example would be a therapist telling a client she was angry with him. Do you think a therapist should do this? What are some implications for counseling if he or she does?

_____

_____

_____

_____

_____

_____

_____

Exercise 2.4

Some believe that touching a client in therapy can be a manifestation of empathy. Do you think mental health professionals should ever touch their clients? What circumstances would be present in therapy to make you feel that touching a client was appropriate? What circumstances would dictate that touching was inappropriate?

_____

_____

_____

_____

_____

_____

Part B

ETHICAL AND LEGAL DIMENSIONS

Chapter 3

IN AN ETHICAL CONTEXT

Ethical and legal concerns go hand-in-hand. In fact, an ethical violation can be a legal violation. For example, a mental health professional who knows (or should know) that a teenager is going to commit suicide and does nothing to prevent it may be guilty of an ethical and legal transgression. For heuristic purposes, however, the focus of this chapter will be on an ethical perspective. As Huber and Baruth (1987) noted, "Ethics is concerned with the conduct of human beings as they make moral decisions" (p. 37). Beauchamp and Childress (1994) defined it this way: "Ethics is a generic term for various ways of understanding and examining the moral life" (p. 4).

ETHICAL CODES

Ethical codes are the written set of ethical standards for the professional mental health provider. Each profession (psychologists, social workers, counselors, etc.) has a code specific to its particular client relationships. Mental health professionals have an obligation to behave in ways that do not violate these codes. The codes are both national and regional. Violations of the standards by a mental health worker can result in sanctions or loss of licensure.

The primary obligation of mental health professionals is to promote the well-being of their clients; ethical codes were developed to protect the integrity of the process. They allow mental health professionals to police their own members, thus reducing the need for government regulation of the profession. These codes are normative in nature, in that they prescribe what mental health professionals ought to do. If a counselor finds him- or herself facing an ethical dilemma, he or she can refer to the codes for guidance.

ETHICAL PRINCIPLES

Should ethical codes not be specific or thorough enough to answer a question, one should employ *ethical principles* to the dilemma. These are used to make decisions about moral issues inherent in a particular ethical dilemma. An ethical dilemma is a situation in which one must make a choice between competing and contradictory ethical mandates. The ethical codes do not and cannot always provide solutions to such dilemmas. Ethical principles establish a moral structure to solve dilemmas and guide future ethical thinking.

The ethical principles described in this section are based on the work of Beauchamp and Childress (1994) and Kitchener (1984). They have their roots in commonsense morality, and they detail a structure of *prima facie* obligation—that is, they are considered adequate to solve ethical dilemmas unless they are refuted. If they prove to be inadequate, given the complexity of the dilemma, one must consult ethical theory.

Autonomy

The principle of autonomy says that individuals are free to direct the course of their lives as long as their choices do not interfere with the autonomy of others. If people want to be treated as autonomous beings, they must also respect and treat others as autonomous. Autonomy also implies the freedom to make one's own judgments. The concept of autonomy assumes the ability to make rational judgments. Autonomy provides the foundation for many psychological tenants. Mental health professionals must enter practice with respect for:

- the client and individual differences,

- the client's ability to make his or her own decisions,

- the client's right to privacy,

- the client's autonomous nature, and

- the client's competence.

Beneficence

Sound ethical practices require that mental health professionals work for the health and welfare of their clients. Clients who contract for professional psychological services must be able to expect positive benefits from the interactions. This assumes an expectation of competence. Thus, *mental health professionals should never contract with clients whose problems are outside their areas of expertise.* They should also be careful not to become paternalistic with their clients. Paternalism assumes that one knows what is best for another and attempts to regulate behavior according to one's personal prejudices.

Justice

The meaning of justice as an ethical principle is said to have originated with Aristotle (Beauchamp & Childress, 1979), who suggested that justice means treating equals equally and unequals unequally but in proportion to their relative differences. Thus, equal people have the right to be treated equally, and nonequal people have the right to be treated differently if the inequality is relevant to the issue in question. For example, politicians may be equal as persons but have different party affiliations. Should these politicians need medical care, they should be treated equally and fairly. Should they ascribe to office and run for reelection, they may be treated differently by their constituents.

Nonmaleficence

The principle of nonmaleficence requires that one not intentionally inflict harm or take actions that might harm another. Nonmaleficence, like the Hippocratic Oath, requires that one, first, do no harm.

Fidelity

Issues of fidelity arise for mental health professionals when two people voluntarily enter into a client—counselor relationship. Fidelity involves keeping promises; it also involves issues of faithfulness and loyalty.

ETHICAL THEORY

Not all ethicists agree that the ethical principles have equal weight and importance. Ethical theories differ in their basic assumptions or premises. For example, a major distinction can be seen between ontological and teleological perspectives. For an *ontologist*, certain values are considered intrinsic to the nature of human beings. For instance, veracity is considered positive regardless of circumstance. In a *teleological* perspective, morality lies outside the action itself. For example, in *utilitarianism* the ideal is to achieve the greatest good for the greatest number, and potential decisions are weighed and balanced accordingly. In a theory of *liberal individualism,* on the other hand, respect for the rights and autonomy of the individual is paramount.

Consequently, ethical decisions are weighted and balanced according to basic premises. A theorist's assumptions about what is moral may make ethical decisions even less obvious. Kohlberg (1984) and Gilligan (1979) offer two contemporary examples of theorists espousing primary principles.

Kohlberg and Justice

Kohlberg (1984) argued for the concept of justice as the dominant principle in moral decision making. He developed six stages of moral decision making, and posited that the latter stages exemplify more sophisticated moral thinking. The final stage represents those who employ principled thought in their decision making. Thus, people whose decision-making processes fall into the final stage are said to be rational and impartial; they would likely organize social cooperation more fairly than those represented by earlier stages. For Kohlberg, moral behavior emanates from the construct of justice. In this view, the more education one receives, the more principled one becomes in terms of making fair and just decisions. Kohlberg's stages of moral development are:

1. *Punishment:* An act is good if one is not punished for it. Young children tend to be in this stage. They perceive an act as bad if they are punished for it. They typically do not consider the possibility that the person doing the punishing may be bad.

2. *Instrumental egoism:* An act is fair if it serves the desires and interests of an individual. One should obey the law only if it is prudent to do so. This stage is characterized by simple exchange. The interaction between drug dealers and drug users represents this kind of transaction. Let's make a deal, as long as we don't get caught.

3. *Interpersonal concordance:* In this stage, one is preoccupied with being considerate and nice to other people. This is different from stage 2 because there is a general understanding rather than an explicit agreement. Acts are moral if they are based on a prosocial motive, and being moral implies a concern with others' approval.

4. *Law and duty to the social order:* Everyone is obligated and protected by the law. A person in this stage has a societal orientation.

Social order can be achieved only if *right* is defined by categorical rules that fix shared expectations and are binding on all. This does not necessarily mean that the law is just, only that it is to be obeyed. Respect for delegated authority is part of one's obligation to society, and values are derived from and subordinated to the social order.

5. *Societal consensus:* Obligation is incurred by whatever arrangements are agreed to by due process. Moral obligation derives from voluntary commitments to cooperate. Procedures for selecting laws that maximize justice are discerned as the will of the majority. Basic rights are preconditions to social obligations.

6. *Nonarbitrary social cooperation:* This is the manner by which rational and impartial people would organize cooperate. (Rational and arbitrary cooperation would take into account any and all parties that would be affected by the fair and just decision.)

Gilligan and Fidelity

Gilligan (1979) developed her ethical emphasis from the responsibility inherent in a special relationship, in which parties in a relationship owe a special responsibility to one another on the ethical principal of fidelity. For Gilligan, morality is determined by the responsibility to the other based upon the substance of the relationship.

> Sensitivity to the needs of others and the assumption of responsibility for taking care lead women to attend to voices other than their own and to include in their judgment other points of view. ... In this conception, the moral problem is seen to arise from conflicting responsibilities rather than from competing rights and to require for its resolution a mode of thinking that is contextual and inductive rather than formal and abstract. (Gilligan, 1979, pp. 440, 442)

Summary

Ethical principles are used to solve ethical dilemmas. First, one must determine which principles are relevant to the situation. If principles are in conflict, one must balance them in deciding how to solve the conflict. Ethical theories may differ in their assumptions of which principles are most important. For example, if one believes justice is the most important principle, all actions will be weighed to determine if they lead to the most just decision for everyone involved. The same procedure holds if one believes that fidelity is the most important principle. If the theorist believes all the principles are equally important, then each principle is weighed equally in terms of solving the dilemma.

Today more than ever students and practitioners of psychology and social work are called upon to make ethical decisions on a day-to-day basis. The ethical codes that inform these decisions are not always adequate, because the dilemmas often are too complex for a simple application of codes. When this situation arises, the mental health professional must rely on ethical principles or ethical theory.

LEARNING FACILITATION AND FOCUS

Ethical Dilemmas and Principles: A Paradigm

The most popular approach for solving ethical dilemmas is to juxtapose the competing claims (i.e., beneficence, nonmaleficence, autonomy, fidelity, and justice). This allows the counselor to identify the fullest range of options for solving the dilemma in the most ethical manner. This form of ethical decision making is the "paradigmatic center of moral reflection" (Hauerwas, 1981, p. 114). To this end, we have developed the following paradigm.

The paradigm is divided into two parts. The first covers ethical dilemmas in counseling situations; the second, ethical dilemmas in research situations.

Here's how the paradigm works:

1. Read the dilemma.

2. Write down the problem(s) inherent in the dilemma.

3. Place a X on the scale to show the importance each principle plays in solving the dilemma.

4. Decide what you would do if faced with the dilemma.

5. Before you start, read the example for the first dilemma.

Ethical Dilemmas and Principles

The Dilemma. A school counselor has a 13-year-old male client who confides that he and some of his buddies sniff glue at night in the ballpark. This behavior initially happened once a week, but now it happens almost every night. That afternoon the boy's mother comes to the school and asks the counselor if she knows anything about the boy, because he seems to have changed in the last month. The mother says that sometimes he is listless and inattentive.

Recognition of the Problem. First, who is the client? Is there a school law concerning this problem? Are there any laws against sniffing glue? Is it ethical to tell the mother? Did the counselor inform the boy that she would tell his parents under certain conditions? Is the boy in danger? Will he come back for future sessions? What if something happens to the boy as a result of the counselor's not revealing the information? Does the boy have ethical rights? Does the mother have ethical rights?

Specifying and Weighing the Ethical Principles.

Beneficence	1	2	3	4	5
	Not Important	Somewhat Important	Important	Very Important	Absolutely Important

Nonmaleficence	1	2	3	4	5
	Not Important	Somewhat Important	Important	Very Important	Absolutely Important

Autonomy	1	2	3	4	5
	Not Important	Somewhat Important	Important	Very Important	Absolutely Important

Justice	1	2	3	4	5
	Not Important	Somewhat Important	Important	Very Important	Absolutely Important

Fidelity	1	2	3	4	5
	Not Important	Somewhat Important	Important	Very Important	Absolutely Important

My Decision (underline the principles used in your narrative). I would not tell the mother based mainly on the principles of *beneficence* and *fidelity*. I think the greatest good for the boy would be to cultivate his trust. I also like him and respect him. I feel loyal to him. I don't know if there is some possible harm that might happen (*nonmaleficence*), but I think that the potential good of emphasizing *fidelity* outweighs the potential harm of losing his trust. I don't think *autonomy* plays a big role here because of his age (i.e., competence). Also I'm not sure what role *justice* plays. I would like to discuss the role of *justice* in class.

Client Situation. Exercise 3.1

The Dilemma. Harry T. is a social worker who works in several hospitals in the area. While reviewing the records in a client's file, he comes across the name of a pedophile who was a client of his five years ago. He remembers that the client was compulsively drawn to young children and had several convictions that were thrown out of court. He also notices that the former client is in the hospital for a routine check-up.

That afternoon, while shopping in a local food mart, Harry T. chats with a friend of his. His friend has a large house, and occasionally rents rooms out. Harry T. learns that his friend, who has three small children, is considering renting a room to the pedophile. His friend is not aware of the man's history. Should Harry T. tell his friend about the man's history? Apply the ethical principles in this case to decide what decision you would make if you were Harry T.

Recognition of the Problem._____

_____

_____

_____

_____

Specifying and Weighing the Ethical Principles.

Beneficence	1	2	3	4	5
	Not Important	Somewhat Important	Important	Very Important	Absolutely Important

Nonmaleficence	1	2	3	4	5
	Not Important	Somewhat Important	Important	Very Important	Absolutely Important

Autonomy	1	2	3	4	5
	Not Important	Somewhat Important	Important	Very Important	Absolutely Important

Justice	1	2	3	4	5
	Not Important	Somewhat Important	Important	Very Important	Absolutely Important

Fidelity	1	2	3	4	5
	Not Important	Somewhat Important	Important	Very Important	Absolutely Important

My Decision. _____

_____

_____

_____

_____

Client Situation. Exercise 3.2

The Dilemma. Harriet T. has her master's degree in clinical psychology. She is presently finishing her course work, and is doing her research project in the department of counseling psychology. She has completed a two-year internship as a counseling psychology student.

Harriet also works as a research assistant for Dr. U. Her job is to interview participants in a research project three separate times to learn the child-rearing philosophies of different cultural groups. She asks questions such as, "Do you think children should have a bedtime?"

One of the participants, Mr. V., is in his third interview. When the interview is about two-thirds completed, Mr. V. tells Harriet that he plans to kill his wife when he goes home. Harriet has noticed some violent tendencies in Mr. V. She certainly does not consider him her client, because she has not been doing therapy with him. Yet, she has been trained as a clinician and has all the skills a professional clinician should have.

What principles should be involved in her reaction to this disclosure? What would you do if you were Harriet T.?

Recognition of the Problem. _____

_____

_____

_____

_____

Specifying and Weighing the Ethical Principles.

Beneficence	1	2	3	4	5
	Not Important	Somewhat Important	Important	Very Important	Absolutely Important

Nonmaleficence	1	2	3	4	5
	Not Important	Somewhat Important	Important	Very Important	Absolutely Important

Autonomy	1	2	3	4	5
	Not Important	Somewhat Important	Important	Very Important	Absolutely Important

Justice	1	2	3	4	5
	Not Important	Somewhat Important	Important	Very Important	Absolutely Important

Fidelity	1	2	3	4	5
	Not Important	Somewhat Important	Important	Very Important	Absolutely Important

My Decision. _____

_____

_____

_____

_____

Client Situation. Exercise 3.3

The Dilemma.   Professor X supervises the master's degree program in counseling at the university. Student Y has been a student in the program for 18 months. Student Y has an excellent grade point average and has received high recommendations from his supervisors in clinical practice. Professor X is somewhat bothered by Student Y because of an incident that happened a year ago.

It was a cold day and Professor X had stopped by a campus establishment to have a glass of wine and a sandwich. Student Y was also in the establishment and, in the opinion of Professor X, had had too much to drink. Student Y sat down with Professor X and, among other things, voiced his extreme dislike for homosexuals.

After the meeting Professor X was perplexed about how to react to the outburst. Ultimately, he did nothing about it. What principles should determine what Professor X should do in this situation? What would you have done?

Recognition of the Problem._____

_____

_____

_____

_____

Specifying and Weighing the Ethical Principles.

Beneficence	1	2	3	4	5
	Not Important	Somewhat Important	Important	Very Important	Absolutely Important

Nonmaleficence	1	2	3	4	5
	Not Important	Somewhat Important	Important	Very Important	Absolutely Important

Autonomy	1	2	3	4	5
	Not Important	Somewhat Important	Important	Very Important	Absolutely Important

Justice	1	2	3	4	5
	Not Important	Somewhat Important	Important	Very Important	Absolutely Important

Fidelity	1	2	3	4	5
	Not Important	Somewhat Important	Important	Very Important	Absolutely Important

My Decision._____

_____

_____

_____

_____

Client Situation. Exercise 3.4

The Dilemma. Supervisor X is supervising the clinical work of Student Y in the college counseling center. During a supervision session, Student Y reveals that he is counseling Harriet, a first-year student at the college. Harriet has revealed to Student Y that she was sexually seduced by her previous therapist. At the end of that session, Student Y says he hugged Harriet and made a new appointment for her. Supervisor X admonishes Student Y, telling him that hugging a client who has been seduced by a previous therapist is inappropriate.

Harriet leaves the college at the end of her first semester. Supervisor X continues to supervise Student Y, and he becomes convinced that Student Y was narcissistic and manipulative in his dealings with Harriet. Yet Supervisor X does not feel he has enough hard evidence to stop or fail Student Y. At the same time, he believes Student Y will ultimately attempt to seduce clients. What principles should be involved in Supervisor X's reaction? What would you have done?

Recognition of the Problem._____

_____

_____

_____

_____

Specifying and Weighing the Ethical Principles.

Beneficence	1	2	3	4	5
	Not Important	Somewhat Important	Important	Very Important	Absolutely Important

Nonmaleficence	1	2	3	4	5
	Not Important	Somewhat Important	Important	Very Important	Absolutely Important

Autonomy	1	2	3	4	5
	Not Important	Somewhat Important	Important	Very Important	Absolutely Important

Justice	1	2	3	4	5
	Not Important	Somewhat Important	Important	Very Important	Absolutely Important

Fidelity	1	2	3	4	5
	Not Important	Somewhat Important	Important	Very Important	Absolutely Important

My Decision. _____

_____

_____

_____

_____

Client Situation. Exercise 3.5

The Dilemma. At the age of 31 Dr. Rachel graduates with her Ph.D. in counseling psychology and lands a job in a counseling psychology program on a small college campus. She quickly learns that the other faculty, who are all much older, are not receptive to her socially, although they treat her as a professional in the department. Eventually Dr. Rachel begins to attend student parties, takes students with her to national conferences, and attends basketball games with them. Through these activities Dr. Rachel hears gossip about faculty and students. Occasionally, when she has too much to drink, she reveals her thoughts and feelings about students and faculty.

Given that Dr. Rachel must evaluate these students and carry on a professional relationship with her colleagues, what ethical considerations does she face in this situation?

Recognition of the Problem. _____

_____

_____

_____

_____

Specifying and Weighing the Ethical Principles.

Beneficence	1	2	3	4	5
	Not Important	Somewhat Important	Important	Very Important	Absolutely Important

Nonmaleficence	1	2	3	4	5
	Not Important	Somewhat Important	Important	Very Important	Absolutely Important

Autonomy	1	2	3	4	5
	Not Important	Somewhat Important	Important	Very Important	Absolutely Important

Justice	1	2	3	4	5
	Not Important	Somewhat Important	Important	Very Important	Absolutely Important

Fidelity	1	2	3	4	5
	Not Important	Somewhat Important	Important	Very Important	Absolutely Important

My Decision. _____

_____

_____

_____

_____

Research Situation. Exercise 3.6

The Dilemma. Susan Straight has worked hard for her educational goals. She comes from a poverty-stricken family, and from the time she has been legally able to work, she has done so. She attended college on an academic scholarship.

Upon graduation, Susan applies to graduate school. She knows she can attend the program only if she can get a graduate assistantship. Dr. Ready, aware of Susan's talent, offers her a graduate assistantship, telling Susan that she will need to be as meticulous as ever to make sure that his research results are in line with his previous work. Susan has heard that some of Dr. Ready's former graduate assistants were relieved of their duties when they produced results that were not in line with his previous work. She also knows that some of his assistants have adjusted research data to ensure the results meet Dr. Ready's approval.

Susan knows she can contribute a great deal to the profession of psychology if she receives her graduate degree. Should Susan take the job?

Recognition of the Problem._____

_____

_____

_____

_____

Specifying and Weighing the Ethical Principles.

Beneficence	1	2	3	4	5
	Not Important	Somewhat Important	Important	Very Important	Absolutely Important

Nonmaleficence	1	2	3	4	5
	Not Important	Somewhat Important	Important	Very Important	Absolutely Important

Autonomy	1	2	3	4	5
	Not Important	Somewhat Important	Important	Very Important	Absolutely Important

Justice	1	2	3	4	5
	Not Important	Somewhat Important	Important	Very Important	Absolutely Important

Fidelity	1	2	3	4	5
	Not Important	Somewhat Important	Important	Very Important	Absolutely Important

My Decision. _____

_____

_____

_____

_____

Research Situation. Exercise 3.7

The Dilemma.   Dr. Green has spent years trying to perfect a treatment for depression in adolescents. Her treatment consists of psychodynamic therapy. Dr. Green is sure that her therapy has helped the adolescents with whom she has worked. In order to prove her theory, she wants to institute a research experiment in the clinic in which she works. Dr. Green wants to provide her treatment to a randomly selected group of patients, provide a placebo treatment to another randomly selected group of patients, and place a final randomly selected group in a control group. Keep in mind that patients seek treatment thinking they will receive help for their problems. Is it ethical to deceive those in the placebo group who believe they are getting one treatment but are receiving another?

Recognition of the Problem. _____

_____

_____

_____

_____

Specifying and Weighing the Ethical Principles.

Beneficence	1	2	3	4	5
	Not Important	Somewhat Important	Important	Very Important	Absolutely Important

Nonmaleficence	1	2	3	4	5
	Not Important	Somewhat Important	Important	Very Important	Absolutely Important

Autonomy	1	2	3	4	5
	Not Important	Somewhat Important	Important	Very Important	Absolutely Important

Justice	1	2	3	4	5
	Not Important	Somewhat Important	Important	Very Important	Absolutely Important

Fidelity	1	2	3	4	5
	Not Important	Somewhat Important	Important	Very Important	Absolutely Important

My Decision. _____

_____

_____

_____

_____

Research Situation. Exercise 3.8

The Dilemma. Randy is a doctoral student who is conducting research on adolescent suicide. He has acquired three scales that have been proven to identify students who are at-risk for suicide. Studies have shown that school districts which have administered these scales to their students and given counseling to identified at-risk students have had significantly lower suicide rates than school districts nationwide. Randy wants to replicate these studies in school district X.

School officials at school district X review Randy's proposal and decide that he can administer the scales and compare the number of identified at-risk students to the national norm. However, he cannot make public the names of any students, nor will any counseling be permitted. School officials feel that, although the reliability and validity of the scales are more than adequate, those students identified as at-risk should not be stigmatized by the label. They feel that singling out students on the basis of the scales alone would be unethical and could provoke negative reactions in the community. Should Randy conduct the research given these conditions?

Recognition of the Problem._____

_____

_____

_____

_____

Specifying and Weighing the Ethical Principles.

Beneficence	1	2	3	4	5
	Not Important	Somewhat Important	Important	Very Important	Absolutely Important

Nonmaleficence	1	2	3	4	5
	Not Important	Somewhat Important	Important	Very Important	Absolutely Important

Autonomy	1	2	3	4	5
	Not Important	Somewhat Important	Important	Very Important	Absolutely Important

Justice	1	2	3	4	5
	Not Important	Somewhat Important	Important	Very Important	Absolutely Important

Fidelity	1	2	3	4	5
	Not Important	Somewhat Important	Important	Very Important	Absolutely Important

My Decision. _____

_____

_____

_____

Research Situation. Exercise 3.9

The Dilemma. Dr. Lookout is a psychologist who has a government grant to study high blood pressure. He advertises in the newspaper for people who want to share their opinions on the death penalty. Through an initial interview and screening process, Dr. Lookout selects participants who are vehemently against the death penalty. When they come for their second interviews he tells participants he will study their voice modulation as they talk to an interviewer about the death penalty. He attaches a small wire to each person's arm which measures blood pressure.

During the second session a trained interviewer talks with the participants, using techniques designed to be provoking, belittling, and disdainful of the participants' views. Some participants storm out of the interviews before they are completed. Afterward, Dr. Lookout and his staff explain the purpose of the experiment to the participants who completed the interviews. Is this research ethical?

Recognition of the Problem._____

_____

_____

_____

_____

Specifying and Weighing the Ethical Principles.

Beneficence	1	2	3	4	5
	Not Important	Somewhat Important	Important	Very Important	Absolutely Important

Nonmaleficence	1	2	3	4	5
	Not Important	Somewhat Important	Important	Very Important	Absolutely Important

Autonomy	1	2	3	4	5
	Not Important	Somewhat Important	Important	Very Important	Absolutely Important

Justice	1	2	3	4	5
	Not Important	Somewhat Important	Important	Very Important	Absolutely Important

Fidelity	1	2	3	4	5
	Not Important	Somewhat Important	Important	Very Important	Absolutely Important

My Decision. _____

_____

_____

_____

_____

ETHICAL VIRTUES

A virtue is a quality that is socially or morally valued. As such, virtues involve more than just actions; they are ideals and moral habits embedded in the traditions and practices of a culture. Using these ideals to guide one's life develops character. The ideals may be different in different cultures. Virtue ethics focus on the *actor* not the act.

Moral virtue denotes the qualities of a person that are perceived as worthy of merit in the context of issues related to ideal conduct. For instance, *integrity* describes a character trait that has a certain quality of inner strength. *Public spiritedness* could be described as a virtue that expects one to do good for the community. Some of the more salient virtues found in the literature are integrity, discretion, prudence, respectfulness, benevolence, hope, humility, perseverance, and courage.

Virtue and Culture

Virtues are meritorious qualities that are specific to communities and cultures. They constitute the expectations of behavior in a community that has a shared set of purposes and assumptions. For example, in certain cultures it is expected that women will defer to men. In other cultures, however, this behavior is seen as disrespectful. Edel, Flower, and O'Connor (1994) reported that those who have a Western perspective of morality often are not aware of the clear distinctions they draw between right and wrong. But the view that something is either right or wrong is not the ideal found in North African/Mediterranean cultures. People in these cultures are more interested in preserving the honor of others. Virtues are not always totally relative to culture; views of courage and cowardice, for example, are shared across cultures. Mental health professionals who work with cultures different from those in which they were nurtured should be keenly aware that different cultures may have different hierarchies of values.

Virtue and Ideals

Proponents of virtue ethics believe that mental health professionals should do more than simply learn rules and regulations. They assert that counselors should also be dedicated to cultivating traits and dispositions that motivate them to excellence. The therapist who is motivated to do what is right because it is right—not simply out of fear of reprisal—is a virtuous therapist. Aspiration to the moral ideal is inextricably linked to the aspiration for ideal moral action.

According to this view, the pursuit of ideals must be important for the mental health professional. The therapist has an imperative to approximate the ideal with respect to these virtues (Jordan & Meara, 1990). Proponents of virtue ethics believe that focusing only on principle ethics has severe limitations. As Jordan and Meara (1990) noted, "Case studies risk becoming primarily abstract thought puzzles to be analyzed according to specialized rules. Other critical psychological dimensions, such as human pain, pathos and historical particularity, tend to be underestimated or forgotten" (p. 108). Perhaps the recent emphasis on the formal and abstract dimensions of ethical problem solving, to the exclusion of other dimensions, is what prompted the following criticisms of the current code of ethics by the American Psychological Association (APA):

> The current APA code (1995), which was the result of a massive, careful consultative effort, has been sharply criticized for a number of problems, including being "too lawyerly," ... not being as sensitive to minority issues as former codes, ... being more concerned about the profession than the public, ... and having mediocre expectations for teaching psychologists. (Meara, Schmidt, & Day, 1996, p. 5)

Virtue and Skill

Hauerwas (1981) described virtues as "specific skills required to live faithfully to a traditional understanding of the moral product in which its adherents participate" (p. 115). Jordan and Meara (1990) demonstrated how the virtues of prudence and discretion translate into skills that help the mental health professional in his or her therapeutic endeavors:

> In the psychotherapeutic context, prudence enables the professional to hear the client's history, current life situation, and future hopes, but he or she does this with cautious attentiveness to the client's natural and subtle but self-serving distortions of memory, identity, and expectation. Discretion enables the therapist to make genuine responses to these distortions. In addition, prudence and discretion encourage an alert realization that the psychotherapeutic interaction is in part always open-ended and unpredictable. (p. 112)

Another example of virtue helping to develop demonstrative skills can be shown in a counselor's responsibility for informed consent. While much attention has been given to *what* should be disclosed to a client so as to properly obtain informed consent, little attention is paid to *how* the client should be informed. How the client is informed, and how he or she is treated, are as important as the information involved (May, cited in Jordan & Meara, 1990).

Limitation of Virtue Ethics

Bersoff (1996) questioned whether decisions actually are made by virtue ethics:

> The difference between virtue and principle is not clear to my mind. What shall I do? and Who shall I be? are not competing questions. The answers to both are inextricably woven. Who I am is determined by what I do.
>
> Character traits, although potentially malleable, are developed as a result of genetics. Not even years of professional training, in which students are sensitized to ethics, will necessarily produce a virtuous agent able to employ virtuous ideals. Intensive therapy over many years often fails to accomplish this goal. Secondly, if acting ethically depends on one's character, I wonder if the outcomes of professional training will be too individualized and idiosyncratic. An ethical code and ethical conduct, I would assert, rely on consensual decision making about the integrity of the profession, not the singular vagaries of a psychologist's character. (pp. 88–89)

Kitchener (1996) wondered how character traits differ from the more common construct of personality traits. She asserted that psychologists need a better understanding of what character traits are and how they relate to psychological constructs already understood before educators begin to develop them.

Summary

Proponents of virtue ethics believe that ethical training for mental health professionals should include virtue ethics. They assert that mental health professionals should learn traits of character or qualities that approach the ideal way of being with a client. Such training emphasizes the question, "How shall I be?" In contrast, ethical principle proponents emphasize the question, "How should I behave?" The controversy over virtue ethics includes three basic questions:

1. What exactly are they?

2. How are they different from principles?

3. Can they be taught?

LEARNING FACILITATION AND FOCUS

The Virtuous Therapist Preference Scale

Proponents of virtue ethics believe that mental health professionals can develop character traits, and that these traits can be translated into demonstrative skills that exemplify the ideal way to be and behave with a client. To this end, we have developed *The Virtue Ethics Preference Scale.*

How to Use the Scale.

1. Read the client statement that follows the identified client type.

2. Respond to the client using the selected counseling technique.

3. Explain how you would be and behave cognitively, nonverbally, and emotionally. Also, describe your voice tone.

4. Explain how you think the ideal mental health professional would be and behave in the same situation.

5. Before you start, read the example given for the first client statement.

Exercise 3.10. Angry Husband

Client statement: "I don't care what anybody says. If I'm the one who provides the income in my house, my wife will vote the way I do. I know what will keep the economy on track."

Selected counseling technique: *Confrontation*—defined as pointing out inconsistencies, labeling irrational thinking, and questioning self-defeating behaviors.

Therapist response: "Look here, you are equating economics with your wife's right to think for herself. That's like mixing apples and oranges. Do you really want your wife to be a "Stepford Wife" or one who has a vitality she can bring to your relationship?"

How I Would Be and Behave

Cognitively: I would be wondering if the technique had value.

Nonverbally: My hands would be shaking a little bit. I may be sweating. In confrontations, sometimes my lower lip trembles.

Emotionally: I would be a basket case. Not so much because of the confrontation but because of what this client reminds me of—men who like to pull rank on women. I really have to work on this issue.

Voice tone: My voice would be low and subdued.

How the Ideal Therapist Would Be and Behave

Cognitively: I think the ideal therapist would be assertive. I also believe he or she should have an accepted rationale for this technique. The rationale should have empirical proof of its effectiveness.

Nonverbally: I think the ideal therapist would be sitting up straight and making direct eye contact with the client. Have eye-to-eye contact with the client.

Emotionally: The therapist should be calm and be in control of his or her emotions. Certainly anger should not accompany this technique.

Voice Tone: The therapist voice should be even-keeled. The therapist should use an authoritative tone.

Exercise 3.11. Child Client

Client statement: John is a 7-year-old boy you have seen three times in play therapy. In the fourth session, John says, "I think your rules are terrible. I don't want to follow them!" John takes his playdough, pulls it into shreds, and throws it on the floor. You have already established that this behavior is against the rules.

Selected counseling technique: *Confrontation*—defined as pointing out inconsistencies, labeling irrational thinking, and questioning self-defeating behaviors.

Therapist response: _____

_____

_____

_____

How I Would Be and Behave

Cognitively:_____

_____

Nonverbally:_____

_____

_____

Emotionally: _____

_____

_____

Voice tone:_____

_____

How the Ideal Therapist Would Be and Behave

Cognitively:_____

_____

Nonverbally:_____

_____

_____

Emotionally: _____

_____

_____

Voice tone:_____

_____

Exercise 3.12. Geriatric Client

Client statement: "Yes, I know you told me of your expectation that I follow a proper diet and do my exercises. But, let me tell you, as long as my daughter sends me these sweets, I'm going to eat them. And, quite frankly, I didn't exercise when I was young and I'm not going to exercise when I'm old."

Selected counseling technique: *Confrontation*—defined as pointing out inconsistencies, labeling irrational thinking, and questioning self-defeating behaviors.

Therapist response: _____

_____

_____

_____

How I Would Be and Behave

Cognitively:_____

_____

Nonverbally:_____

_____

_____

Emotionally:_____

_____

_____

Voice tone:_____

_____

How the Ideal Therapist Would Be and Behave

Cognitively:_____

_____

Nonverbally:_____

_____

_____

Emotionally:_____

_____

_____

Voice tone:_____

_____

Exercise 3.13. Acting-Out Adolescent

Client statement: "Last night I had five beers. After that I picked up Mary and went for a drive. She made me mad, so I just put the pedal to the metal. I had that sucker up to 105 miles an hour. That sure ticked her off. I told her I figured we were even."

Selected counseling technique: *Confrontation*—defined as pointing out inconsistencies, labeling irrational thinking, and questioning self-defeating behaviors.

Therapist response:_____

_____

_____

_____

How I Would Be and Behave

Cognitively:_____

_____

Nonverbally:_____

_____

_____

Emotionally:_____

_____

_____

Voice tone:_____

_____

How the Ideal Therapist Would Be and Behave

Cognitively:_____

_____

Nonverbally:_____

_____

_____

Emotionally:_____

_____

_____

Voice tone:_____

_____

Exercise 3.14. Adolescent Female

Client statement: "I don't know. I thought about it for a long time—I mean, telling him I didn't like it when he talked like that. So I told him. He got up and stomped out of the house. After he left I felt like I don't know him, even though I've known him for a long time. I didn't eat that night I felt so down, you know."

Selected counseling technique: *Empathy*—defined as accurately reflecting what the client is thinking and feeling.

Therapist response: *(Sample)* "Let's see. You became assertive and he stomped out of the room. Then I guess, you didn't feel assertive anymore. Sounds like you got sad or depressed."

Therapist response: _____

_____

_____

_____

How I Would Be and Behave

Cognitively: _____

_____

Nonverbally: _____

_____

_____

Emotionally: _____

_____

_____

Voice tone: _____

_____

How the Ideal Therapist Would Be and Behave

Cognitively: _____

_____

Nonverbally: _____

_____

_____

Emotionally: _____

_____

_____

Voice tone: _____

_____

Exercise 3.15. Adolescent Boy

Client statement: "She kept it up. That's my mother, you know. She just kept it up. 'You will never amount to anything. You're lazy and you don't care about anybody but yourself.' Someday I'm going to hit her when she starts that stuff."

Selected counseling technique: *Empathy*—defined as accurately reflecting what the client is thinking and feeling.

Therapist response: _____

_____

_____

_____

How I Would Be and Behave

Cognitively: _____

_____

Nonverbally: _____

_____

_____

Emotionally: _____

_____

_____

Voice tone: _____

_____

How the Ideal Therapist Would Be and Behave

Cognitively: _____

_____

Nonverbally: _____

_____

_____

Emotionally: _____

_____

_____

Voice tone: _____

_____

Exercise 3.16. Divorced Woman

Client statement: "Yea, yea. I know she's right. I really shouldn't be dating him. He's really a first-class bum. But, I don't know, at times, he can just say and do the nicest things."

Selected counseling technique: *Empathy*—defined as accurately reflecting what the client is feeling and thinking.

Therapist response: _____

_____

_____

_____

How I Would Be and Behave

Cognitively:_____

_____

Nonverbally:_____

_____

_____

Emotionally: _____

_____

_____

Voice tone:_____

_____

How the Ideal Therapist Would Be and Behave

Cognitively:_____

_____

Nonverbally:_____

_____

_____

Emotionally: _____

_____

_____

Voice tone: _____

_____

Exercise 3.17. Geriatric Male

Client statement: "I went to the movies last night. All of a sudden, I felt very vulnerable."

Selected counseling technique: *Clarification*—defined as obtaining more details about a client's statement.

Therapist response: *(Sample)* "Can you be more specific as to what was making you feel that way?"

Therapist response: _____

_____

_____

_____

How I Would Be and Behave

Cognitively: _____

_____

Nonverbally: _____

_____

_____

Emotionally: _____

_____

_____

Voice tone: _____

_____

How the Ideal Therapist Would Be and Behave

Cognitively: _____

_____

Nonverbally: _____

_____

_____

Emotionally: _____

_____

_____

Voice tone: _____

_____

Exercise 3.18. Potentially Violent Client

Client statement: "You know, I meant to tell you. Well, it has happened before. I didn't mean to do it. If someone keeps pushing me like that, someone may get more than they bargained for."

Selected counseling technique: *Clarification*—defined as obtaining more details about a client's statement.

Therapist response: _____

_____

_____

_____

How I Would Be and Behave

Cognitively: _____

_____

Nonverbally: _____

_____

_____

Emotionally: _____

_____

Voice tone: _____

_____

How the Ideal Therapist Would Be and Behave

Cognitively: _____

_____

Nonverbally: _____

_____

_____

Emotionally: _____

_____

_____

Voice tone: _____

_____

Exercise 3.19. Potentially Suicidal Client

Client statement: "Sometime when it gets this bad I don't know what to do. I mean, I really get down. Everything seems so futile. I think, 'What's the use?'"

Selected counseling technique: *Clarification*—defined as obtaining more details about a client's statement.

Therapist response: _____

_____

_____

_____

How I Would Be and Behave

Cognitively: _____

_____

Nonverbally: _____

_____

_____

Emotionally: _____

_____

_____

Voice tone: _____

_____

How the Ideal Therapist Would Be and Behave

Cognitively: _____

_____

Nonverbally: _____

_____

_____

Emotionally: _____

_____

_____

Voice tone: _____

_____

Chapter 4

IN A LEGAL CONTEXT

In chapter 3, we discussed the idea that understanding virtue ethics and ethical principles is a major and necessary responsibility for the mental health professional. The therapist's relationship, in its essence, demands ethical responsibility. The trust invested in the helping professional by clients demands that he or she observe the highest moral and ethical standards. Because ethical violations often are legal violations, we will examine ethical standards in this chapter as well.

LEGAL TERMINOLOGY AND LAWS

American cinema offers a classic depiction of the advent of justice from the American frontier. Two gunfighters square off in the street. Before they draw, the bad guy snarls, "Your days are over." To which the good guy responds, "The difference between you and me is, I know it." In short the good guy knows that the days for settling disputes by violence are coming to an end—that disputes can only be settled by law. Through the years societies have learned that consistency, predictability, and fairness are harbingers of "life, liberty, and the pursuit of happiness"; without them, life is chaotic.

The law, as arbitrated through the court system, is society's attempt to ensure predictability, consistency, and fairness. Its purpose is to offer an alternative to private action in settling disputes. As Swenson (1997) noted,

> The question is not whether mental health professionals will interact
> with laws and legal professionals; it is *how* they will interact both
> now and in the future in which intercessions by legal professionals
> into mental health practice become even more intrusive. (p. 32)

Therefore, it is imperative that mental health professionals understand the legal system.

The Law

The law should be viewed as dynamic, not as static. It is not an entity that rigidly adheres to historically derived rules, but neither does it deny their relevance to current disputes. Legal principles derive from social interactions. At the same time, the law places a great deal of importance on precedence. Many laws are based on *natural law*—that is, law promulgated by prominent philosophers as an expression of man's innate moral sense. Natural law is considered absolute and unconditional. Courts usually accept prior judicial decisions as truths when they fit or appear to fit natural law (Horowitz & Willging, 1984).

As enforced through the legal system, the law can be seen as an instrument of concern by the state for the social well-being of the people. Its primary concerns are predictability, stability, and fairness; at the same time, the system must be sensitive to expansion and readaptation. Laws are a consensus of rules to be followed in a civilized society.

Classifications of the Law

Laws are classified as constitutional, statutes passed by legislatures, regulations, and case laws.

- *Constitutional laws* are those found in state constitutions and in the United States Constitution.

- *Statutory laws* are those written by legislatures.

- Statutory laws may have enabling clauses that permit administrators to write *regulations* to clarify them. Once written, these regulations become laws.

- Finally, decisions by appeals courts create *case laws* for the people who reside in their jurisdictions. If a legal problem manifests itself, and parties differ on how to solve it, they may go to a *trial court*. The decision made in the trial court is not published and does not become law. However, if lawyers do not believe the trial court (the lower court) interpreted the law correctly they may appeal to an *appeals court* (a higher court). The function of the appeals court is to determine whether the trial court applied the law correctly. The members of the appeals court publish the decision, and the majority decision becomes the law for that jurisdiction. The appeals court is said to have set a precedent for that jurisdiction.

Types of Laws

Laws are enacted to settle disputes that occur in society. They arise out of social interactions as members of society develop values that are necessary to the maintenance of order and justice. They come into being based on the common thoughts and experiences of people. They are antecedents to judgments regarding right and wrong.

The person who claims to have been wronged is called the *plaintiff;* the person accused of committing the wrong is the *defendant.* The dispute is known as a *lawsuit.*

Functionally, we can define three types of law: civil law, criminal law, and mental health law (Swenson, 1997).

1. *Civil law* is applicable, for the most part, to disputes between or among people. Losing the lawsuit usually means losing money. If a person fails to obey the stipulations made as a analogue to a civil lawsuit, he or she may be subject to a criminal charge called *contempt of court.* An example would be a mother or father who does not pay child support.

2. *Criminal law* is applicable to disputes between the state and people. Losing defendants often face a loss of liberty. The standard of proof is higher in a criminal case than in a civil case.

3. *Mental health law* regulates how the state may act regarding people with mental illnesses. These laws enact a permission from the state to protect people from serious harm to themselves or others. They allow the state to act as a guardian for those with mental disorders, and to institutionalize them if necessary. Most experts believe mental health law is part of civil law.

Steps in a Lawsuit

A lawsuit proceeds through standard steps. Each step has serious legal consequences and rules that must be followed. It is important to remember that most lawsuits do not go to trial; instead, they are settled at an earlier stage.

First, the plaintiff files a complaint through a lawyer to a court in the appropriate jurisdiction. *Jurisdiction* is determined by geographical and substantive factors. Filing this complaint initiates the legal proceeding.

Once the complaint is filed, the plaintiff must make a judicial effort to inform the defendant of his or her intentions (legal notice). This preceding is called *due process*. The reason for this procedure is to allow the defendant to rebut the accusation.

Once valid due process is accomplished, a *discovery process* is in order. At this point the lawyers involved investigate the facts of the case.

In order to obtain the facts, the lawyers may use a subpoena. The *subpoena* demands access to the facts and to the presence of witnesses at court hearings. Based on this information, the two sides may settle the dispute, or they may proceed to litigation.

If the attorneys and clients decide to proceed with the lawsuit, the next step is to have *pretrial hearings*. At this step the judge determines how the laws apply to the facts. The lawsuit may be settled at this point. "The general policy of most courts is to promote settlements and, in fact, disputants settle about 90% of all cases" (Swenson, 1997, p. 46).

In the trial phase, each side presents evidence and attempts to discredit the evidence of the opponent.

Ultimately the lawsuit is decided by a judge or jury. If either party is dissatisfied with the verdict, he or she may claim that the law was not correctly applied and appeal to a higher court (Swenson, 1997).

THE SPECIAL RELATIONSHIP

In this section we will outline the rationales that define the legal responsibilities of professional mental health workers.

Initially, in Anglo-American law injuries were considered to have occurred when someone inflicted harm on another. This situation is called *misfeasance*. Injuries occurring from nonaction (*nonfeasance*) did not entertain legal remedy. Eventually the concept of no penalties for nonfeasance eroded, and those who were in public callings could be held liable for nonfeasance. The courts now hold that anyone who voluntarily assumes responsibility for another is in a *special relationship* with that person. Furthermore, people in special relationships have a duty to care for those for whom they have assumed some responsibility.

Innocent people often get hurt when a certain duty of care is not maintained. Consequently, if one who has a duty to care does something he or she should not do, or does not do something he or she should do, as it pertains to the relationship, that person has breached the duty to care. In short, such persons have been negligent in their responsibilities. Typically this duty is described as the care that an ordinary or average person would exercise under similar circumstances.

Mental health professions are like other members of society. However, because they are professionals and have received more training and education than the average person, and because they typically are governed by licensure or certification laws, they must act under terms of a more demanding social contract. Those who deliver psychological services owe a duty to care that is defined more stringently than it is for the average member of society. For mental health professionals who offer their skills and talent to the general public, the legal test for negligence compares their behavior with the behavior of their peers.

Negligence and the Special Relationship

Most malpractice suits brought against mental health professionals are related to issues of negligence. The plaintiff must prove that the defendant behaved in a way that did not meet the standard of care for the profession. If a therapist is deemed to have violated that standard of care, he or she may be held to be negligent. The standard of care can be defined as what the average or prudent mental health professional would have done (or not done) under the same circumstances.

Mental health professionals usually use a standard that is universal to their profession. Thus, because their training is more comprehensive, psychiatrists generally are held to a different (higher) standard of care than counselors. Psychiatrists should know more about physical symptoms than school counselors, who may not be trained in biology. Mental health professionals are not expected to be compared to the most erudite and esoteric members of their profession; rather, they are compared to the average member of their field.

Mental health professionals also may be evaluated by comparison to the standards of their community. The standard of care may be evidenced by reference to germane literature in journals, supervisors, ethical codes, ethical guidelines, ethical standards, peers, case law (within the appropriate jurisdiction), general statutes, licensing boards, and certification boards.

ELEMENTS OF MALPRACTICE

As a legal term, *malpractice* describes complaints in which a professional is accused of negligence within a special relationship. The law of malpractice refers to torts. A *tort* is a wrongful act, injury, or damage (not including a breach of contract) for which a civil action can be brought.

To win a malpractice or tort law claim, the plaintiff must prove the following:

1.   A legal duty of care was owed by the defendant to the plaintiff. A professional (special) relationship was formed between the mental health professional and the client.

2.   There is a standard of care, and the mental health professional breached that duty.

3.   The client suffered harm or injury (demonstrated and established).

4.   The mental health professional's breach of duty was the proximate cause of the harm or injury. Thus, the harm or injury was a reasonably foreseeable consequence of the breach.

When does the special relationship begin? A formal contract is not necessary. The legal theory to establish duty comes from the *theory of contracts*. In the eyes of the law, an implicit act can create a contract (a special relationship). Payment is not necessary to determine the relationship. Ministering to clients admitted to a hospital (voluntarily or involuntarily), making notes on charts, or giving treatment in emergency rooms can be construed as behavioral manifestations of contract creation. In a Utah case in which a mental health professional provided therapy to a postsurgery patient, the state supreme court said that one hour of therapy was enough to create a special relationship (*Farrow v. Health Services Corp., 1979*, cited in Swenson, 1997).

Why Clients Sue

We live in a litigious society. Mental health professionals do therapy with clients who are emotionally distraught. Clinical expertise is needed on the part of the mental health professional (Bednar, Bednar, Lambert, & Waite, 1991). Good relationships with clients reduce the likelihood of lawsuits. Counselors should use their skills in creating positive feelings between themselves and the clients they serve. People do not want to sue someone they like or someone who is acting in their best interests.

Suicide is a factor in 50% of psychiatric malpractice actions (Hirsch & White, 1982). Because blaming and anger are nearly universal reactions by family survivors, the mental health professional is particularly vulnerable. As Swenson (1997) noted, "Between 1974 and 1976, insurance companies received about 1 malpractice claim for every 200 mental health professionals" (p. 167). The parties settled most of these claims out of court, or the courts dismissed them (Schwitzgebel & Schwitzgebel, 1980). Psychiatric litigation accounts for only 3% of medical malpractice suits (Hirsch & White, 1982).

Other Reasons to Sue

Breaking a contract is essentially the same as breaking a promise. If the breach causes damage or injury, the law may provide a monetary remedy. A client who is angry does not have to show negligence on the part of the mental health professional, only that the therapy did not achieve the purpose it was intended to achieve (Schwitzgebel & Schwitzgebel, 1980). Damages typically involve at least the cost of the therapy.

Injury to a person's reputation may occur when derogatory words or written statements are made to a third party about the person. This is called *defamation of character*. *Slander* is spoken defamation; *libel* is written defamation. In a recent unpublished case, a trade school counselor made a public remark to the effect that a student had missed classes because she had a venereal disease contracted while working as a prostitute. In fact, the disease was the result of a rape. Because of stress related to gossip, the girl quit school, went into therapy, and sued the school district. The school settled the case, paying $50,000 in damages for the injury. The school also fired the counselor (Swenson, 1997).

Mental health professionals should be extremely careful about information given in letters of recommendation, notes on educational records, or any other oral comments to students. Communication of an opinion, when it can be said to imply a false and damaging statement, could be judged as slanderous or libelous (*Milkovich v. Lorain*, 1990).

PREPARING FOR THE SPECIAL RELATIONSHIP

Policy Development

Before a mental health professional begins to see clients, he or she should think through and articulate a policy toward various situations that may manifest themselves in counseling relationships. One's attitudes and values concerning advertising, client referral, termination, billing, and record keeping are some examples. Naturally, these policies must conform to the accepted ethical and legal standards. Therefore, if one is not familiar with these standards, one must make the effort to become so. When one is employed in an agency or school, these policies should already be extant. However, the potential for conflict between one's own ethical standards and institutionalized standards is always present.

Advertising and Soliciting Clients

Mental health providers are permitted to market their services. They must, however, be familiar with ethical guidelines, state laws, and Federal Trade Commission regulations. Not long ago it was considered unethical and unprofessional to advertise. Advertising today is accepted as long as it meets legal and ethical guidelines. Claims of therapy effectiveness and misrepresentation of professional status or qualifications should not be made in advertising (Schwitzgebel & Schwitzgebel, 1980). Statements made to the public about services must not mislead or give the wrong impression (Hass & Malouf, 1989). The following are examples of statements regarding advertising as manifested in ethical codes:

> Psychologists do not make public statements that are false, deceptive, misleading, or fraudulent, either because of what they state, convey, or suggest or because of what they omit, concerning their research practice, or other work activities or those of persons or organizations with which they are affiliated. As examples (and not in limitation) of this standard, psychologists do not make false or deceptive statements concerning (1) their training, experience, or competence; (2) their academic degrees; (3) their credentials; (4) their institutional or association affiliations; (5) their services; (6) the scientific or clinical basis for, or results or degree of success of, their services; (7) their fees; or (8) their publication or research findings. (APA, 1995, 3, 303)

* * * *

There are no restrictions on advertising by counselors except those that can be specifically justified to protect the public from deceptive practices. Counselors advertise or represent their services to the public by identifying their credentials in an accurate manner that is not false, misleading, deceptive, or fraudulent. Counselors may only advertise the highest degree earned which is in counseling or a closely related field from a college or university that was accredited by one of the recognized accrediting bodies. (ACA, 1995, C,3,a)

* * * *

Marriage and family therapists assure that advertisements and publications in any media (such as directories, announcements, business cards, newspapers, radio, television , and facsimiles) convey information that is necessary for the public to make an appropriate selection of professional services. Information could include: (a) office information, such as name, address, telephone number, credit card acceptability, fees, languages spoken, and office hours; (b) appropriate degrees, state licensure and/or certification, and AAMFT Clinical Member status; and (c) description of practice. (American Association for Marriage and Family Therapy, 1991, 2)

* * * *

Social workers should ensure that their representations to clients, agencies, and the public of professional qualifications, credentials, education, competence, affiliations, services provided, or results to be achieved are accurate. Social workers should claim only those relevant professional credentials they actually possess and take steps to correct any inaccuracies or misrepresentations of their credentials by others. (National Association of Social Workers, 1997, 4.06,c)

An Unethical Advertisement

Overweight, depressed, not satisfied with your job? Come on down for therapy. Guaranteed results in 10 weeks. Call 412-555-1212. Ask for Tracey.

An Ethical Advertisement

Psychological Services. Ph.D. in counseling psychology from Butler University. Specializing in Cognitive Therapy, fluent in Spanish. Call 412-555-1212.

Client Referral

A therapist may have a legitimate reason for terminating a client's therapy. It is not unusual for a professional to make a valid conclusion that he or she is not helping a client and refer that client to another professional. Mental health professionals must be careful that the referral is made not only in the best interest of the client but also with concern for lawsuit exposure. Once a contract is formed, the therapist has an ethical and legal duty not to abandon the client. Breach of contract suits are not as prevalent as negligence suits, but sometimes the mental health professional is sued for both. Mental health professionals are legally obligated to do more than simply tell a client to call a public agency if a referral is not found.

> Social workers should take reasonable steps to avoid abandoning clients who are still in need of services. Social workers should withdraw services precipitously only under unusual circumstances, giving careful consideration to all factors in the situation and taking care to minimize possible adverse effects. Social workers should assist in making appropriate arrangements for continuation of services when necessary. (National Association of Social Workers, 1997, 1.16,b)

* * * *

> Prior to termination for whatever reason, except where precluded by the patient's or client's conduct, the psychologist discusses the patient's or client's views and needs, provides appropriate pretermination counseling, suggests alternative service providers as appropriate, and takes other reasonable steps to facilitate transfer of responsibility to another provider if the patient or client needs one immediately. (APA, 1995. 4.09,c)

* * * *

> Counselors do not abandon or neglect clients in counseling. Counselors assist in making appropriate arrangements for the continuation of treatment, when necessary, during interruptions such as vacations, and following termination. (American Counseling Association, 1995, A.11,a)

Fees for Counseling

Therapists must make sure their clients have the ability to pay for services and understand the laws governing billing and bill collection in their states and localities. Above all, they must not engage in fee splitting. *Fee splitting* is an arrangement whereby "part of a sum for a product or service is returned or paid out because of a prearranged agreement or coercion" (Keith-Spiegel & Koocher, 1985, pp. 158–159). Fee splitting is unethical because, in effect, it implies that financial considerations are more important to the management of the case than is the welfare of the client (Keith-Spiegel & Koocher, 1985). It is wise to request prompt payment from clients and not allow bills to accumulate. It is important that therapists can justify why they charge or do not charge a particular fee. If they are receiving third-party payments from an insurance company, they must know their contractual obligations regarding these payments.

Being sued is a traumatic experience and can have serious professional and financial consequences. In one case, a therapist's conscious disregard for an insurance company's rules about copayments gave the company relief from making any copayments and awarded it punitive damages as well (*Weisman v. Blue Shield of California*, 1985). A counselor cannot legally waive the collection of copayments in order to keep a client in therapy. Also, mental health professionals who see clients on a *pro bono* basis should realize that the same practice guidelines apply to the treatment of paying and nonpaying clients. Complete and accurate records should be maintained for both. Below are some examples of fee guidelines for mental health professionals:

> Counselors clearly explain to clients, prior to entering the counseling relationship, all financial arrangements related to professional services, including the use of collection agencies or legal measures for nonpayment. In establishing fees for professional counseling services, counselors consider the financial status of clients and locality. In the event that the established fee structure is inappropriate for a client, assistance is provided in attempting to find comparable services of acceptable cost. (American Counseling Association, 1995. A1.0,a,b)

* * * *

> As early as is feasible in a professional or scientific relationship, the psychologist and the patient, client, or other appropriate recipient of psychological services reach an agreement specifying the compensation and the billing arrangements.

> Psychologists do not exploit recipients of services or payers with respect to fees.

> Psychologists' fee practices are consistent with the law.

> Psychologists do not misrepresent their fees. (APA, 1995. 1.25.a, b, c, d)

Dual Relationships

Mental health professionals play many roles in society, including therapist, friend, neighbor, and business associate. It is improbable that a mental
health professional could matriculate through psychological practice without
some dual relationships. Overlapping relationships are nearly inevitable in small
communities. A dual relationship occurs whenever a therapist interacts with a
client in more than one capacity: for example, as a therapist *and* a business
partner, teacher *and* investor. Any dual relationships that could interfere with
the autonomy of the client or the objectivity of the counselor should be avoided.
Therapists are considered to be in a professional service by the very structure
of their relationship with their clients (Pope, 1985). Therapy is a contractual
relationship, and the exploitation of the client's trust is unethical and perhaps
illegal. Consider the following example:

> Cohen (plaintiff's attorney) asked, "Is it a commonly acceptable
> practice for a psychiatrist to employ a patient after therapy sessions
> for the purpose of typing letters or doing stenographic work?" "No,
> it is not," said Dr. Gaylin. "Can you tell us why?" "That would go
> back to the heart of transference. You have to lean over backward
> not to take advantage of the patient when you have a feeling that he
> is clearly not as free in his judgments as he would be if he weren't a
> patient of yours. So you don't make contracts with them." (Free-
> man & Roy, 1976, pp. 162–163)

Following are some other examples of dual relationships taken from calls
reported to the APA ethics committee and described by Pope. The cases are
fictionalized and names have been changed.

> Ian Shaky, a doctoral student in a clinical psychology program, was
> experiencing serious depression. He asked one of his professors to
> see him privately. The professor agreed. Several weeks later, Shaky
> made a serious suicidal gesture. The professor told the program di-
> rector about it. Shaky was then asked to leave the program until he
> could resolve his problems. Shaky brought ethics charges against
> the professor for violating the confidentiality provisions of the
> therapy relationship. The professor claimed he was not acting un-
> ethically because the student/client was a "clear danger" to himself.
> (Pope, 1985, p. 277)

* * * *

> S. R. Mod, Ph.D., agreed to give his best friend's daughter a series
> of behavioral therapy sessions to control her nail-biting. He explained

to her father that some aversive conditioning was involved, but the father's enthusiasm remained undaunted. When the girl complained about the procedures, the father stormed over to Dr. Mod's house, demanding to know what was going on. When Mod noted that all of this had been described to him prior to the session, the friend retorted: "Well, I certainly didn't think you would do anything painful to your best friend's daughter. I guess I don't know you that well after all." (Pope, 1985, p. 277)

Sexual intimacy with clients is a dual relationship that is potentially destructive to both parties, yet statistics show that 90% of mental health professionals have been tempted by the possibility at least once (Rutter, 1989). Ethical standards prohibiting sexual activity with clients date as far back as the Hippocratic Oath: "In every house where I come, I will enter only for the good of my patients, keeping myself far from all intentional ill-doing and all seduction, and especially from the pleasures of love with women and men" (Dorland, 1974, p. 715).

Sweeney estimated that 70% of clients who have had sex with a therapist were harmed (cited in Swenson, 1997). Many are depressed and feel powerless to seek a new therapist. In a survey by Borys and Pope (1989), professionals from several mental health fields were questioned: .2% of the women and .9% of the men admitted to sexual contact with clients. There is an ongoing discussion in the field as to whether having a sexual relationship with a client is proper after therapy has been terminated. In the survey by Borys and Pope (1989), 68% of respondents rated sex with former clients unethical. California law requires a 24-month break between therapy and a sexual relationship.

Interrupted Therapy

Mental health professionals can no more control every aspect of their lives than can a nonprofessional. Emergencies occur, batteries go dead, and it may be necessary to change appointments. The mental health professional who is absent from a session may be seen by patients as having abandoned them. Consequently, staff should be trained in appropriate procedures should an emergency arise, and clients should be informed of one's policies relevant to emergencies and other reasons for absence.

Client Records

Naturally, mental health professionals should keep records for each client. Records provide an excellent inventory of information for assisting the mental health professional in managing client cases. They also serve as documentation of a therapist's judgments, type of treatment, recommendations, and treatment outcomes.

Therapists must also keep financial records. These are necessary to obtain third-party reimbursement for the counselor or the client. The content of records may be defined by agency policy, state licensing laws, statutory laws, or regulation laws. Records may be read in open court, and derogatory comments about clients should never be included.

In most jurisdictions, the paper belongs to the agency, but the information on the paper belongs to the client. Clients can request copies of their records. Some jurisdictions limit access to records if such access would be harmful to a client's mental health.

The evolving standard of practice is to keep records for seven years, although some suggest they should be kept forever. The appropriate regulatory agencies in one's jurisdiction should be consulted regarding record retention and disposition. Below are some types of information that should be kept in client records:

1. Basic identifying information, such as the client's name, address, telephone number; also, if the client is a minor, the names of parents or legal guardians

2. Signed informed consent for treatment

3. History of the client, both medical and psychiatric, if relevant

4. Dates and types of services offered

5. Signature and title of the person who rendered the therapy

6. A description of the presenting problem

7. A description of assessment techniques and results

8. Progress notes for each date of service documenting the implementation of the treatment plan and changes in the treatment plan

9. Documentation of sensitive or dangerous issues, alternatives considered, and actions taken

10. A treatment plan with explicit goals

11. Consultations with other professionals, consultations with people in the client's life, clinical supervision received, and peer consultation

12. Release of confidential information forms signed by the client

13. Fees assessed and collected

Computers

Data on clients can be stored in word processors and database program files. In addition, the computer can be used to store information on grants, payroll accounts, fiscal planning, payments, and preparation of research. With macros and style sheets, computer programs can reduce the need for reentry of information and make updating a client's files much faster and easier. Computer technology provides increased convenience for mental health professionals, but also commands new responsibilities, knowledge, and accountability.

The use of computers also allows the mental health professional to access diagnostic categories and to offer computerized versions of various personality tests. Professionals who use these new electronic programs must be careful not to violate federal or state copyright laws that police the use of software. "A conviction for violating a computer crime statute may result in a fine, imprisonment, or both" (Atcherson, 1993, p. 36). Atcherson listed the following behaviors that may be considered illegal:

1. Unauthorized access to or alterations of electronic communication

2. Unauthorized use of or access to computer resources or information

3. Unauthorized disclosure of computer-based information obtained by wiretapping, eavesdropping, or browsing through personnel data

4. Unauthorized modification or destruction of computer resources (hardware, software, or data)

5. Theft of storage media or printouts

6. User misuse, such as unauthorized copying of software or use of computer resources in committing a misdemeanor or felony

7. Misuse of local communication links or other communication links

8. Intentional spread of computer viruses

Mental health professionals who use computers are held ethically responsible for making sure the information their clients receive is accurate. Psychological tests administered by computer programs must be treated like any other tests. They should not be used by untrained personnel. Also, data entries must be made carefully so inaccurate results do not result. Ethical codes also stress the responsibility of mental health professionals in their use of computers:

> Counselors are responsible for the appropriate application, scoring, interpretation, and use of assessment instruments, whether they score and interpret such tests themselves or use computerized or other services. (American Counseling Association, 1995, E,2,b)

> Psychologists select scoring and interpretation services (including automated services) on the basis of evidence of the validity of the program and procedures as well as on other appropriate consideration (American Counseling Association, 1995, E,2,b).

> Psychologists retain appropriate responsibility for the appropriate application, interpretation, and use of assessment instrument, whether they score and interpret such tests themselves or use automated or other services (American Counseling Association, 1995, E,2).

* * * *

> Certified counselors must ensure that computer-generated test administration and scoring programs function properly, thereby providing clients with accurate test results. (National Board for Certified Counselors, 1997, C,12)

Liability Insurance

All mental health professionals should purchase liability insurance before they begin practice.

> An *occurrence-based policy* covers incidents no matter when the claim is made, as long as the policy was in force during the year of the alleged incident. Thus, if a therapist is accused today of an infraction alleged to have occurred two years ago (when the policy was in effect) he or she is covered even if the policy is not in force at present.

A *claims-made policy* covers only claims made while the policy is in force.

If a counselor previously had a claims-made policy, he or she may purchase *tail-coverage insurance*, which covers him or her if an alleged incident occurring during the period the policy was in effect is reported after the policy has expired.

Avoiding Burnout and Stress

Mental health professionals who cannot function effectively will not be able to meet their ethical, professional, and possibly legal responsibilities. Two important variables contributing to ineffectiveness are stress and burnout. Deutsch (1984) reported three common preconceptions that produce stress for mental health professionals, all of which pertain to doing perfect work with clients:

1. I should always work at my peak level of enthusiasm and competence.

2. I should be able to cope with any client emergency that arises.

3. I should be able to help every client.

Deutsch (1984) also listed client behaviors that are stress-producing:

- suicidal statements
- anger toward the therapist
- severely depressed clients
- apathy or lack of motivation
- client's premature termination

Farber (1983) found similar client behaviors stressful to mental health professionals:

- suicidal statements
- aggression and hostility
- premature termination of therapy
- agitated anxiety
- apathy and depression

Burnout is characterized by physical, emotional, and mental exhaustion and by feelings of physical depletion, helplessness, and hopelessness. Victims of burnout often experience a negative attitude toward themselves, others, and work (Pines & Aronson, 1981). Because they face constant pressures in their work, therapists should develop strategies to cope with potential burnout. They should learn to set limits, to see the humor in situations, and to express negative feelings about their work. In addition, they should cultivate a circle of colleagues with whom they can discuss their concerns and develop activities and interests outside their profession (Corey, Corey, & Callanan, 1988).

IMPLEMENTING THE SPECIAL RELATIONSHIP

Contracting for Therapy

Not long ago, most contracts between mental health professionals and clients were oral. More formalized contracts were seen as alienating to the client. Also, common law principles, under which those agreements were governed, did not require written forms (Bednar et al., 1991). In 1985, only 29% of therapists in private practice reported using written contracts (Handelsman & Galvin, 1988). Numerous lawsuits, based on the absence of informed consent, have since changed that (Bednar et al., 1991). Counselors inform their clients in writing of the relevant facts about therapy. The clients must understand the information and sign any forms voluntarily.

Informed Consent

A written informed consent form is a contract and a promise by the mental health professional to perform the therapy competently. There are three basic legal elements of informed consent.

1. The client must be competent. Competence refers to the legal capacity to give consent. If, because of age or mental ability, a client does not have the capacity to give consent, the therapist should consult another person or a judicial body who can legally assume responsibility for the client.

2. Both the substance of the information regarding therapy and the manner in which it is given are important. The substance of the information should include the relevant facts about therapy. This information should be presented to the client in a manner that is easily understood.

3. The client must volunteer for therapy and must not be coerced or forced to participate.

Some common themes in consent forms that should be explicated prior to therapy include these:

1. The client should be given a description of the services to be provided, including their goals and procedures. This should be done in simple language to inform the client exactly what the mental health professional will attempt to do in the therapy sessions. The client should be appraised as to what, if any, behavior or action will be required of the client, such as homework. Clients also should know how interruptions in therapy will be handled.

2. Any anticipated results—beneficial *and* negative—should be explained. The therapist should state that there is no guarantee of success, but that specific behaviors will be targeted and goals will be set. If more than one type of therapy seems appropriate, the therapist should describe the various types.

3. The therapist should estimate the duration of the therapy and the frequency of appointments.

4. A timetable for review of client progress should be established. The client should be informed that he or she has the right to withdraw from therapy at any time and that no additional costs will result, unless such costs have been previously explicated.

5. The basis for services should be explained to the client. A timely system for collecting fees should be established.

6. The therapist should give a statement regarding confidentiality and privileged communication. (These issues are dealt with in more detail below.)

7. A statement acknowledging the client's informed consent should be signed by the client, parent, or legal guardian.

Release of Information

The essence of a counseling relationship is trust. Mental health professionals must protect the information they receive from clients. They must keep confidential communications secret unless a well-defined exception applies.

Confidential information may be disclosed if the client (or the client's parent or legal representative) agrees and signs a consent form for such a disclosure. A *consent to waiver* does not always have to be in writing, but it is best if it is. The client should be informed of any and all implications of the wavier.

Confidentiality

Therapists should provide an environment in which their clients feel they can communicate honestly about their thoughts, feelings, and behaviors. In order to feel safe in this process, most people want information about their private lives to be kept confidential. Confidentiality is the foundation of effective therapy. Should there be no prior consent or legal mandate, the only disclosure of confidential information that is ethical is that which promotes the welfare of the client. Hass and Malouf (1989) listed some of the situations in which a decision to breach confidentiality may be made:

1. Court subpoena

2. Duty to warn, protect, or report

3. Requests for information from family members

4. Seeing clients in groups

5. When there are problems defining the "client"

6. Sharing information with other staff members within one's agency

7. Personal or professional needs of practicality (consultation, teaching, support) (p. 30)

Privileged Communication

When a competent client presents for therapy, any disclosure he or she makes may be protected from legal disclosure. Such communication is considered privileged. The issue at hand is the conflict between the individual's right to privacy and the need of the public to know certain information. The client is considered the holder of the privilege, and he or she is the only one who can waive that right.

Privileged communication is established by statutory law enacted by legislators. Client communication with a specified group of mental health professionals may be privileged in some states but not in others. Also, statutes may specify a wide range of exceptions to privileged communication. For instance, privileged communication laws are abrogated, in all states, by an initial report of child abuse.

Mental health professionals generally do not have legal grounds for maintaining confidentiality if they are called upon to testify in court, unless they are asked to provide communication protected by privileged communication statutes. Clients should be told whether any information they reveal will be protected by privileged communication laws before therapy begins. In the following examples, the therapist (an intern) implies that the information the client is about to reveal is privileged. The court later ruled it was not. Had the client been informed that his communications were not privileged, he may not have revealed what he did.

> "Can I ask for this to be strictly confidential?" he said. The graduate student replied, "Okay, I can say this much, Reid … whatever … you say here is confidential; and we're real selective about what the courts have access to." [The client then said,] "It's just not [like] myself to be thinking like this, to ah … I think a lot about, ah, rape. … I think a lot about killing somebody." He then added that the impulse to kill someone with a knife was "so strong I wonder sometimes if I wouldn't actually do it, you know, if the situation was ever right. … and then later on I'll feel terrible about it [these feelings]." (Kane & Keeton, 1985, pp. 52–53)

Ten months later Donna Lyn Allen was killed. Reid Hall's fantasies, acquired from the graduate student's tape recording of the session, were read in open court and were described by his lawyer as the most damaging evidence leading to his conviction for murder. The judge ruled that, because the counselor was a graduate student and not a licensed professional, Hall's communications were not covered by privileged communication law. Informed consent forms at the University of Georgia now state that client-therapist privileged communication may not apply to students-in-training (Kane & Keeton, 1985).

Being a Courtroom Witness

Increasingly mental health professionals are called on to testify in court or at depositions. Typical cases involve personal injury, child custody, and child abuse. This exposure provides an opportunity for mental health professionals to expand their social effectiveness and educate the public (Forge & Henderson, 1990). The role of therapists in the courtroom is to educate (Deutsch & Parker, 1985). Their obligation is to present information that is accurate and objective, and to share with the judge or jury the basis of their opinions (Weissman, 1984).

It goes without saying that mental health professionals appearing as witnesses must carefully prepare their testimony before arriving at a deposition or courtroom setting. This preparation allows them to identify the major facts and consider how they will strengthen or damage the case (Dorn, 1984). A *deposition*—a search for legally binding information—normally precedes a courtroom hearing. A deposition is made in the presence of attorneys for both sides, and a written transcript or audiovisual record is produced (Dorn, 1984).

To be considered as an expert witness, one must have education, training, and experience well beyond the norm in dealing with mental health issues. Mental health professionals should not accept employment as expert witnesses unless they are qualified to do so. Academic education, training, and experience directly related to the subject matter of the case should be a prerequisite (Swenson, 1997).

Once in court, expert witnesses may be questioned about their qualifications and about accuracy and credibility issues (Humpreys, 1987). It is important to remember that answers to questions should reflect one's expertise (Weikel, 1986). The opposing side can easily attack any expert who misstates information regarding authoritative tests (Friedman, 1985). It is the opposing attorney's job to discredit the expert witness and weaken his or her testimony. Once on the witness stand, the mental health professional should not be defensive (Swenson, 1997).

Receiving a Subpoena

Therapists may receive a subpoena for any number of reasons. A subpoena can come from a client's attorney, from an attorney representing a spouse or former spouse of a client, or from an attorney representing another party. One must be careful to respond appropriately to a subpoena to ensure legal compliance. For instance, the therapist must know if client-counselor communications are considered privileged. Even if they are protected by privilege law, the law may be abrogated to a duty-to-report statute. Child abuse reporting laws are a good example of this.

When a therapist receives a subpoena regarding a client, he or she should immediately contact the client and the clients' attorney. Once this contact has been made the therapist should petition the client and attorney for guidance to determine how to respond to the subpoena. Implications of the disclosure of the requested information should be discussed. If the client and his or her attorney determine that they will allow disclosure of the information requested, an informed consent form must be signed. The consent form must identify exactly what information is to be disclosed and to whom. The mental health professional must obtain the signed permission of all people associated with the counseling. For example, in marriage counseling both spouses must sign.

If the client or the client's attorney do not want to respond to a subpoena, they will file a motion for such. If the motion is granted by the judge, the mental health professional is prevented from responding to the subpoena. In any case therapists are advised to retain copies of all documents and to document all discussions germane to the disposition of the subpoena with the client or the client's attorney in their records.

Being Named in a Lawsuit

Counselors named in lawsuits should immediately notify their insurance companies in writing. The notification should include all the factual information about the incident for which the counselor is being sued.

If the counselor is contacted by the person who has initiated the suit or that person's lawyer, he or she should respond that an appropriate person will address their inquiry. Client information should *never* be revealed except to the appointed attorney. In fact, the counselor should avoid discussing anything about the case with anyone except his or her appointed attorney. The mental health professional should never admit negligence.

SUMMARY

Mental health professionals increasingly are being subjected to interactions with the legal system. For this reason students of psychology are expected to know not only the clinical aspects of their profession but also the legal ramifications of their behavior. Those who are not aware of their legal responsibilities can easily make mistakes that result in litigation. Most lawsuits against mental health professionals are for malpractice. Counselors who do things they should not do or don't do things they should may be found guilty of negligence and incompetence. The counseling relationship is seen in the eyes of the law as a special relationship that has special responsibilities.

LEARNING FACILITATION AND FOCUS

Exercise 4.1

Dr. Mason, an M.D., prefers to take the bus to work each morning. Over time he becomes acquainted with Lauren, who waits at the same bus stop. One morning Lauren tells Dr. Mason she has an extreme case of bronchitis and asks him if he can help her. Dr. Mason prescribes a certain medicine for her, and Lauren has the prescription filled at the local pharmacy.

Dr. Hanson, a psychologist, also takes the bus to work. Over time Dr. Hanson becomes acquainted with Fred, who waits at the same bus stop. One morning Fred tells Dr. Hanson of the behavior problems his 6-year-old daughter is manifesting. Dr. Hanson tells Fred of some behavior modification techniques Fred might use with the child. Fred goes home and tries these techniques.

1. Was either doctor in a special relationship with his bus-stop acquaintance? _____

    _____

2. Are there legal implications in the behaviors of the doctors? _____

    _____

3. Is there a difference legally or ethically in the doctors' behaviors? If so, what is it?_____

    _____

    _____

    _____

Exercise 4.2

Dr. Peggy is a social worker in private practice. When clients present for therapy, she discusses with them the financial arrangements. She explains that her fee is $100 a session, which can be paid for through insurance and a client copayment. Many of Dr. Peggy's clients have insurance policies that pay one-half of the doctor's fee. The client is expected to pay the other half. Some of Dr. Peggy's clients negotiate fee schedules that include only part of the copayment.

For instance, some patients pay $20.00 as a copayment. Dr. Peggy collects $50.00 from the insurance company, $20.00 from the client, and carries $30.00 per session as owed in her records. Dr. Peggy and her clients know that the $30.00 per session will never be paid.

1. Is this kind of fee schedule legal?_____

2. Does the fact that Dr. Peggy knows her colleagues routinely employ the same procedures change the situation? _____

   _____

3. Could Dr. Peggy change her fee schedule for some clients to $200 a session, so the insurance company will pay the total bill?_____

   _____

Exercise 4.3

Kenneth Blaus is the director of a psychological facility that sees 100 patients a week. Mr. Blaus employs a secretary to bill insurance companies for these services. The secretary routinely uses a inked stamped replica of Mr. Blaus's signature to verify that the billing is accurate. One day Mr. Blaus comes to the office early and opens the mail, an activity normally handled by the secretary. He notices a payment made by the insurance company to the secretary's husband for therapy received at the center. Upon inspection of records Mr. Blaus cannot find any record of the secretary's husband receiving treatment.

1. Should Mr. Blaus confront the secretary about this issue? What should he say to her? _____

   _____

   _____

2. Given no reasonable explanation by the secretary, what should Mr. Blaus do? Should he call the police? Should he simply ask her to leave?_____

   _____

   _____

3. What should Mr. Blaus do with the money received from the insurance company? Is the fact that his stamped signature appeared on the bill an issue?_____

_____

_____

Exercise 4.4

Evette is a psychologist and administrator in the human services division of a large multifaceted company. The company provides many services, including primary care for pregnant teenagers, dieting groups, childcare services, and individual and group therapy. A new computerized phone system is installed by the company. One of the functions of the new system is to allow administrators to evaluate the accessibility, use, capacity, and production of the various departments. Using a routine computer scan, Evette finds that the names, addresses, and phone numbers of anyone receiving individual therapy under her direction are available throughout the company to certain executives and their secretaries.

1. Could this be a legal/ethical issue?_____

_____

2. Can you see potential problems with this situation? What are they?

_____

_____

_____

3. What solutions might you offer to change the situation?_____

_____

_____

_____

_____

Exercise 4.5

Henry is a licensed counselor in private practice. He has been seeing Barbara as a client for about 18 months. She is in the process of making some major life decisions. One day Barbara announces she has lost her job and can no longer pay for Henry's services. She pleads with Henry to keep her in counseling on a *pro bono* basis until she finds another job. After a week of reflecting on the problem, Henry decides he must reject Barbara's request and replace her with another paying client. When Barbara comes to counseling, he explains to her that he already has three *pro bono* clients and suggests several charitable organizations Barbara can contact for help. Barbara becomes incensed and storms out of Henry's office.

1. Is Henry legally or ethically bound to continue to see Barbara?____

_____

2. What should Henry do after Barbara's stormy exit?_____

_____

_____

_____

Exercise 4.6

Mark is a career counselor. In the state were he practices there is no statute that proclaims client communication to career counselors as privileged. However, there is a law that declares information given during therapy as privileged communication. Mark spends a lot of time with client John, interpreting test results as they pertain to appropriate career choices. Mark also spends several sessions with John working through John's anxiety and paranoia about job selection. John is suing an airline company because he tripped over an improperly placed piece of luggage and injured his knee. The airline company subpoenas Mark's records.

1. Should John claim the records contain privileged communication?

_____

_____

2. Can career counselors claim they are conducting therapy when they are trained primarily for job placement counseling?_____

_____

_____

Exercise 4.7

Maria is counseling a 16-year-old client named Bryant. One day, Bryant's mother accompanies him to session and tells Maria that Bryant is being harmed by the actions of his English teacher. The teacher requires all students to do their work at the blackboard. Working in front of his peers causes the boy extreme anxiety. The school principal refuses to move Bryant to another English class. Bryant's mother asks Maria to intervene and explain to the principal that, because of his high anxiety, the boy should be allowed to change classes.

In order for Maria to do this, she must obtain Bryant's written consent. She then must send a copy of the following consent form to the principal, keeping the original form with Bryant's records.

1. Should Maria intervene?_____

_____

_____

2. How should the consent form be filled in before any intervention takes place?_____

_____

_____

Consent for the Release of Confidential Information

I _____
(name of client)

authorize _____
(name of counselor)

to disclose to _____
(name of person or organization to whom disclosure is to be made)

the following information: _____
(nature of the information, as limited as possible)

_____

_____

_____

The purpose of the disclosure authorized herein is to: _____

_____
(purpose of disclosure, as specific as possible)

_____

_____

_____
(specification of the date, event, or condition upon which this consent expires)

Date: _____ Signature of participant: _____

Signature of parent, guardian, or authorized representative:

_____

Part C

MULTICULTURAL CONTEXT

Chapter 5

THE MENTAL HEALTH PROFESSIONAL IN A MULTICULTURAL CONTEXT

CHANGING DEMOGRAPHICS

Statistics from the U.S. Bureau of the Census (1992) indicated that the multicultural makeup of the county will be quite different in the year 2050 than it is today. Between 1992 and 2050, the African-American population will grow from 32 million (12% of the population) to 62 million (16%); the Hispanic population, from 24 million (9%) to 81 million (21%); the American Indian, Eskimo, and Aleut population, from 2.2 million (0.8%) to 4.6 million (1.2%); the Asian and Pacific Islander population, from 9 million (3%) to 41 million (11%); while the non-Hispanic White population will grow much more slowly—from 191 million (75%) to 202 million (52%).

Other projections detail an even more rapid transformation. Sue (1991) reported that by the year 2010, racial and ethnic minorities will be the majority, with White Americans making up 48% of the U.S. population. Counselors and teachers in our schools already are encountering different student populations. In California, White students constitute less than 50% of school enrollment (Athinson, Morten, & Sue, cited in Sue, Arredondo, & McDavis, 1992). Mental health professionals increasingly will find themselves working with clients who are culturally different from themselves (Sue et al., 1992).

MULTICULTURAL TERMINOLOGY

Ethnicity can be defined as a sense of identity that is taken from common ancestry, race, religion, or nationality. According to Shibutani and Kwan (1965), *ethnic groups* can be viewed "as those who conceive of themselves as alike by virtue of their common ancestry, real or fictitious, and who are so regarded by others" (p. 23). An ethnic group shares a cultural heritage that is passed from generation to generation, and many ethnic groups are unified by a sense of belonging (Axelson, 1985). Ethnic groups share an ancestry, and *ethnic minority groups* often are viewed as those other than Caucasians who have not been treated equally in American society (Preli & Bernard, 1993). Others define minority groups as people who have been subordinated, powerless, or dominated by the majority culture. These groups include gay and lesbian people, the elderly, the physically handicapped, and the behaviorally delinquent (Lum, 1986).

Culture is a broader term than ethnicity. According to Pedersen (1986), culture includes three factors:

1. *Demographic variables,* including age, gender, and place of residence.

2. *Status variables,* including social, economic, and educational background.

3. *Formal and informal afflictions,* including language, institutions, values, and religion.

Barth (1969) described culture as those things that are opposed to communication across some kind of social boundary. Preli and Bernard (1993) noted, "One is born into one's ethnicity, but one can move in and out of cultural context" (p. 6). The *majority culture* in the United States is defined by historical experiences, expectation, and assumptions that are shared by many White citizens of European ancestry. Majority culture can be used interchangeably with *mainstream culture* (Preli & Bernard, 1993).

DEFINITIONS OF MULTICULTURAL COUNSELING

At present, there is no agreed-upon definition for what multicultural counseling should encompass. Some scholars assert that multiculturalism should be defined broadly (an *etic* approach); others say it should be viewed from a cultural-specific perspective (an *emic* approach) (Essandoh, 1996). Scholars who favor an etic perspective claim that, to some degree, all clients exemplify a multicultural dimension. Sociodemograpic variables, gender, and sexual orientation all have different cultural explications. Those who favor an emic perspective believe that, if the definition of multiculturalism is too general or broad, specific cultural groups will be affected in a negative way.

This phenomenon is one of inclusivity versus exclusivity. Those who favor inclusivity aver that race, ethnicity, sexual orientation, gender, age, and religion are all multicultural issues. Others believe that the term *multiculturalism* should be limited to the visible racial and ethnic minority groups: African-American, Native American, Asian-American, and Hispanic.

They claim, for example, that some issues (such as gender) simply dilute a more dominate issue (such as race). According to emic scholars, each non-White race sees its relationship to the dominant White structure as *the* crucial variable in the relationship (Essandoh, 1996).

> While acknowledging that to some extent all counseling is cross-cultural, the term can be defined so broadly it dilutes the focus on racial and ethnic concerns (a primary one being racism) and allows counseling professionals to avoid and omit dealing with the four major minority groups in our society. (Sue et al., 1992, p. 66)

Still others assert that excessive devotion to cultural issues can lead to decreased sensitivity to the feelings and needs of the individual (Trimble, 1981). Mental health professionals, they caution, should be careful about placing people in categories on the basis of perceived cultural differences. As Kluckhohn and Murray (1953) noted, "Every man is in certain respects like all other men, like some other men, and like no other man" (p. 58). Lloyd (1987) agreed, noting that differences *within* culture groups can be even greater than differences *between* cultural groups.

Niles (1993) offered this prescription for a balanced approach:

> It seems that more culture-specific approaches to counselor education combined with sensitivity to individual differences in a cultural framework is appropriate. Bias can be eliminated best through better understanding of culture and cultural differences. What we need to ensure, however, is that counselors are educated toward increased awareness, understanding, and appreciation of human diversity, without prejudice or a diminished ability to perceive each individual as a unique person who belongs to a cultural group. (p. 16)

Whitfield (1994) suggested:

> Until there is a clear and accepted definition of multicultural coun-
> seling, counselor educators may continue to teach counselors to help
> others in a monocultural context. Whereas the definitions suggested
> by [various] authors have merit, I suggest a more comprehensive,
> inclusive definition of multicultural counseling, which includes the
> effective counseling of persons or groups of persons who differ from
> the counselor culturally, socioeconomically, ethnically-racially,
> sexually (including sexual orientation), religiously, ecologically, and
> educationally. This includes persons who are physically challenged
> such as persons who are blind, deaf, and paraplegic. (p. 241)

VALUES AND MULTICULTURALISM

Scholars are quick to note a great deal of difference between Western and non-Western approaches to living in the world. These differences are not necessarily regarded as geographical but, rather, as concepts representing social, political, and cultural values that guide a people to a way of being in the world. Yet, most contemporary Western psychological practice uses theories developed by White men of European heritage. For example, while most Western therapists would describe a family as nuclear or extended, most non-White ethnic minority cultures value more collateral relationships (Aponte, Rivers, & Wohl, 1995; Ivey, Ivey, & Simek-Morgan, 1993). In collateral relationships non-blood relatives are valued, treated, and regarded as significant family members. In the African community the family never has been nuclear. It has always been multigenerational and transgenerational, and it has always included several different networks, including friends, teachers, neighbors, and priests (Hines & Boyd-Franklin, cited in Essandoh, 1996, p. 135).

Predominant Western cultural values include choice, individualism, the uniqueness of the individual, and assertiveness to promote the self. As a result, therapy promotes these characteristics and considers them to be valued and healthy. Teaching clients to change their environments, develop coping skills, manage stress, and learn assertiveness are some examples. Some non-Western philosophies, on the other hand, do not see a dichotomy between the self and the environment. Rather, finding and losing oneself in the totality of the cosmos is the more common way of seeing one's life experience. Understanding and accepting one's position in the environment is most highly valued.

How one treats clients in a social context and the expectations for treatment outcome also vary between cultures. For instance, Gabbard (cited in

Vasquez, 1996) described how offering a client something to drink or eat could create a dilemma in therapy, because the client then might not feel free to express hostility or negative feelings toward the therapist. Gabbard believed it was not the goal of the therapist to gratify clients so that he or she would be seen in a positive way. Vasquez (1996) disagreed:

> Mutual respect and adherence to cultural values may predispose a Latina psychologist from the Southwest to offer her clients something to drink on a regular basis, choosing the behavior from the southern and Latino cultural norms of politeness and respect and deprioritizing the belief that this may prevent the patient from expressing anger toward the therapist when necessary. A therapist who engages in behaviors from a perspective of mutual respect and adherence to cultural values may also facilitate direct, honest, and genuine expressions of anger and conflict. (p. 101)

A curriculum survey of graduate training programs conducted by McFadden and Wilson (cited in Sue et al., 1992) revealed that less than 1% of those responding included instructional requirements for the study of racial and minority groups. Other surveys have reported a stronger multicultural emphasis. Hills and Strozier, (cited in Sue et al., 1992) reported that 89% of counseling psychology programs offered a course in multicultural issues. They noted, however:

> [T]hese surveys, however, fail to give us any indication about (a) their integration in the overall counseling curriculum, (b) the multicultural perspective of the course, and (c) the degree of commitment by the department to multicultural issues. Indeed, the greatest fears among multicultural specialists are (a) that program professionals continue to see multicultural courses as less legitimate than other counseling requirements, (b) that they are taught primarily by junior-level faculty or adjuncts, (c) that they are haphazard and fragmented without a strong conceptual framework linked to specific competencies, and (d) that they tend to deal with cultural differences from a purely intellectual perspective without reference to the sociopolitical ramifications of counseling (oppression, discrimination, and racism). ... In reality, most counselors do not have enough practical experience in training, nor in their daily lives, with racial and ethnic minorities. (Sue et al., 1992, p. 65)

Indeed, we don't have to look far to find criticism of those who set the policies that ultimately mold behavior regarding multicultural issues. Ivey (1986) concluded that ethical codes were not fully ethical and proposed these changes:

- Multicultural awareness should be more focused in the codes, thereby enabling them to be a starting point for psychological practice.

- Multicultural practice should be a central issue in publications and research journals.

- Programs that explicate awareness of ourselves as cultural beings should be initiated.

- Ethical codes and practice should be opened to more involvement with the general public.

Pedersen and Marsella (1982) offered several criticisms of multicultural education in counseling:

- The ethical crisis of cross-cultural counseling is the result of mental health assumptions that were developed in one cultural context and implemented in a totally different one.

- Ethical guidelines often are insensitive to clients' cultural values. The dominant culture's values often color its descriptions of people in other cultures, without demonstration that these descriptions can be generalized to a minority culture.

- It should be regarded as unethical for a counselor to counsel people from cultural backgrounds different from his or hers, if he or she is not trained or competent to work with that group.

- The multiplicity of cultural values in our society has been neglected.

Often, mental health professionals are culturally biased, and their services are more suited to the dominant culture than to the unique needs of various ethnic groups. Ibrahim (1986) proposed the following revisions to the APA *Ethical Codes*:

1. In the Preamble, it should be emphasized that much of human behavior is learned in a social context. People understand themselves and others through the perspective of their own beliefs, values, assumptions, and world views.

2. Principle 1 (Responsibility) should incorporate the psychologist's responsibility to understand the role of cultural factors in shaping human behavior, resulting in different philosophies and world views.

3. Principle 2 (Competence) should have a stronger statement regarding the need for appropriate education and training to work with diverse populations. Unless practitioners have been educated about cultural differences, they cannot determine whether they are competent to work with certain populations.

4. Principle 4 (Public Statements) should be revised to require practitioners to specify their level of training to work with diverse populations.

5. Principle 5 (Confidentiality) should state that people from different cultural backgrounds have different concepts of the limits of confidentiality, and this matter must be appropriately communicated to clients from diverse cultures.

Other writers have noted significant gains in psychology regarding multicultural counseling theory. Several journals have dedicated articles and entire issues to the rationale for a multicultural perspective. Counseling psychology has paid more attention to multicultural counseling than some of the other professions (Essandoh, 1996). As Pedersen (1991) noted, the profession of psychology is "moving toward a generic theory of multiculturalism as a fourth force position, complimentary to the other three forces of psychodynamic, behavioral, and humanistic explanations of human behavior" (p. 7).

On the other hand, Cheatham (1994) asserted, "Proclaiming multiculturalism as a forth force in psychotherapy does not make it so" (p. 290).

Essandoh (1996) agreed:

> Although some progress has been made toward enhanced multicultural awareness ... many unanswered questions still remain ... will this progress achieve the kind of impact realized by the first three forces? Is multiculturalism just a fad that will pass away in due time? (p. 128)

THE CULTURALLY SKILLED COUNSELOR

Sue et al. (1992) reported that most attempts to identify cross-cultural counseling competencies have listed three dimensions:

1. beliefs and attitudes,

2. knowledge, and

3. skills.

These three dimensions all contain characteristics that must be acquired by a culturally skilled counselor. A brief summary of this matrix reported by Sue et al. (1992) is detailed below. Some of the beliefs and attitudes of culturally skilled counselors are these:

- They demonstrate sensitivity to clients' cultural heritage and how it affects their lives.

- They are comfortable with culturally different clients, are aware of their own negative emotional reactions, respect clients' religious or spiritual beliefs, recognize minority community efforts, and value bilingualism.

- They understand how their own cultural heritage may contribute to their biases and how racism may effect their personality and work.

- They have information about the group with whom they are working and the institutional barriers they may face, minority family structures, and pertinent discriminatory practices in the community.

- They can seek consultative help, are familiar with relevant research, are actively involved with clients outside the counseling setting, and can send and receive verbal and nonverbal communications accurately and appropriately.

Acquiring Multicultural Counseling Skills

A review of the professional literature by Ponteretto and Cass (cited in Preli & Bernard, 1993) revealed that many counselors embrace a pluralistic philosophy as a prerequisite for training, because it engages an attitude of openness to other cultures and a realization that all cultural perspectives contain positive and thought-worthy dimensions. Others have suggested several qualifications for students of multicultural counseling:

- Gardner (cited in Preli & Bernard, 1993) suggested that the absence of bias be an admission standard for counseling training programs.

- Webb (cited in Preli & Bernard, 1993) cited cultural knowledge as an important training variable.

- Petersen (cited in Preli & Bernard, 1993) advised consciousness raising.

- Stewart (cited in Preli & Bernard, 1993), noting that the majority culture tends to have *sympathy* rather than *empathy*, suggested that one goal of consciousness training should be to increase student empathy while confronting the motives of sympathy.

- Boyd-Franklin, Mio, Parker, and Davis (cited in Preli & Bernard, 1993) asserted that contact with minorities is crucial. Preli and Bernard (1993) agreed, noting that as society grows more diverse, it becomes more and more incongruous for trainees to feel they can conduct therapy without some association with people from minority groups.

After trainees gain knowledge and awareness of other cultures, they should practice the skills that will allow them to work in a multicultural context, using videotape and feedback, role-playing, and other experiential techniques.

Fundamentally, however, the mental health profession still cannot agree on exactly what skills, knowledge, and experiences are essential to the culturally skilled counselor. Everyone seems to agree that counselors who are delinquent in cross-cultural skills need to expand their knowledge of such skills. Yet, as Whitfield (1994, p. 247) noted, "Counselors must be careful ... in assuming that everyone who is culturally different from the counselor wants to be counseled differently." Ivey (1986, p. 169) agreed, noting, "Counseling skills and techniques are to be used differently with different groups, but within each group is immense individual variation." Vasquez (1996, p. 99) asked the telling question, "For example, who defines what community virtues are? What constitutes a 'community'?"

Finally, the profession needs to take up the issue of training culturally diverse counselors themselves. As McNeill, Hom, and Perez (1995) noted, "Despite the increasing attention given to issues of multicultural training in counseling programs, there is a dearth of information available on the unique training needs of racial and ethnic consulting minority trainees" (p. 246).

McRoy, Freeman, Logan, and Blackmon (1986) reported on the experience of social work interns and their supervisors in cross-cultural dyads: More problems than positive outcomes were identified—both by supervisors and by interns. White supervisors saw minority interns as defensive. They also cited language barriers, prejudice or bigotry, and lack of knowledge of cultural differences as problems with communication and disclosure. African-American supervisors working with White interns reported similar problems. A number of Black supervisors reported that White students questioned their competence and were unwilling to accept their supervision. Latino supervisors reported language differences and issues with authority as communication barriers.

White interns reported problems with supervisors' accents, differences in values, prejudices, and an inability to be honest and direct about problems in communication and learning. African-American trainees related that White supervisors were not aware of racism, were ignorant of their culturally different background experiences, and tended to minimize racial differences. Supervisors tended to report they had effectively addressed problems with the interns, while students said they avoided discussing problems about cultural issues and expressed discomfort if they did so. These perceptions persisted despite the fact that 47% of the students believed their supervisors were very sensitive to racial and cultural differences; in fact, only 5% viewed their supervisors as insensitive to racial and cultural differences.

Heppner and O'Brien (1994) used a qualitative design to determine how students experienced the impact of a multicultural course. The participants were 20 master's and doctoral students enrolled in an elective beginning course in multicultural counseling. The students were rated on perceived changes in thinking and feeling. The most often reported changes were an increased awareness and more openness to and interest in multicultural issues. Students rated interpersonal exchanges that occurred in class as the most helpful in achieving change. Below are some responses typical of this category (interpersonal exchanges):

> "The more I hear people speak of their lives, the more my safe and provincial world begins to enlarge."

> "Talking with individuals who are African American—because where I was raised, I had almost no contact with them before this class."

> "To hear life stories of oppression and abuse by people whom I call friends—their lifestyle gets them branded as nearly subhuman. My awareness of this helps me to be able to help and act in their behalf."

> "I think the panel discussions were most helpful. I have in a way found it difficult to learn about minority issues from those who are not minority." (p. 13)

Formally presented lectures were rated second most important in helping change student perceptions, understanding, and awareness of cultural differences. One student reported, "reflecting on the readings and trying to find an interconnectedness with the readings on psychotherapy and my personal experiences have allowed me to become more open to change" (p. 15). Most of the students cited personal issues or biases as hindering change.

Heppner and O'Brien (1994) also reported that cognitive and attitudinal changes in respect to self and others were unexpected benefits from the course.

> "I had expected to learn about different cultures, but I hadn't expected the introspection and self-discovery that goes along with becoming culturally skilled. I did not expect to be surprised at all the new things I am learning, I'm glad to begin uncovering my ignorance; I find [I] became really excited by this stuff, I haven't been this turned on to new learning in a long time."(p. 14)

Heppner and O'Brien (1994) concluded that, although students felt they could perceive changes in their multicultural awareness and knowledge, a primary concern was whether they could integrate the new awareness and knowledge into clinical behavior.

In a survey of 225 African-American, Latino, Asian-American, and Native American trainees, Cook and Helms (1988) reported on levels of satisfaction with cross-cultural supervision. African-American, Latino and Native American trainees had perceived lower satisfaction levels than Asian-Americans. Native American trainees were more uncomfortable with their supervisors than the other three groups.

Another reason multicultural training may pose difficulties is that stereotypes of cultural differences are formed very early, and may have to be readjusted by both trainers and trainees. Ausdale and Feagin (1996) broke from Piaget's (1926) thinking about cognitive development and focused on how very young children create and assign meaning for racial and ethnic concepts. The following are conversational excerpts that demonstrate their ideas:

1. *How racial and ethnic concepts are used to exclude others:*

> "No, only people who can speak Spanish can come in." ... Elizabeth frowns and says, "I can come in." Rita counters, "Can you speak Spanish?" Elizabeth shakes her head no, and Rita repeats, "Well, then you aren't allowed in." (p. 781)

> "I need to move this," explains Carla. "Why?" asks the teacher. "Because I can't sleep next to a nigger," Carla says, pointing to Nicole on a cot nearby. "Niggers are stinky. I can't sleep next to one." (p. 782)

2.   *How racial and ethnic concepts are used to include cultures*:

> "They called character, you know." She points out several. "What does that say?" Debi asks, pointing to one. "Cat!" Ling beams. Debi and Ling spend some time reading from Ling's book. (p. 783)

3.   *How racial and ethnic concepts are used to define oneself*:

> "Chinese people prefer Chinese food." When David asks for a taste, she hesitates. "Well," she offers, "you probably won't like it. You're not Chinese." (p. 784)

4.   *How racial and ethnic concepts define others:*

> "For goodness sake, can't you see that you aren't pink?" ... "Debi," Cathie continues to insist, "you have to make her see that she's brown." Cathie is exasperated and takes Taleshia by the arm. "Look," she instructs, "you are brown! See?" (p. 786)

In noting the problems of minority students, McNeill et al. (1995) related the following:

> White professors and supervisors often present themselves as being extremely culturally sensitive and aware. Consequently, they may overcompensate in their interactions with minority trainees through excessive praise and avoidance of criticism, both publicly and privately, connoting the racist view that the minority trainee has achieved beyond anyone's expectations. ... On the other end of the scale, there are White professors who are blatantly culturally insensitive ... they do claim to be color-blind, refusing to acknowledge cultural differences. This perspective is often rationalized as having the right intention, but the consequence is that culturally diverse trainees are then faced with a struggle to assert their unique needs and make others aware of the multicultural implications of course material, counseling theories, and interventions. Most often, however, students are forced to attend to and accept this insensitivity for fear of repercussion because of the power differential between professor and student. (p. 253)

The identification and solidification of a bicultural identity is a crucial developmental task for ethnic minority trainees. They must incorporate their own ethnic identity with a professional identity. This may mean going through a reconciliation stage that delineates aspects of their own cultural identity with aspects of the culture of psychology that are in conflict with their cultural background. The process reaches successful culmination when they are able to compartmentalize or integrate aspects of the culture of psychology, while at the same time holding in esteem aspects of their own culture (Vasquez & McKinley, 1982).

Ponterotto, Alexander, and Grieger (1995) developed a multicultural competency checklist that counseling training programs can use to examine their comprehensiveness. The checklist includes 22 items organized around six major themes. A summary of the list follows:

1. *Minority representation:* African-Americans, Hispanic-Americans, Asian-American, Pacific Islanders, and Native Americans constitute at least 30% of students, faculty, and program support staff.

2. *Curriculum issues:* Multicultural issues are incorporated into all facets of the curriculum.

3. *Counseling practice and supervision:* All trainees have caseloads with at least 30% minority clients.

4. *Research:* At least one faculty member is interested in multicultural research.

5. *Student and faculty competency evaluation:* Multicultural issues are included in exams.

6. *Physical environment:* Multicultural art is actively displayed in the campus environment.

SUMMARY

Proponents of multicultural counseling seem to be saying that psychological services may be *for* the people but not *of* or *by* the people they ascribe to serve. In the next 50 years, the majority of people in the United States will not be of European ancestry. Yet, the predominate psychological theories and research practices to which they will be subjected were developed in a European male culture which not only is foreign but represents structures that are oppressive to them. Western psychological structures value the individual, assertiveness, nonconformity, competition, freedom, individual responsibility, expression of feelings, innovation, and individualized morality. Non-Western psychological structures, on the other hand, may emphasize the primacy of relationships, compliance, conformity, cooperation, security, collective responsibility, control of feelings, conservatism, and morality. Professional psychologists and those who train mental health professionals must be responsive to these differences and address them in their ethical standards and training practices.

LEARNING FACILITATION AND FOCUS

Exercise 5.1

The literature on multicultural counseling reveals a split between the etic approach and the emic approach. Some assert that, to some degree, all clients exemplify a multicultural dimension, and that an excessive devotion to culture may lead to a decreased sensitivity to the feelings and needs of individuals. As Kluckhohn and Murray (1953) noted, "Every man is in certain respects like all other men, like some other men, and like no other man" (p. 58). Others believe that the thrust of multicultural education should be toward the ethnic and racial concerns of African-Americans, Native Americans, Asian-Americans, and Hispanics.

Consider and articulate below which emphasis should be given in mental health professional training programs. In your answer, consider whether multicultural concerns should be housed in particular courses or whether they should permeate the curriculum. Also, what particular knowledge, experience, and skills should be emphasized? Finally, does the location of the training area have any bearing on what cultures should be emphasized? For example, if most of the clients in an area are Hispanic, should that culture receive more attention than others?

_____

_____

_____

_____

_____

_____

Exercise 5.2

Most educators believe that a student who aspires to counsel others should be aware of his or her own biases and prejudices. With this in mind, consider your culture of origin and comment on the following.

1. Has your culture experienced prejudice or racism. If so, what form does/ did it take? _____

   _____

   _____

2. What religion is valued in your culture? _____

   _____

   _____

3. What occupations are valued and devalued in your culture? _____

   _____

   _____

4. How are those outside of your culture viewed? _____

   _____

   _____

5. Are there specific cultural groups that are valued or devalued by members of your culture? _____

   _____

   _____

   _____

Part D

RELATIONSHIPS WITH SPECIAL POPULATIONS

Chapter 6

CLIENTS WHO ARE DANGEROUS TO THEMSELVES OR OTHERS

THE CLIENT WHO IS POTENTIALLY HARMFUL TO SELF

Definition of Suicide

Beauchamp (1985) defined suicide this way:

1. The person intentionally brings about his or her own death;

2. others do not coerce him or her to the action; and,

3. death is caused by conditions arranged by the person for the purpose of bringing about his or her own death.

Training Regarding Suicide

When working with suicidal patients, the mental health professional is held to a standard of care that says he or she has acquired the appropriate clinical and legal education to perform such a function. Mental health professionals cannot claim lack of training as a defense for negligent actions because a court may claim they "should have known." The appropriate education implies competence (Barron, 1987). Clinicians rank working with suicidal patients as the most stressful aspect of their work (Deutsch, 1984):

> Losing a patient to suicide is so personally and professionally impactful, that almost half of the psychologists who lost a patient reported intrusive symptoms of stress in the weeks that followed the suicide ... stress comparable to individuals who had suffered the death of a close family member. ... Patient suicide should be acknowledged as an occupational hazard for psychologists, not only because of its frequency but also because of its impact on psychologists' professional and personal lives. ... Training programs do not currently have established protocols for helping trainees to deal with the aftermath of a patient's suicide; therefore, trainees and their supervisors are left to their own devices (pp. 419–420).

The average psychologist working in direct patient care has a greater than 20% chance of losing a patient to suicide; the odds are better than 50% for psychiatrists (Chemtob, Hamada, Bauer, Kinney, & Torigoe, 1988). Yet, Bongar and Harmatz (1989) reported that the number of formal suicide training curriculums in member departments of the Council of University Directors of Clinical Psychology was just a little more than one-third. Little formal training in suicide prevention is conducted in psychiatric residencies, social work schools, or nursing programs (Berman, 1986). Apparently, suicide training is lacking in continuing education as well; fewer than one in four psychologists and psychiatrists in the Washington, D.C., area had postinternship graduate training in suicide assessment (Berman & Cohen-Sandler, 1982).

By contrast, 77% of school counselors indicated they had special training in suicide, but only 32% reported that this training took place in counselor education programs. Most received their training in professional workshops (59%) or school service programs (Nelson & Crawford, 1990).

Legal, ethical, and moral tenets impose on mental health professionals the obligation to seek the best treatment for their clients. Concern for the client's welfare is always the primary priority. Therefore, all mental health professionals should make sure they understand four things:

1. their ethical responsibilities regarding potentially suicidal clients,

2. their legal mandates regarding potentially suicidal clients,

3. presenting characteristics of danger to self, and

4. the skills to counsel clients who are a danger to themselves.

Ethical Mandates and Danger to Self

The ethical codes from several professional organizations clearly address the welfare of clients as paramount, as shown in the statements that follow:

> [The school counselor] informs the appropriate authorities when the counselee's condition indicates a clear and imminent danger to the counselee or others. This is to be done after careful deliberation and, where possible, after consultation with other professionals. The counselor informs the counselee of actions to be taken so as to minimize confusion and clarify expectations. (American School Counselor Association, 1992, p. 10)

* * * *

> Marriage and family therapists may not disclose client confidences except (a) as mandated by law; (b) to prevent a clear and immediate danger to a person or persons; (c) where the therapist is a defendant in a civil, criminal, or disciplinary action arising from the therapy (in which case client confidences may be disclosed only in the course of that action); or (d) if there is a waiver previously obtained in writing, and then such information may be revealed only in accordance with the terms of the waiver. In circumstances where more than one person in a family receives therapy, each such family member who is legally competent to execute a waiver must agree to the waiver required by subparagraph (d). Without such a waiver from each family member legally competent to execute a waiver, a therapist cannot disclose information received from any family member. (American Association for Marriage and Family Therapy, 1991, 2.1)

* * * *

> Psychologists disclose confidential information without the consent of the individual only as mandated by law, or where permitted by law for a valid purpose, such as (1) to provide needed professional services to the patient or the individual or organizational client, (2) to obtain appropriate professional consultations, (3) to protect the patient or client or others from harm, or (4) to obtain payment for services, in which instance disclosure is limited to the minimum that is necessary to achieve the purpose. (APA, 1995, 5, 501)

Social workers should protect the confidentiality of all information obtained in the course of professional service, except for compelling professional reasons. The general expectation that social workers will keep information confidential does not apply when disclosure is necessary to prevent serious, foreseeable, and imminent harm to a client or other identifiable person or when laws or regulations require disclosure without a client's consent. In all instances, social workers should disclose the least amount of confidential information necessary to achieve the desired purpose; only information that is directly relevant to the purpose for which the disclosure is made should be revealed. (National Association of Social Workers, 1997, 1., 105)

* * * *

Exceptions. The general requirement that counselors keep information confidential does not apply when disclosure is required to prevent clear and imminent danger to the client or others or when legal requirements demand that confidential information be revealed. Counselors consult with other professionals when in doubt as to the validity of an exception. (American Counseling Association, 1995, B.1.d.)

Legal Mandates and Danger to Self

Again, the mental health professional's special relationship with the client creates the context for the legal accountability for negligent malpractice with potentially suicidal patients. A therapist is assumed to possess superior knowledge and skills beyond those of the average person and may be considered by the courts to be responsible for the suicide of his or her patient. The client's dependence on the counselor is enough to shift some of the weight of the responsibility for the client's actions to the mental health professional. This was not always the case.

In England, toward the latter part of the nineteenth century, suicide was considered self-murder, and authorities buried the bodies of those who committed suicide at the side of the road with a stake through the heart (Bednar et al., 1991). Today a mental health professional who does not take appropriate action to prevent a suicide can be sued. The most important consideration for the courts is this: Was the suicide foreseeable? Look at this case as an example:

A medical patient experienced hallucinations after surgery. The patient requested psychiatric help, and a therapist conducted an hour of therapy and made no recommendations to the hospital staff. Sometime later, the patient jumped from a sixth-floor window. Injuries from the fall left him a quadriplegic. The Utah Supreme Court concluded that after an hour of therapy, a special relationship was formed. It held the therapist liable for negligently failing to accurately diagnose the patient's condition and for failing to take appropriate protective steps (*Farrow v. Health Services Corp.*, 1979).

On the other hand, liability has not been found when apparently cooperative patients suddenly attempt suicide (*Carlino v. State*, 1968; *Dalton v. State*, 1970), or when an aggressive patient does not reveal any suicidal symptoms (*Paridies v. Benedictine Hospital*, 1980). In determining liability, courts also must decide whether the recommendations of a mental health professional were followed. In one case, a hospital was found liable when the staff did not follow the psychiatrist's recommendations (*Comiskey v. State of New York*, 1979).

Liability may be imposed if a therapist is negligent in his or her treatment of a patient. Negligence is found when the mental health professional does not perform his or her duties according to the standard of care for that particular profession. Consequently, mental health professionals should adhere to the following model, similar to the one presented later in a section on *Tarasoff*.

1. *Make an assessment of the danger.* This assessment is based on the client interview.

2. *Determine what action is reasonable.* The therapist may need to intensify treatment, change medication, advise voluntary commitment, or authorize involuntary commitment.

3. *Make sure the recommendation is followed.*

Characteristics of Potential Harm to Self

> Suicidal behavior is an increasing concern in the U.S. By the end of 1993, approximately 28,500 people will have committed suicide. (Dixon, Heppner, & Rudd, 1994, p. 91)

> * * * *

> Studies of persons in the general population who commit suicide have shown both social and psychiatric risk factors ... national statistical evidence shows increased suicide risk in the elderly, unmarried, unemployed, and those living alone ... [Researchers] collected a consecutive series of 134 suicide cases in St. Louis and systematically interviewed relatives and others who had had contact with the

person before the suicide. Ninety-four percent were judged to have been psychiatrically ill at the time of suicide. They found that 60 of the suicides (45%) were suffering from an affective disorder and 31 (23%) from alcoholism, and that the known prevalence of notable physical disease was 51% ... 114 consecutive suicide cases in Seattle found comparable figures. In England, ... 64% had an affective disorder at the time of suicide ... a significantly larger proportion of the suicides with affective disorder and alcoholism were living alone compared with the US population aged 23 years and over. (Roy, 1982, p. 1089)

In a review of the literature, Fujimura, Weis, and Cochran (1985, p. 613) listed characteristics of potentially suicidal clients, including these:

1. *Previous suicide attempts:* A previous suicide attempt is the single best predictor of lethality. Suicide attempts by family member or close friends exert an influence as well.

2. *Sleeping disruption:* Sleeping disruptions may increase the intensity of depression. The person may be hallucinating, possibly from an excess of drugs such as stimulants and depressants.

3. *Definitiveness of plan:* The suicidal individual must be asked to talk about this, and he or she almost always will if asked. The more definitive the plan, the more serious the intent.

4. *Reversibility of plan:* Time span is an important consideration. Using a gun or jumping from a high place are irreversible methods most of the time. Taking pills is less lethal because there is a better chance for reversibility.

5. *Proximity of others:* A person who really does not want to die will rely on intervention from other people. A person truly intent on committing suicide will ensure that no one can intervene.

6. *Giving possessions away:* The suicidal individual is likely to give away prized possessions, finalize business affairs, or revise a will.

7. *A history of severe alcohol or drug abuse:* An individual who is dependent on drugs or alcohol is at greater suicide risk.

8. *A history of psychiatric treatment or hospitalization:* The suicidal individual is likely to have received previous psychiatric treatment or to have been hospitalized.

9. *Availability of resource and support systems:* The suicidal person may not recognize the existence of support systems available.

10. *Willingness to use resource and support systems:* A suicidal person not using these systems signifies a cutting off of communication and makes the intent more serious.

Interventions

Listed below are some techniques generally recognized by therapists to facilitate the counseling process for suicidal clients:

1. Listen intelligently, sensitively, and carefully to the client.

2. Accept and understand the client's suicidal thoughts.

3. Don't give false assurances. Don't say things like, "Everything is going to be all right."

4. Be supportive.

5. Assure the client of your availability.

6. Be firm and caring at the same time.

7. Don't use euphemisms. Ask direct questions like, "Would you like to kill yourself?" rather than using vague expressions.

8. Bring out any ambivalence the client has. Try to increase his or her choices.

9. If the client is in crisis, don't leave him or her alone.

10. Intervene to dispose of any weapons the client has.

11. Tell others, especially those who would be concerned and can help. (You already have informed the client of the limits of confidentiality.)

12. Help the client develop support systems.

13. Trust your own judgment.

14. Know the suicide hotline numbers.

15. Be aware of commitment procedures in your area.

16. Have the client sign a nonsuicide contract.

If you determine that the client is potentially suicidal and he or she will not consent to hospitalization, the case may be serious enough to warrant attempting an involuntary commitment to a treatment center. The procedures for commitment, whether voluntary or involuntary, vary a great deal from area to area. Laws on commitment procedures are different from state to state. Mental health professionals should be familiar with the legal aspects of commitment in their areas.

Childhood Depression

Stress, once identified with adolescents, is becoming more prevalent in elementary school children. Today the literature on suicide and children reveals a more prevalent sense of suicidal behaviors and ideation in children. As stress in the lives of children increases, symptoms such as anxiety, depression, helplessness, and hopelessness increase as well. Research has revealed that, while suicide in very young children is rare, suicidal thoughts, threats, and attempts are not. Clinicians are beginning to believe that depression in very young children is a real and often unrecognized problem (Connell, 1972; Philips, 1983). Estimates of the prevalence of childhood depression are erratic, ranging from less than 2% to as many as 30% of elementary school children (Annell, 1971; Tueting, Koslow, & Hirschfield, 1983).

> Through research, a strong familial component of depression has been uncovered. Investigators have found that a large percentage of depressed children have a close relative, often a parent, who is depressed. Conversely, many depressed parents have children who are impaired. … School counselors and other educators play significant roles in the lives of children. Therefore, it is imperative that counselors be aware of the existence and features of the disorder. Counselors, with their training and skills, and with the consultative functions they serve in schools, can assume roles of child advocates. This can be accomplished by bringing the phenomenon of childhood depression to the attention of school personnel and parents and by bringing depressed children to the attention of those individuals who can aid them. To fight the battle against childhood depression, counselors must be armed with knowledge and keep on hand a vast storehouse of compassion and concern. (Lasko, 1986, pp. 285–287)

Intervention in the Schools

Suicide among American youth is growing at an alarming rate. Currently, it is the fastest growing cause of death among adolescents in the U.S. (Sheeley & Herlihy, 1989). Suicide is the third leading—in some states the second leading—cause of death among young people (Rosenberg, Smith, Davidson, & Conn, 1987; Strother, 1986). Although the number of adolescent suicides has increased 300% in the past 30 years (Peach & Reddick, 1991), actual cases are considered under-reported because of the tendency to disguise these cases as accidents (Capuzzi & Golden, 1988). Some researchers believe suicides to be under-reported by a ratio of 4 to 1 (Davis, 1985).

The tragedy of suicide is further complicated by the strong possibility that it can be prevented (Eisenberg, 1984). Professionals concur that most potential suicide victims want to be saved and often send out signals for help. Considering the magnitude of this problem, schools have a moral imperative to develop suicide prevention programs (Celotta, Golden, Keys, & Cannon, 1988). These are most effective when they are comprehensive and systematic—in short, when they are *proactive* (Kush, 1990).

Given the enormity of the problem, schools have not been active enough in developing procedures to confront youth suicide. There are a number of reasons for their procrastination: First, school personnel usually are not exposed to suicide prevention procedures as part of their normal in-education training. This lack of education is true for school personnel across the board—administrators, teachers, counselors, and school psychologists. Also, suicide prevention proposals often are met with fear, denial, and resistance in the community (Poland, 1990). Some educators acknowledge the need for programs but express concern at the limitations of school systems already overburdened (Grob, Klein, & Eisen, 1982; Sandoval, 1985; Wise, Smead, & Huebner, 1987).

There are also those who do not support active suicide prevention efforts in the schools. Their argument is that talking about the problem somehow causes it; this is much the same argument those opposed to sex education use. Some community members profess that suicide is not a significant problem and that any recognition of it should be addressed in the church or at home (Barrett, 1985). Additionally, some professionals resist developing suicide prevention programs because of the many ethical and legal issues involved, and because many states do not have laws that address the unique moral issues raised by youth suicide (Celotta et al., 1988). For this reason, teenage suicide too often is viewed as a "hands-off" subject.

However, because school and college personnel have direct and continuous contact with a large population of adolescents, schools can be a strategic setting for suicide prevention, intervention, and postintervention programs. Mental health professionals who counsel children in school should be prepared to assess lethality because of both professional and legal obligations.

The literature suggests that, to be effective, school-based programs must be comprehensive and systematic and include strategies for suicide prevention, intervention during, and postintervention following a completed suicide. Comprehensive and systematic programs also must be ongoing, intact, and continuously updated. This position is shared by many researchers who have developed models of school-based programs. A review of recent literature reveals the following components as those most often recommended for school-based adolescent suicide prevention and intervention programs:

1. A written, formal policy statement for reacting to suicide and suicidal ideation

2. Staff in-service training and orientation for the program

3. Mental health professionals on site

4. A mental health team

5. Prevention materials for distribution to parents

6. Prevention materials for distribution to students

7. Psychological screening programs to identify at-risk students

8. Prevention-focused classroom discussions

9. Mental health counseling for at-risk students

10. Suicide prevention and intervention training for school counselors

11. Faculty training for detection of suicide warning signs

12. Postintervention component in the event of an actual suicide

13. Written statement describing specific criteria for counselors to assess the lethality of a potential suicide

14. Written policy describing how the program will be evaluated

To determine the number of schools that included these components of effective programs, we surveyed a nationwide random sample of 1,000 secondary school counselors who were currently members of the American School Counselors Association (ASCA). Of those surveyed, 325 (32.5%) were used in the study. Participants were asked to note the presence or absence of each component (in the list above) in their school programs. Of the respondents used in the survey, 43% had 0 to 5 years of experience as a school counselor; 22% had 6 to 10 years; 15% had 11 to 15 years, 14% had 16 to 20 years; 6% had 21 to 30 years, and 6% did not respond to this category. Also, 67% had a master's degree plus additional credits; 24% had a master's degree; 4% had a doctoral degree; 3% had a bachelor's degree; and 2% had postdoctoral training. (This study appeared in *The School Counselor* in November of 1994, pp. 130–136. It is reprinted with permission.)

Results.   Responses to the survey revealed that three components were present in over 65% of the school programs: mental health counseling for at-risk students, a mental health team, and a mental health professional onsite.

Nine components were present in less than 65% but more than 40% of the schools: a written formal suicide policy statement, written procedures to address at-risk students, staff in-service training and orientation, prevention materials for distribution to students, prevention-focused classroom discussion, suicide prevention and intervention training for school counselors, faculty training in recognition of suicide warning signs, and a postintervention component to be used in the event of an actual suicide.

Finally, four components were used by the schools less than 4% of the time: prevention materials for distribution to parents, psychological screening programs to identify at-risk students, a written statement describing criteria for counselors to assess the lethality of a potential suicide, and a written policy describing how the program would be evaluated. All of the components were found more often in schools with written suicide policies, with the exception of psychological screening programs to identify at-risk students and mental health counseling for at-risk students.

The majority of schools responding to the survey included some form of mental health counseling for students at-risk (87% had mental health counseling for at-risk students). However, about one-half of the schools did not employ the other components. One might argue that the absence of such components limits the effectiveness of these school programs. Nonetheless, schools still have both ethical and legal mandates to ensure the health and safety of their students.

In our study, only 51% of respondents provided suicide reference materials for school counselors; 35% had a written statement describing specific criteria for counselors to assess the lethality of a potential suicide; and only 47% provided faculty training in detection of suicide warning signs. The absence of these components should be warning signs for counselors and school administrators of legal vulnerability for counseling practice.

For instance, schools have been found legally liable for negligence when not reporting a student's suicidal threats to his or her parents. It is particularly disheartening to see that, although most teen suicides occur in the home, only 28% of the schools responding used distributed prevention materials to parents, even though this component could be included with minimum economic hardship to the school system.

The results of this survey strongly indicate that schools employing a written policy are considerably more comprehensive and systematic in their approach to intervention and prevention of suicide. With the exception of two components, a written suicide policy authorized by the school enhances the probability that the other components will be developed. Mental health counseling was found in a significant number of the schools.

Psychological screening in schools is fraught with ethical and legal issues, and school systems often are not prepared to grapple with them. Counselors should review available literature regarding the importance and necessity of including comprehensive and systematic suicide prevention and intervention programs in the school and seek advice to assure that these programs meet the ethical, moral, and legal standards applicable to them. School personnel should be made aware of court rulings stating that school counselors have a legal duty to protect children when the counselor foresees or should have foreseen that students were potentially dangerous to themselves. If a school system does not have a written formal suicide prevention and postintervention policy, the board and community should be petitioned to enact one. Systematic and comprehensive suicide prevention and intervention programs can save lives and protect counselors and the school from liability.

School counselors also must realize that certification or licensure in counseling does not necessarily qualify them to practice counseling in all areas. Professional organizations and the law now require counselors to have appropriate credentials and training to perform specific counseling functions and activities. It is imperative, therefore, that school counselors attend workshops, classes, and training sessions to gain the knowledge and develop the clinical skills to counsel at-risk students and to learn to identify situations requiring legal or psychological counsel. We have developed a checklist to help school counselors compare their programs with ideal programs as recommend in the literature. This checklist appears on pages 129–131.

Intervention Strategies

More and more, the courts have been called upon to decide liability issues in relation to suicidal clients and the responsibility of school counselors. The Maryland Court of Appeals ruled that school counselors have a legal duty to prevent the suicide of a student client if the counselor foresees a danger of suicide (Pate, 1992). Appropriate intervention steps cannot be implemented, however, until lethality is determined. The following process should be followed as soon as a student is suspected of being suicidal:

1. *Ask directly during a session.* Ask the student, without hesitation, if he or she is thinking about killing him- or herself. If the student claims to have had suicidal ideation, the strength of the intent should be determined. Continue with the questioning.

2. *Ask if he or she has attempted suicide before.* If so, how many times were attempts made and when were they made? The more attempts and the more recent the attempts, the more serious the situation becomes.

3. *Ask how the previous attempts were made.* If the student took aspirin, for example, ask how many. One? Six? Twenty? Then ask about the consequences of the attempts. For example, was there medical intervention?

4. *Ask why.* Why did the student attempt suicide before? Why the suicidal thoughts now?

5. *Does the student have a plan?* Ask about the details. The more detailed the plan is, the more lethal it is. Does the student know when and how the attempt will be made? Assess the lethality of the method. This assessment is critical. Does the student have a weapon? Using a gun or hanging oneself leaves little time for medical help.

6. *Ask about the student's preoccupation with suicide.* Does he or she think about it only at home or during a particular incident—or does it go beyond all other activities?

7. *Ask about drug use.* Drug use complicates the seriousness of the situation because people tend to be less inhibited when under the influence of drugs. Although the student may deny drug use, try to get as much information as possible.

8. *Observe nonverbal actions.* Is the student agitated, tense, or sad? Is he or she inebriated? Use caution if the student seems to be at peace. This peaceful state may be the result of having organized a suicide plan, with completion being the next step.

9. *Try to gauge the level of depression.* A student may not be depressed because he or she is anxious about completing the plan.

This process will help you determine the level of suicide risk for a student. A low-risk student may have thought about suicide but has never attempted suicide in the past, does not have a plan, is not taking drugs, and is not preoccupied with the ideation. Most students at low risk will agree to the therapist's contacting their parents, which should be done. The statements must be monitored closely, however, as a low-risk student can quickly become a high-risk student.

A typical high-risk student has a plan but may or may not have attempted suicide in the past. Of course, a previous attempt is an important factor in assessing lethality, especially if the attempt was recent. But counselors should remember that many first-time attempts are successful. The current situation must never be minimized. The plan of a high-risk student usually is detailed and the ideation is frequent. At this point, other people need to become involved, including the counselor's supervisor, principal, and school nurse.

Ideally, the school will have some type of suicide intervention policy. The goal in a high-risk situation is to have the student undergo a psychiatric evaluation as soon as possible, whether by voluntary or by involuntary commitment. The student's parents must be notified; confidentiality is not an issue if the limits of confidentiality were explained previously via informed consent. Although confidentiality laws vary from state to state, a counselor usually is not bound if the client intends to harm him- or herself or someone else (Kane & Keeton, 1985). It is absolutely imperative, however, that school counselors discuss confidentiality limits at the beginning of every client intake session.

Mental health professionals may encounter crisis situations in three different ways, and each requires some specific guidelines.

First, the student may attempt suicide on school premises. The counselor should refer to the school's policy regarding this intervention.

Second, the student may disclose suicidal ideation directly to the therapist. In this case, the counselor should assess lethality using the process outlined above.

Third, peers may inform the counselor of a suicidal student. Seven out of 10 students will tell a peer about suicide ideation before telling anyone else. It is especially important to take this information seriously. The decision by the Maryland Court of Appeals mentioned above involved a peer's informing a counselor of another student's intention to kill herself. The counselor confronted the teen, but she denied any problems, so the counselor did not notify her parents. The failure to inform the parents was deemed negligence (Pate, 1992).

Below are some guidelines for each of the situations listed above:

1. *If a suicide attempt occurs on the premises:* Involve appropriate school personnel, then notify police and an ambulance service. Also notify the parents (or guardian). Let them know where their child is being taken. If the parents (or guardian) are not available, notify the next closest relative. See to it that the student receives proper medical and psychiatric care. Often, the hospital will send the student back to the school after the crisis without a psychiatric evaluation. Counselors should guard against this phenomenon.

2. *If the student discloses to you.* First, consult your supervisor or another mental health professional. Go over the assessment of lethality with the student. This process will help you establish the standard of care. Call the parents (or guardian) and tell them to go to the appropriate psychiatric facility. Explain to the parents and the student that an evaluation or diagnosis does not necessarily mean commitment. If the parents resist this process, you may need to contact Children and Youth Services for assistance. Be sure to contact the parents in the presence of the child, to eliminate the "he said/she said" phenomenon.

3. *If a peer tells you.* Confront the student. If the student admits the suicidal ideation, follow the procedure outlined above. If the student denies the ideation, notify the parents (or guardian). Of course, you must inform the student about this disclosure.

College Student Suicide

Obtaining accurate data on suicide rates of college students is difficult. Most colleges and universities employ ineffective record-keeping systems, and the data that exist tend to be inconsistent. Because of concern about negative publicity, colleges may under-report or mislabel suicides (Westefeld, Whitchard, & Range, 1990).

College students face certain issues that are unique to this setting. Striving for academic success, having unclear vocational goals, and being away from home may cause students to become depressed (Mathiasen, 1988). Also, research has shown poor problem-solving skills under high stress to be influential with suicidal college students (Fremouw, Callahan, & Kashden, 1993).

Middle and secondary schools today are taking more responsibility for preventing student suicides. Colleges and universities also have an obligation to respond to and prevent suicides. Campus seminars on suicide prevention and programming efforts can be beneficial. Workshops on dealing with stress, academic concerns, career planning, and problem solving can help students deal with the major life stresses of college. Educating faculty, staff, students, and administrators about the signs of depression and suicide should be a component in any prevention program. Residence hall staff, especially, should be educated in this area, as their exposure to students is extensive (Philips, 1983).

Intervention with College Students

Mental health professionals who deal with the college population face some special considerations. The main difference between college-aged students and those who are younger is the requirement for parental notification. Some college students are minors, but the majority are over 18 years old. Legally, a mental health professional is not obligated to contact the parents of a potentially suicidal client if the student is not a minor. However, in 1992, *Gallagher's National Survey of Counseling Center Directors* revealed that 63.8% had notified a third party in regard to a potentially suicidal student. This statistic has increased 5% since 1991.

Residence provides another complication in this matter. Out-of state and international students sometimes are turned away from psychiatric hospitals because they have out-of-state insurance policies. This can put responsibility back on the university, even if students are of legal age. In this circumstance, the counseling center must take a more active role in helping the student receive proper psychiatric attention. Contacting the parents or guardian is necessary in this situation.

Summary

Working with potentially suicidal clients is a serious responsibility. Mental health professionals have a legal and ethical responsibility to seek clinical training and education in this area. Faced with a client who is a potential harm to him- or herself, the counselor should follow the steps listed below:

1. *Make an assessment of the danger.*

2. *Determine what action is reasonable.*

3. *See that the course of action reaches fruition.*

LEARNING FACILITATION AND FOCUS

Exercise 6.1. Counselor Checklist for School-Based Suicide Programs

Assess your school program in each category. Place a check in the appropriate box. After completing the assessment for each component, add the checks in each column. Determine how your school compares with the literature review in regard to comprehensive and systematic school-based suicide programs.

Program Components	Yes	No	Not Sure
Program Construction			
The administration supports the program.	___	___	___
The district school board has approved the program.	___	___	___
The school has published a policy describing explicit procedures for intervention with potentially suicidal students.	___	___	___
Community mental health resources for referral, training, and consultation have been identified.	___	___	___
A needs assessment has been conducted to determine the knowledge and attitudes of teachers and students regarding youth suicide.	___	___	___

Program Components	Yes	No	Not Sure
Multidisciplinary teams have been formed as part of the program.	____	____	____
An outside mental health consultant has been made available.	____	____	____
In-service training on suicide has been implemented for teachers, counselors, and staff. Qualified professionals with a special focus on adolescent suicide are available in the event of a crisis.	____	____	____

Crisis Prevention

	Yes	No	Not Sure
The administration conducts psychometric screening to identify at-risk students and conducts appropriate follow-up with these students.	____	____	____
Students with substance, academic, or family problems are identified.	____	____	____
Supportive counseling for at-risk students is available.	____	____	____
Suicidal students are immediately referred to a mental health professional.	____	____	____
Classroom and group discussions on teen suicide are conducted by mental health professionals.	____	____	____
Handouts, pamphlets, and wallet cards with suicide prevention information are distributed to students and parents.	____	____	____

Postintervention

	Yes	No	Not Sure
Individual and group counseling is provided for students.	____	____	____
A specialized consultant works with the school's prevention team.	____	____	____

Program Components	Yes	No	Not Sure
A single spokesperson addresses the media.	_____	_____	_____
A prepared statement regarding the death is read to the students by the teachers.	_____	_____	_____
Memorial activities do not exceed the school's custom for acknowledging the death of a student.	_____	_____	_____
Assemblies to discuss the death are not held.	_____	_____	_____
Students who want to attend the funeral may do so with parental permission.	_____	_____	_____
The school stays open during the funeral for those students not attending the funeral.	_____	_____	_____
Referrals for counseling are made for survivors.	_____	_____	_____
TOTAL:	_____	_____	_____

This checklist appeared in *The School Counselor*, in January, 1994, pp. 191-194. Reprinted with permission.

Exercise 6.2

Using the outline listed earlier and the information in this section, choose a person to role-play an adult client with suicidal characteristics and symptoms. Conduct a clinical interview with this client. Then assume you believe he or she is suicidal. Detail below the exact procedural sequence you would employ to ensure the safety of your client.

Step 1: _____

_____

_____

_____

Step 2: _____

_____

_____

_____

Step 3: _____

_____

_____

_____

Step 4: _____

_____

_____

_____

Exercise 6.3

Repeat Exercise 6.2, this time assuming the client is a minor.

Step 1: _____

_____

_____

_____

Step 2: _____

_____

_____

Step 3: _____

_____

_____

_____

Step 4: _____

_____

_____

_____

THE POTENTIALLY DANGEROUS CLIENT

The *Tarasoff* Case

Prosenjit Poddar was a graduate student at the University of California—Berkeley. In 1968, Poddar attended dancing classes at the International House in Berkeley, where he met a woman named Tatiana (Tanya) Tarasoff. This meeting quickly led to an obsessive, one-sided love affair. After a friendly New Year's Eve kiss under the mistletoe, Poddar began harrassing Ms. Tarasoff, calling and pestering her continually. He was consistently and repeatedly rebuffed by the young woman.

In the summer of 1969, Tanya Tarasoff went to Brazil. When she returned, Poddar went to her home and again was rebuffed. Tanya Tarasoff became emotional and screamed at him. Poddar drew a pellet gun and shot at her. Desperate, the young woman ran from the house, only to be chased down and caught by Poddar, who fatally stabbed her with a kitchen knife. This tragic chain of events unleashed some unforeseen and shocking consequences for mental health professionals.

While Tanya Tarasoff was in Brazil, Poddar sought help for depression at Cowell Memorial Hospital, an affiliate of the University of California—Berkeley. His intake interview was conducted by Dr. Stuart Gold, a psychiatrist, and his therapy was conducted by a psychologist, Dr. Lawrence Moore.

In August of 1969, Poddar told Dr. Moore he was going to kill Tanya Tarasoff when she returned from Brazil. Moore immediately consulted his supervisor, and they agreed that Poddar should be involuntarily committed. Dr. Moore called the police, who detained Poddar; but after questioning the man, police officials decided he was rational and released him. His freedom led directly to Tanya Tarasoff's death.

In late 1974, the California Supreme Court ruled there was cause for action for negligence against the therapist, the university, and the police for the failure to warn (*Tarasoff v. Regents of the University of California,* 1974). This case is commonly known as *Tarasoff I.* The court, apparently under pressure from various professional groups, agreed to a rehearing in 1976 (*Tarasoff v. Regents of the University of California,* 1976). This case is commonly known as *Tarasoff II.*

Whenever we mention the *Tarasoff* case throughout this book, we are citing *Tarasoff II.* In the court's final decision—presented in *Tarasoff II* on July 1, 1976—it set a new standard for therapists. The mandate was clear: *"Therapists who know or should know of patients' dangerousness to identifiable third persons have an obligation to take all reasonable steps necessary to protect the potential victims"* (Appelbaum, 1985, p. 425: emphasis ours).

Various writers on the subject of *Tarasoff* have defined the term *therapist* to include psychologists; counselors; child, marriage, and family therapists; and community mental health counselors. As Stone (cited in Waldo & Malley, 1992) noted:

> Many mental health professionals and paraprofessionals, including social workers, psychiatric social workers, psychiatric nurses, occupational therapists, pastoral counselors, and guidance counselors, provide some form of therapy. ... How many of these millions of therapist-patient contacts each year are intended to be covered by the court's decision is unclear. (p. 539)

What *Tarasoff* Did Not Require.   Researchers have looked extensively at what the *Tarasoff* ruling requires of mental health professionals, and what it does not. VandeCreek and Knapp (1993) addressed this issue head on:

> Because the *Tarasoff* decision has been subject to so many misinterpretations, it is important to know what the *Tarasoff* court did

not say. The court did not require psychotherapists to issue a warning every time a patient talks about an urge or fantasy to harm someone. On the contrary, the court stated that "a therapist should not be encouraged routinely to reveal such threats ... unless such disclosure is necessary to avert danger to others" (*Tarasoff*, p. 347). Finally, the court did not specify that warning the intended victim was the only required response when danger arises; on the contrary, the court stated that the discharge of such duty may require the therapist to take one or more of various steps. (p. 6)

Past *Tarasoff.* Since the *Tarasoff* trial, other courts have ruled that liability should not be imposed on the therapist if a victim was not identified (*Thompson v. County of Alemeda*, 1980). However, other courts have ruled that the potential victim need only be foreseeably identifiable (*Jablonski v. United States*, 1983) or that the danger need only be foreseeable (*Hedlund v. Superior Court of Orange County*, 1983; *Lipari v. Sears Roebuck*, 1980). Mental health professionals have been found liable for not using prior patient records to predict violence (*Jablonski v. United States*, 1983) and for keeping inadequate records (*Peck v. The Counseling Service of Addison County*, 1985). A Florida appellate court ruled that *Tarasoff* should not be imposed because the relationship of trust and confidence, necessary for the therapeutic process, would be harmed if mental health professionals were required to warn potential victims (*Boynton v. Burglass*, 1991).

It is the special relationship between mental health professionals and clients that sets the stage for therapist liability. The *Tarasoff* case is binding only in California, and it is impossible to predict what courts in other states will do. Some states have expanded the *Tarasoff* reasoning, while others have rejected it.

> In jurisdictions in which appellate courts have not yet ruled on the question, the prudent clinician is well advised to proceed under the assumption that some version of *Tarasoff* liability will be imposed. The duty to protect, in short, is now a fact of professional life for nearly all American clinicians and potentially for clinical researchers as well. (Appelbaum & Rosenbaum, cited in Monahan, 1993, p. 243)

Assessing Danger

Appelbaum (1985) presented a model for fulfilling the *Tarasoff* obligation, urging that clinicians treating potentially dangerous patients should undertake a three-stage process of assessment, selection of a course of action, and implementation.

- The first stage, *assessment*, has two components: First, the therapist must gather the data to evaluate the level of danger; then, he or she must make a determination of dangerousness on the basis of that data.

- In the second stage, the clinician who has determined a patient is likely to be dangerous must choose a course of action to protect potential victims.

- In the third stage, the therapist must *implement* his or her decisions appropriately. This requirement has two components:

  1. First, the therapist must take action to protect potential victims.

  2. Second, he or she must monitor the situation on a continuing basis to assess the success or failure of the initial response, the likelihood that the patient will be violent, and the need for further measures (Applebaum, 1985, p. 426).

The First Stage: Assessment.   Information needed to assess the level of danger can be found in the client's past and current records or gathered in the counseling interview. Use the following questions and guidelines to help determine the potential for violent behavior.

1. Does the client have a history of violent behavior? Past violence is the best predictor of future violence.

2. Does the client have a history of violent conduct with a previous assessment or diagnosis of mental illness?

3. Does the client have a history of arrests for violent conduct?

4. Does the client have a history of threats associated with violent conflict?

5. Has the client ever been diagnosed with a mental disorder for which violence is a common symptom?

6. Has the client had at least one inpatient hospitalization associated with dangerous conduct, whether voluntary or involuntary?

7. Does the client have any history of dangerous conduct, apparently unprovoked and not stress-related?

8. If the client has a history of dangerous conduct, how long ago was the incident? The more recent the dangerous behavior, the more likely it is that the behavior will be repeated.

9. If you consider the client dangerous to someone else, note any threats and your observations, and notify the person you think might be harmed. Those acts that have a high degree of intent or intensity are most likely to recur.

10. Determine if any serious threats, attempts, or acts harmful to others have been related to drug or alcohol intoxication.

11. Ask the client direct and focused questions, such as, "What is the most violent thing you have ever done?" and "How close have you come to becoming violent?" (Monahan, 1993, p. 244).

12. Use the reports of significant others. Often, family members can provide valuable information about a client's potential for violence. Again, ask direct questions, such as, "Are you worried that your loved one is going to hurt someone?"(Monahan, 1993, p. 244).

13. Has the client threatened others?

14. Does the client have access to weapons?

15. What is the client's relationship to the intended victim(s)?

16. Does the client belong to a social support group that condones violence?

The Second Stage: Selecting a Course of Action. Once the mental health professional has assessed the danger a client poses to others, he or she must decide what to do. Use the guidelines below to help form an action plan.

1. *If you don't consider the danger to be imminent, keep the client in intensified therapy.* Deal with the client's aggression as part of the treatment. However, if the client does not adhere to the treatment plan—that is, if he or she discontinues therapy—the danger level should be considered higher.

2. *Invite the client to participate in the disclosure decision.* This process often makes the client feel more in control. It also is prudent to

contact the third party in the presence of the client. This may vitiate problems of paranoia over what has been communicated.

3. *Attempt environmental manipulations.* Medication may be initiated, changed, or increased. Have the client get rid of any lethal weapons.

4. *Keep careful records.* When recording information relevant to risk, note the source of the information (e.g., the name of the spouse), the content (e.g., the character of the threat and the circumstances under which it was disclosed), and the date on which the information was disclosed. Finally, include your rationale for any decisions you make.

5. *If warning a third party is unavoidable, disclose only the minimum amount necessary to protect the victim or the public.* State the specific threat, but reserve any opinions or predictions.

6. *Consult with your supervisor.* Your agency or school should have a contingency plan for such problems that is derived in consultation with an informed attorney, an area psychiatric facility, and local police.

The Third Stage: Monitoring the Situation.   You should constantly monitor any course of action to ensure the objectives of the initial implementation are satisfied. Follow-up procedures should be scrupulously adhered to and well-documented.

Patient's Past Criminal Acts

Applebaum and Meisel (1986) reported that therapists' legal obligations to report past criminal acts differ under state and federal laws. Under federal law, therapist obligations fall under a statue of "misprision of a felony." Applebaum and Meisel (1986) noted these conditions as necessary to establish guilt for a misprision of a felony:

1. The principle committed and completed the felony alleged.

2. The defendant had full knowledge of the fact.

3. The defendant failed to notify authorities.

4. The defendant took an affirmative step to conceal the crime.

The mere failure to report the crime does not appear to meet the criteria of affirmative concealment. If the mental health professional is questioned by law enforcement officials, he or she must respond truthfully, but is not obligated to break confidentiality; it does not appear that the mental health professional has an obligation to say anything at all. Few states have statutes addressing misprision of a felony. Most do require the reporting of gunshot wounds, child abuse, or other specified evidence of certain crimes. The strong trend is for courts to reject the crime of misprision (Applebaum & Meisel, 1986).

Summary

Mental health professionals who counsel potentially violent clients have a duty to protect potential victims from serious and imminent danger. Assessment of a client's potential danger to others should be based on an inspection of past and current records, an interview with the client, and interviews with significant others. If it is determined that the client is dangerous to others, the mental health professional must choose a course of action to prevent the danger. The course of action must be implemented and carefully monitored.

LEARNING FACILITATION AND FOCUS

Exercise 6.4

Rich (1988) conducted a survey using eight case studies. Two of the case studies had one variable: an identifiable victim. Two had two variables: an identifiable victim and a clear threat. Two had three variables: an identifiable victim, a clear threat, and imminent behavior. Two had four variables: an identifiable victim, a clear threat, imminent behavior, and serious danger.

The case studies were sent to 600 randomly selected mental health professionals, including 200 clinical psychologists, 200 social workers, and 200 mental health counselors. Of those 600, 199 responded. Among other questions, respondents were asked if they would break confidentiality in each case.

Read each case study below and determine (a) if you would break confidentiality and (b) what reasonable care would be. After you have completed your assignment, you can compare your answers with those of the respondents (see Table 6.1).

Case #1. Charles is 38 years old, single, and employed. He has been in therapy for four sessions. His presenting problem is his obsession with Karen Jones. Charles and Karen ended their six-month relationship shortly before Charles came for treatment. He is having difficulty accepting Karen's wish to end the relationship.

Today, Charles talks repeatedly of possessing Karen. He tells you he has begun following her, going through her mail, and calling her at different times during the night to see if she is alone. He tells you that Karen has called the police and they have told him to stay away form her. Charles says he can't stop himself. He has missed the last three days of work because he's been hanging around Karen's apartment, waiting to catch Karen with another man. Charles tells you that he's going to kill Karen and stop his torment. He says he has a gun.

___ I would break confidentiality.

___ I would not break confidentiality.

Reasonable care in this case would be:

_____

_____

_____

_____

_____

_____

Case #2. Helen is 41 years old, single, and unemployed. She has been seen by two other therapists and has a history of making threats. You have seen her for four sessions. At today's session, Helen tells you she is still having trouble sleeping and eating. She says she feels old. She then looks at you and says, "I'm going to kill someone at the end of two months."

___ I would break confidentiality.

___ I would not break confidentiality.

Reasonable care in this case would be:

_____

_____

_____

_____

_____

_____

Case #3. Joe is 26 years old, married, and the father of two young children. He is employed as a dishwasher at a local diner. He is a machinist by trade, but has been unable to find work since he was laid off three years ago. He has had four sessions with you. Joe's presenting problem is trouble coping with his underemployment. He has become isolated from his family and says he feels more and more like a failure. Lately, Joe has become increasingly hostile toward the world.

At today's session, Joe tells you he has just been turned down for a good-paying job, which would have solved all of his financial problems. He says that he lost out because of affirmative action. He is very agitated. Joe tells you he's fed up and he's going to take matters into his own hands. He says, "If things don't change, I'm going to kill someone."

___ I would break confidentiality.

___ I would not break confidentiality.

Reasonable care in this case would be:

_____

_____

_____

_____

Case #4. Susan is 37 years old, recently divorced, the mother of three young children, and unemployed. She has come to four sessions. Her presenting problem is her struggle coping with her divorce. During today's session, Susan begins crying uncontrollably and screaming that she's going to kill her husband when he returns from a business trip in three weeks. She says she can't deal with all of the emotional and financial burdens any longer. She says her husband makes a lot of money and has a girlfriend, and that this makes her furious. Susan tells you this torture has to stop and she doesn't see any alternative.

___ I would break confidentiality.

___ I would not break confidentiality.

Reasonable care in this case would be:

_____

_____

_____

_____

_____

_____

Case #5. Sam is 51 years old, married, the father of five children, and employed at a local mill. He has been in treatment for four sessions. Sam's presenting problem is poor impulse control and violent outbursts, both at home and at work. His wife has threatened to leave him and he has had verbal and written warnings at work.

Two days ago, Sam came to the session in a very agitated state. He had just been notified that he was going to be laid off from his job indefinitely. Sam blames his supervisor, Mr. Bennett, for his layoff. You were able to talk Sam through his anger, and he agreed to come in today for another session. He has not shown up for his session. He is 15 minutes late when he calls. Sam tells you that he won't be coming in for his session. He says he's bought a gun and he is going to kill Bennett. He says he's not going to let Bennett get away with what he's done. He hangs up the phone.

___ I would break confidentiality.

___ I would not break confidentiality.

Reasonable care in this case would be:

_____

_____

_____

_____

_____

_____

Case #6. Mary is 30 years old, single, and unemployed. She is serving a one-year sentence for burglary. She has six months left to serve. Mary has a history of violent behavior. She has become angry and abusive with the guards and other inmates. You have been called in to talk to her. Mary tells you she received a letter from a friend telling her that Mary's boyfriend, Bob Smith, is seeing another woman. Mary is extremely angry and says it is Bob's fault that she is in jail. She says she committed the burglary for him. Mary tells you that as soon as she gets out of jail, she's going to get a gun and kill Bob Smith, and she doesn't care if they lock her up forever.

___ I would break confidentiality.

___ I would not break confidentiality.

Reasonable care in this case would be:

_____

_____

_____

_____

_____

Case #7. Arlene is 45, widowed, and unemployed. She has had four sessions with you. Her presenting problem is that she is having trouble coping with dating and is becoming increasingly frustrated with the various men she is meeting.

During today's session, Arlene tells you that she went out on another date and it was horrible. She says that all her date wanted was to get in bed. She tells you that she isn't going to let men take advantage of her anymore. She says that she's going to carry a gun from now on, and the next date who tries to molest her is going to end up dead, because she is going to shoot him.

____ I would break confidentiality.

____ I would not break confidentiality.

Reasonable care in this case would be:

_____

_____

_____

_____

Case #8. Tom is 18 years old, single, living with his parents, and attending school. He has had four sessions. Tom's presenting problem is his conflict with his father.

At today's session, Tom tells you that, during the past weekend, he was teased by a group of teens and he ran away from the situation. He says the next time he sees them, he's going to kill them.

___ I would break confidentiality.

___ I would not break confidentiality.

Reasonable care in this case would be:

_____

_____

_____

_____

_____

_____

TABLE 6.1
Respondents' Responses

Occurrence of Elements and Case	Break Confidence		Maintain Confidence		Total
	N	%	N	%	N
One Element					
Case No. 2	41	21	158	79	199
Case No. 8	76	38	123	62	199
Two Elements					
Case No. 3	58	29	141	71	199
Case No. 7	51	266	148	74	199
Three Elements					
Case No. 4	76	38	123	62	199
Case No. 6	40	20	159	80	199
Four Elements					
Case No. 1	194	97	5	3	199
Case No. 5	199	100	0	0	199

THE CLIENT WITH AIDS

A client says in therapy that he has a gun in his pocket and the gun is loaded. He also says that when he leaves the therapist's office, he is going to drive to his former place of employment, hold the gun to his boss's head, and "blow his brains out." The therapist knows the client has a history of violent conduct and has been involuntarily committed twice before for violent actions.

If the therapist does not take some reasonable action to protect the intended victim, and if the former employer dies as a result of the client's actions, the therapist almost assuredly will be guilty of an ethical and legal violation. In most jurisdictions, the therapist will be found in violation of the law.

Clients with human immunodeficiency virus (HIV) or acquired immune deficiency syndrome (AIDS) may present mental health professionals with difficult ethical, legal, and moral problems. Unlike the case above, the ethical and legal guidelines regarding AIDS patients infecting third parties are not clear. Those who anticipate definitive ethical and legal guidelines should reflect on the instructions given physicians regarding the tube feeding of an 84-year-old hospital patient:

> I insisted that there are no rules that would replace their prudence and exempt them from the anguishing task of wrestling with the untidy and unpredictable clinical realities of individual cases. Anyone who claims to have a rule that will cut through all of the agonies of ambiguity and uncertainty is involved in deception. (McCormick, 1989, p. 358)

HIV and AIDS

AIDS was first diagnosed in the United States in 1981. The disease spreads when someone with HIV or AIDS directly transfers body fluids to another person. People who get AIDS usually do so within 10 years of being infected with HIV; 75% die within 2 years of developing AIDS, usually of Kaposi's sarcoma, pneumocystic pneumonia, or another opportunistic infection (Kelly, 1987).

Public health laws require health professionals to report specified communicable diseases. Such reporting allows the gathering of epidemiological data on the incidence of diseases (American Medical Association, 1988). Laws in all 50 states and the District of Columbia mandate reporting diagnosed cases of AIDS to state health officials. This information is reported to the Centers for Disease Control (CDC) in Atlanta. More than 20 states have laws saying that positive HIV status is reportable in itself (Dickens, 1990). Current medical knowledge reveals that all HIV seropositive individuals, even those exhibiting no symptoms, are potentially infectious to others. All persons infected with HIV—from those who are asymptomatic seropositive to those with full-blown AIDS—are capable of transmitting the disease to third parties (Harding, Gray, & Neal, 1993).

> As of 1992 about 250,000 Americans have had AIDS, including 100,000 who have already died of AIDS. In addition, about 2 to 2.5 million Americans have the HIV infection. … It is believed that by the [year 2000] at least 1% of the American population will carry HIV or have AIDS. (Knapp & VandeCreek, 1993, p. 5)

Ethical Positions

Generally the literature on HIV and AIDS is divided into ethical and legal discussions. We will look at the ethical considerations first.

A counselor who receives information confirming that a client has a disease commonly known to be both communicable and fatal is justified in disclosing information to an identifiable third party, who by his or her relationship with the client is at a high risk of contracting the disease. Prior to making a disclosure the counselor should ascertain that the client has not already informed the third party about his or her disease and that the client is not intending to inform the third party in the immediate future. (American Counseling Association, 1995. B.1.d)

* * * *

If a patient refuses to agree to change his or her behavior or to notify the person(s) at risk, or the physician has good reason to believe that the patient has failed to or is unable to comply with this agreement, it is ethically permissible for the physician to notify an identifiable person who the physician believes is in danger of contracting the virus. (American Psychiatric Association, Ad Hoc Committee on AIDS Policy, 1988, p. 541)

* * * *

1. A legal duty to protect third parties from HIV infection should not be imposed.

2. If, however, specific legislation is considered, then it should permit disclosure only when (a) the provider knows of an identifiable third party who the provider has compelling reason to believe is at significant risk; and (b) the client/patient has been urged to inform the third party and has either refused or is considered unreliable in his/her willingness to notify the third party.

3. If such legislation is adopted, it should include immunity from civil and criminal liability for providers who, in good faith, make decisions to disclose or not to disclose information about HIV infection to third parties. (American Psychological Association, 1991, p. 1)

* * * *

Social workers should first use the strength of their client-worker relationship to encourage clients with HIV infection to inform their sexual or needle-sharing partners of their antibody status. Clients should be counseled regarding existing partner-notification programs that can be used. If the client cannot or will not inform their sexual or needle-sharing partners, the social workers must inform the clients of the avenues, if any, they are mandated to follow. Social workers have a responsibility to consult with other practitioners and to consider legal counsel if they feel they have a duty to warn. (National Association of Social Workers, 1990, p. 5)

Ethical principles may be applied to the issue of confidentiality with the seropositive client. All clients have the right to have their private business kept confidential. However, the autonomy of a potential sexual partner also must be considered; the principles of beneficence, nonmaleficence, and justice obviously are relevant to parties outside the counseling relationship who may become infected.

Cohen (1990) noted that therapists who keep their clients' HIV status confidential "only permit the clients' grotesque violation of those very same principles" (p. 283). Gray and Harding (1988) agreed:

Given the virulence and fatality of the disease, the increasing rate of prevalence, and the absence of conclusive scientific data regarding transmission, the right of an endangered person to know may overcome any right to privacy regarding individual identification or disclosure to a third party. (p. 221)

However, Harding et al. (1993) recommended that disclosure should occur "as last resort, to use only if no other viable alternatives exist" (p. 303). Melton (1991) agreed, noting that it is better to use clinical interventions designed either to modify client behavior or to help the client warn third parties.

Others have asserted that client confidentiality should not be broken (e.g., Kermani & Weiss, 1989; Wood, Marks, & Dilley, 1990). Kelly (1987) argued that confidentiality is important "for the sake of all potential victims in the future, who will need to believe they can rely on the principle before they disclose information" (p. 336). Morrison (1989) agreed, noting that the therapist who breaks confidentiality may put the therapeutic relationship at risk. And Landesman (1987) argued that disclosing confidential information could influence clients not to get the help they need again.

Breaching confidentiality may have other serious consequences, as Kain noted:

There are, for example, possibilities that (a) permissible disclosure may instill mistrust in the counseling process, (b) some counselor disclosures may be based on fear of civil liability or moral judgment, and (c) reporting of sensitive information to public officials may generate repercussions (e.g., housing discrimination, employment limitation, denial of insurance opportunities, invasion of privacy). (cited in Harding et al., 1993, p. 302)

Legal Positions

Most of a therapist's potential legal duty in breaching confidentiality with an HIV- or AIDS-positive client revolves around the *Tarasoff* case. The arguments in the literature are mostly syllogistic.

- The first position is that a mental health professional may be liable for not warning a third party of serious and foreseeable danger, based on the *Tarasoff* case decision. The person who has HIV and is sexually active may be a serious and foreseeable danger to his or her partner(s). Therefore, a therapist should disclose the danger to the party(s) at risk.

- The second position is the therapist should not be held liable for not warning a third party based on the *Tarasoff* case. The person who is HIV- or AIDS-positive and is sexually active may be a serious and foreseeable danger to his or her partner(s). Although there are similarities between the *Tarasoff* case and sexually active clients who are seropositive, there also are many differences. Therefore, one cannot say that the therapist should disclose the positive danger to a third party at risk. To this date, no case involving confidentiality and an AIDS client has been litigated (Yu & O'Neal, cited in Schlossberger & Heckler, 1996).

Support for reporting communicable sexual diseases is based on historic legal principles. In some states, not warning family members or others in close proximity to a patient of a communicable disease may render physicians negligent in their behavior (Delarosa, 1987). Courts refer to the physician's duty to protect others from communicable diseases, and they define the mental health professional's duty in the same way (Delarosa, 1987; Fulero, 1988).

A case can be made that the physician's responsibility for notifying third parties absolves the mental health professional from responsibility to do so. However, laws requiring the reporting of HIV infection are state-specific. Some jurisdictions do not require reporting of HIV-positive status until patients have a diagnosis of AIDS.

Schlossberger and Heckler (1996) noted that the danger posed to Tanya Tarasoff violated her legal rights. In many states people do not have a legal right to know if their sexual partners are HIV-positive. Consequently, when HIV-positive clients have sexual relationships with others, they have committed no legal wrong. It follows, then, that therapists have no legal responsibility to warn in those states. In fact, Schlossberger and Heckler (1996) continued, any rule that requires the counselor to warn third parties about behaviors that are legal:

> would constitute discrimination against clients of therapists and violate equality under the law: in effect, people in therapy would be held to a different legal standard than everyone else ... we conclude that, unless state law (criminal or tort), directly or indirectly, generally requires seropositive clients to inform their partners, therapists have no legal duty to warn. Although the therapist has a legal duty to warn others subject to an illegal danger, the therapist has no duty to intervene when clients pose dangers that society, through law, grants them the right to pose. (Schlossberger & Heckler, 1996, pp. 32–22)

Some have argued that, since everyone knows about the AIDS epidemic today, the caveat of prudence on the part of sexual partners is in order, comparable to the legal doctrine of assumption of risk (Closen & Isaacman, 1988). However, the caveat may not apply to an unwitting spouse who is married to a sexually active bisexual client (Hoffman, 1991).

Others have argued that third parties should be warned only under certain conditions. Wood et al. (1990), for example, listed the following conditions that must be met before a mental health professional could be held liable for failing to warn a third party:

1. The counselor must know the patient is HIV-infected.

2. The client engages in unsafe behavior on a regular basis.

3. The client intends to continue such behavior even after counseling by the therapist.

4. HIV transmission will be the likely result.

Summary

Mental health professionals face confusing and sometimes conflicting ethical and legal choices when dealing with clients who are HIV-positive and sexually active. Most of the literature pertaining to the legal aspects of this dilemma centers on the question of whether the *Tarasoff* ruling applies. Schlossberger and Heckler (1996) argued that *Tarasoff* does not apply in states that do not have laws requiring seropositive clients to inform their partners. As of this writing, there has not been any litigation to confirm or deny this hypothesis. Mental health professionals should learn the laws in their states, be apprised of the policies and positions of their professions regarding HIV-positive clients, and develop their own ethical thinking on the matter.

LEARNING FACILITATION AND FOCUS

Exercise 6.5

Mary Boturm has been seeing Karen, a social worker, for about six months. Her presenting problem is that she is shy, withdrawn, and very lonely. She has few social skills and doesn't know what to do with her free time. Mary is 27 years old and very attractive. Karen has been trying to improve Mary's self-concept and advising her on social matters. Karen is very empathetic toward Mary. She considers Mary a deeply sincere and honest woman who would be a happy and productive person if she felt better about herself.

Karen has another client named Henry. Henry's presenting problems are two-fold: He is very angry with women and he has AIDS. He believes he acquired the disease from a woman who assured him she was "clean." Henry is 32 years old. He says he wants revenge: If he ever gets the chance, he wants to "play the same sexual game" that was played on him.

As Mary's therapy progresses, she tells Karen that she has a new relationship. Karen has seen Mary chatting with Henry in the waiting room and wonders if he is her new boyfriend.

In one session, Mary debates out loud whether or not she should be sexually intimate with her new friend. Mary believes that sex should be shared only between people who are serious about each other, but she is beginning to think she will become intimate with her boyfriend. Finally, she mentions her boyfriend's name, and Karen realizes it is Henry.

What would you do in this case? Use the ethical principles presented in chapter 4 to make your determination. Write a position paper to support your thinking.

Chapter 7

SEXUAL ABUSE AND HOMOSEXUALITY

THE ABUSED CHILD

Child abuse occurs at an alarmingly high rate. An estimated 2 million children are abused or neglected annually in the United States (General Accounting Office, 1991). The actual number of cases is not known (Gargiulo, 1990), as most professionals believe the crime is significantly under-reported. (Goldman, 1993). Children with special needs are particularly vulnerable to abuse (Gargiulo, 1990; Goldman, 1993).

Presently all states have laws prohibiting child abuse (Besharov, 1988). The instrument for enforcing those laws is an administrative structure commonly known as *child protective services*.

In most states anyone can report suspected child abuse if they do so in good faith. Most states also have *mandated reporters*—professionals who, in the course of their work with children, come upon evidence of abuse. Commonly mandated reporters include doctors, nurses, mental health professionals, social workers, and teachers.

The malicious reporting of child abuse is against the law in all states (Besharov, 1988). The national hotline number for child abuse is 1-800-4-a-child.

Definition of Child Abuse

Definitions of child abuse vary from state to state, but most states have laws addressing four different kinds of abuse:

1. *Physical abuse* is nonaccidental injury received by anybody under the age of 18. It is characterized by unexplained bruises, burns, welts, lacerations, abrasions, skeletal injuries, internal injuries, human bite marks, head injuries, and missing or loosened teeth.

2. *Sexual abuse* includes any act of rape, incest, sodomy, sexual intercourse, oral copulation, penetration of genital or anal openings by a foreign object, or child molestation. Closely related to sexual abuse is sexual exploitation. *Sexual exploitation* is using a child to produce pornographic films, magazines, or books.

3. *Emotional abuse* is blaming, belittling, or rejecting a child. It includes any persistent lack of concern by the parent for the child's welfare (Sloan, 1983).

4. *Neglect* is acting negligently toward a child by a person who is responsible for the child's well-being. The acts can be those of commission or omission. Neglect includes failure to provide for basic needs such as food, shelter, medical care, and appropriate clothing. Placing the child in an unsafe environment also can be considered neglect.

Reporting Child Abuse

Mandated reporters usually are professionals who interact with children in the course of their work. The Federal Child Abuse Prevention and Treatment Act requires that sexual, physical, and mental exploitation of children be reported. *Any circumstance that indicates serious harm or threat to a child's welfare must be reported.* Suspicion alone may not be obligatory. The existence of a *reasonable cause* to believe or suspect triggers the mandate (Besharov, 1988). "Reasonable" is what any prudent professional would do in the situation.

Confidentiality and privileged communication are not legal reasons for failing to report abuse. The laws against child abuse supersede the laws of privilege and the ethical mandates of confidentiality. If the abuse is reported in good faith, most states do not allow retribution; that is, the mental health professional cannot be sued for defamation of character even if the abuse is unfounded.

Child abuse must be reported even if the child does not want it reported and even if the mental health professional does not feel it is in the best interest of the child to do so (Weinstock & Weinstock, 1989). Most states do not have a statute of limitations on child abuse cases, unless the abuse was reported before and the charges were dismissed. "This seems to mean that the mental health professional must report abuse that occurred many years ago" (Swenson, 1997, p. 414). Liability has been imposed on mental health professionals for damages caused by not reporting child abuse (Meyers, 1982; Schroeder, 1979).

Therapists who decide to file a child abuse report typically do so by calling the appropriate social service agency. They must file a written report subsequent to the call. A caseworker will be assigned to the case by the child protective services agency. If the caseworker finds probable evidence that neglect or abuse has occurred, he or she refers the case to a law enforcement agency. At that point, the state either begins a criminal prosecution or takes a civil action. If someone other than a parent or caretaker accuses a parent of sexually abusing a child, authorities may initiate both criminal and civil proceedings simultaneously (Buckley, 1988).

Characteristics of Abusers

There is no such thing as a "psychological profile of a typical molester" (Chaffin & Milner, 1993; Murphy, Rau, & Worley, 1994). Reflecting on her 19 years of psychological practice, Lamson (1995) reported seeing the following characteristics in varying degrees.

1. Immaturity, emotional dependency, and narcissism with an overly strong need for attention and affection

2. Feelings of social or sexual inadequacy with adults

3. Turning to a child for emotional fulfillment that is lacking in adult relationships

4. Impaired empathy

5. Anger toward an adult partner

6. Antisocial personality traits

7. History of childhood emotional/physical/sexual abuse

8. Preoccupation with sex

9. Membership in an extremely strict, sexually repressive religion

10. Substance abuse at the time of the molestation

Erickson, McEnvoy, and Colucci (1984) referred to some general characteristics of child abuse perpetrators. The most widely accepted characteristics of abusing and neglectful parents are these:

1. Were abused as children

2. Are socially and emotionally immature

3. Have low self-esteem

4. Expect children to act as adults

5. Cannot express frustration or anger via acceptable behaviors

6. Have expectations of their children that are not age-appropriate

7. Have a history of violent marital discord

8. Abuse drugs or alcohol

9. Cannot tolerate stress

10. Lack adequate parenting skills

11. Ignore the child's needs

12. Are guarded in discussing family relationships

13. Lack appropriate role models

The problem of psychological abuse has been studied by Garbarino and Vondra (1987), but we do not yet understand its full implications. For example, Brassard, Germain, and Hart (1987) reported that psychological abuse may last longer and have a greater impact than physical abuse. Physically abusive parents also are more likely to inflict verbal abuse (Ney, 1987). Parents who abuse both physically and verbally maximize the trauma the child experiences.

Being abused as a child generally is accepted as a risk factor for being abusive as an adult (Kaufman & Zigler 1987). Kohn (1987) reported that abused boys, especially, tend to be adult abusers. Another report pointing to abused children's potential for future violence was Bross's (1984), who found that abused adolescents in a New York hospital were two to four times more violent than adolescents with no history of abuse.

Characteristics of Abused Children

The most widely accepted characteristics of the abused or neglected child are these:

1. Displays inappropriate hostility, especially toward authority figures

2. Is disruptive and destructive

3. Is passive and withdrawn; cries easily

4. Is fearful at times; displays fear of going home (or to the place where abuse occurs)

5. Is habitually absent from or late to school

6. Dresses inappropriately for the weather

7. Shows symptoms of "failure to thrive"

8. Has bruises, burns, or other unexplainable marks

9. Has chronically untreated medical needs

10. Is constantly hungry

11. Makes sexually oriented remarks

12. Displays sexually suggestive behavior

13. Shows discomfort of the genital areas

14. Shows significant differences from the mean for anxiety levels (Buckner, 1985)

15. Is fearful of physical contact

16. Is fearful of certain places, people, or activities

17. Displays eating or sleeping problems

18. Acts out inappropriate sexual behaviors

19. Is aggressive or rebellious

20. Has extreme mood swings, withdraws, cries excessively

21. Lacks a positive self-image

One must exercise caution in evaluating these general characteristics. The counselor should be concerned when several of the characteristics of the abusive parent and/or the abused child are present. The presence of only a few characteristics may be indicative only of a dysfunctional family. In observing these characteristics, the counselor should keep documented records specifically addressing these issues.

Child Sexual Abuse

Estimated rates of the prevalence of child sexual abuse differ, depending on the definition used. If the definition is broad, the rate of occurrence is higher. If the definition is narrow, the rate is lower (Haugaard & Emery, 1989). For example, using a broad definition, Kilpatrick (1986) found that 55% of females reported they had experienced sexual interactions as children. However, only 2% experienced intercourse. Finkelhor (1979) detailed unwanted sexual experiences in childhood for 19.2% of his study respondents; Fromuth (1986) found a frequency rate of 22%; Alexander and Lupfer's (1987) research showed a rate of 25. Hrabowy (1987) reported rates of 27.9% and 49.1% when he defined abuse differently for two groups—the first more conservatively than the second.

Despite the discrepancy in estimated rates, however, most researchers agree that child abuse is a serious and seriously under-reported problem (Butler 1978; Finkelhor, 1984; Hillman & Solek-Tefft, 1988). Baxter (1986) claimed that a child is sexually abused approximately every two minutes in the United States. In 80% to 90% of cases reported to the authorities, the perpetrator is known to the child; often, the abuser is a member of the child's family (Baxter, 1986). Sanford (1980) noted that the perpetrator rarely is the stereotypical "dirty old man." Usually he (or, less frequently, she) is an average-looking person with no particular distinguishing characteristics and is known and trusted by the victim (Allsopp & Prosen, 1988). And, as Kempe and Kempe (1978) noted, incidents of sexual abuse cross all socioeconomic and cultural conditions.

Most of the literature on sexual abuse has focused on the abuse of female children. However, Etherington (1995) believed that male sexual abuse is not as rare as reported in the literature. In her study, 25 men who identified themselves as adult male survivors of childhood sexual abuse responded to an advertisement to be interviewed. None reported telling anybody of the abuse at the time it happened; a few disclosed later, but were given little positive psychological help. In fact, one respondent claimed that when he did report the abuse, he was told by a social worker that females didn't do that sort of thing.

Over half of the men in Etherington's study reported they had been abused by women. Twenty-three (92%) reported sexual dissatisfaction in their adult lives, 5 (29%) had been convicted of sexual offenses, and 7 (29%) were convicted of other offenses; in all, 12 of the respondents had been convicted of crimes (48%). These statistics are higher than the norm. Looking at these statistics, Etherington (1995) recommended that society widen its perspective on the possible causes of male antisocial behavior.

Elliot (cited in Etherington, 1995) cited a TV program that discussed issues of sexual abuse and offered a hotline so viewers could respond. The hotline was inundated with male callers, 90% of whom had never told anyone about the abuse. In all, 33% of those who called the hotline were men.

Banning (1989) claimed that there is a cultural bias today against recognizing mother-son sexual abuse that is similar to the backlash in Freud's time against his claims of father-daughter incest among his female patients. In fact, most cases of mother-son sexual abuse are revealed in long-term therapy. Such cases rarely are reported to authorities, treated seriously, or included in public statistics. Consequently, abuse surveys do not accurately reflect the prevalence of mother-son sexual abuse (Lawson, 1991).

According to Lawson (1991) there is a dearth of studies that have explored a nonclinical population of males relative to incest. Also, case studies in the literature suggest that male victims and maternal perpetrators may not consider certain types of sexual abuse as abusive at the time of occurrence (Krug, 1989). According to Bross (1991), many young men would rather be executed than admit that they were sexually abused. In a study of the life histories of rapists and child molesters, Groth (1979) found that one-third had experienced some type of sexual trauma in early childhood.

Lawson (1991) defined maternal sexual abuse to include the following:

1. Subtle abuse, which includes behaviors that do not involve coercing, may or may not involve genital contact, and are not intended to harm the child. Examples of subtle maternal abuse are allowing the son to sleep in the mother's bed, massaging the child or allowing the child to massage the mother, and the mother bathing with the child.

2. Seductive abuse is sexual stimulation that is inappropriate for the child's age and is motivated by parental need. Seductive abuse implies conscious awareness on the part of the mother. It is confusing to the child and may be experienced as over-stimulating or pleasurable by the child.

3. Emasculation and humiliation of the child's sexuality may include forcing the boy to wear female clothing. Criticizing one's rate of sexual development and threatening the child with fears of homosexuality would also be included.

4. Overt sexual abuse is defined as overtly sexualized contact between mother and son. Behaviors include attempted intercourse, fellatio, genital fondling, and clothed or unclothed touching of the genitals. (pp. 265, 266)

Mitchell and Morse (1998) reported a study of women who were sexually abused by female perpetrators, mainly mothers and grandmothers. Although prior research is unclear on the prevalence of this phenomenon, the authors asserted that it is more common than has previously been reported.

Interviewing Children Who May Have Been Sexually Abused

The counselor who interviews the suspected sexually abused child must be highly skilled because it is such an intricate matter. The interviewer must not pressure the child; on the other hand, not interviewing at the appropriate time can leave the abuse unattended. The child most often will want to please the therapist. If the therapist is not highly skilled and suggests in any way what answer he or she wants, the child may feel pressure to provide that answer. Yarmey and Jones (1983) reported that 91% of psychologists and 69% of jurors believe a child responds according to the wishes of a questioner. In his review of the literature on suggestibility of children, Baxter (1986) found that most situations that involved strong suggestions were correlated with intense social pressure. Baxter also found, however, that when suggestibility was minimized and steps were taken to maximize accuracy, a child's memory is as accurate as an adult's.

Child Development. Therapists working with young children on possible sexual abuse must be aware that the language, cognition, and logic systems of children are different than those of adults; in other words, children are not miniature adults. A child's vocabulary is much more limited, which means that children understand much more than they can say. Counselors must learn interviewing techniques and clinical skills to work with young children. For instance, the use of pronouns, double negatives, and compound sentences should not be employed in the interview. Instead, the counselor should focus on familiar events: for example, "Did this take place after your birthday or before your birthday?"

Children remember what happened, but their causal connections are not the same as those of adults. If they have been sexually abused, they may think (indeed, they most often do) that they caused the abuse. In addition, children often are afraid they will no longer be loved, are guilty, ashamed, and afraid they will get into trouble, and may even fear harm or death (their own or others') if the sexual abuse is disclosed.

Before the Interview. It is not possible to predetermine how long the interview should be. The ideal time is one that allows the truth of the matter to purge itself. The therapist should have information pertinent to the history of the case before starting the interview. Information such as the child's name, nicknames, family members' names, and when and where the disclosure was made will contribute to the counselor's efficacy before and during the interview.

Interviewing the Child. The main ingredient for veracity in an interview is the introduction of support and rapport. Casual clothes are appropriate most of the time. Anatomically correct dolls, hand puppets with mouths that open, and coloring paper and crayons should be immediately accessible. It is important that the therapist appear on the same level as the child. This requires an atmosphere that is comfortable. The counselor should be able to get down on the floor or on a pillow and make eye contact with the child. Eye contact is essential when communicating to a child he or she is not at fault, and that what happened was an injustice of the worst type. Remember, the effects of sexual abuse are pervasive and emotionally difficult for the rest of the child's life.

The interviewer must not overreact to any statements the child makes. Some interviews may include interested third parties. The third party may even be the perpetrator or someone the child is keeping a secret from. Third parties should be directed to go to the side of the room, where they are not directly part of the interview. The therapist should arrange the parties so that eye contact is not possible between the child and adult. Above all, third parties must be instructed that they are not to be part of the interview.

Therapists must be careful not to ask leading questions. Brainer, Reyna, and Brandse (1996) reported how easy it was to implant memories of events that never happened in 5- to 8-year-old children by suggestion alone. What is more, the implanted false memories often were remembered in more detail than real memories. The biggest danger in examinations of potential sexual abuse is the interviewer who asks leading questions. Questions should be specific; most importantly, they should not suggest an answer. Questions like, "Is it true your Uncle John did this to you?" are leading and may put pressure on the child to answer affirmatively.

If the child says, "Uncle John touched me," a more appropriate response would be: "Where did Uncle John touch you?" Asking, "Did he touch you on your private parts?" is leading the child. Interviewing children is a clinical art form; mental health professionals who conduct such interviews should receive considerable supervised training in this area.

Summary

Child abuse occurs at an alarming rate. The actual numbers are not known, but most professionals believe it is significantly under-reported. Child abuse may be physical, sexual, or emotional. Sexual abuse is considered the worse form of child abuse. Most of the literature focuses on the abuse of female children. However, some professionals believe sexual abuse of young boys is not as rare as reported in the literature.

LEARNING FACILITATION AND FOCUS

Obtain a copy of the child abuse laws in your state. Read and acquaint yourself with the laws. Invite a representative from Child Protective Services to your class. Prepare a list of questions to ask, including these:

1. If a mental health professional is counseling a parent, and the parent admits abusing his or her child, must the counselor report the abuse?

2. What procedures take place after child abuse is reported? How long does the procedure take?

3. What criteria does the Child Protective Services investigator use to determine if abuse actually took place?

4. If it is determined that child abuse did occur, what happens next?

ADULT SURVIVORS OF CHILD SEXUAL ABUSE

> Sexual abuse is any sexual contact between an adult and a child 16 years of age and under. This includes exploitation (using the child for one's own sexual excitement through taking pictures, showing pictures), incest, rape, fondling, oral sex, anal sex, penetration with objects, exposure, forcing a child to commit sexual acts on other adults and/or children, forcing a child to masturbate themselves [sic] or others (adults/children), and satanic sexual rituals including sexual mutilation and torture. (Baladerian, cited in Glantz & Hunt, 1996, p. 327)

Incest may be the most damaging form of child abuse. The abused child may experience ambivalence between hate and love directed at the perpetrator. Incest usually creates emotional scarring that affects the survivor's feelings of safety and well-being throughout life (Cole, 1984–1986). Adults who were sexually abused as children typically need long-term treatment in a trusting and safe environment.

The therapist treating adult survivors of sexual abuse should encourage disclosure and allow clients to access and vent their feelings (Glantz & Hunt, 1996), always keeping in mind that patience is essential. Norris (1986) suggested challenging the survivor's low self-esteem and noted that clients should learn from the beginning that empathy from the therapist does not necessarily mean agreement. Some adult survivors of incest remember the events but have little or no affect regarding the trauma they endured. Dissociation is one primary defense mechanism of the sexually abused client. Other clients may not remember the abuse at all and deny it ever happened. Techniques such as confrontation should be avoided, because they may remind the survivor of the abuse.

> According to the theory [of dissociation], something happens that is so shocking that the mind grabs hold of the memory and pushes it underground, into some inaccessible corner of the unconscious. There it sleeps for years, or even decades, or even forever—isolated from the rest of mental life. Then, one day, it may rise up and emerge into consciousness. (Loftus, 1994, p. 518)

Counseling Adult Survivors of Incest

One critical factor in counseling adult survivors of incest is the relationship between therapist and client. Briere (1989) noted that a therapeutic environment that fosters self-acceptance and a therapist who is accepting are especially effective. Norris (1986) also noted the importance of emphasizing the client's strengths and positive qualities. And Rencken (1989) urged therapists to support clients in their efforts to explore the abuse, confront the abuse, and recognize both their uniqueness and any commonalities with other survivors.

Josephson and Fong-Beyette (1987, p. 478) concluded that mental health professionals "behaving in ways that clients perceive as accepting, validating, encouraging, and knowledgeable" may help clients in their disclosure of incest.

Some researchers advocate writing letters as a safe way for clients to confront their abusers (e.g., Evans & Schaefer, 1987; Rencken, 1989). Other techniques mentioned in the literature include gestalt therapy, transactional analysis and inner child work, hypnotherapy and guided imagery, behavioral techniques, and cognitive education techniques (Pearson, 1994).

Increasingly, the techniques for counseling sexual abuse survivors are being called into question. Therapists should be advised of the legal issues discussed in the latter part of this section.

False Memory Syndrome

The increased attention given to child abuse and incest is monumental. Between 1986 and 1990, the number of cases reported to child protective agencies increased from 83,000 to 375,000 (Darton, Springer, Wright, & Keene-Osborn, 1991). Estimates of the prevalence of incest range from 15% to 38% of all females (Hood, 1994).

This phenomenal increase has lead critics to pronounce that mental health professionals are creating false memories of abuse. In fact, some have asserted that therapists have created a virtual epidemic of these false memories.

> Recently, a new miracle cure has been promoted by some mental health professionals—recovered memory therapy. In less than 10 years' time this therapy, in its various forms, has devastated thousands of lives. Parents have to witness their adult children turn into monsters trying to destroy their reputations and their lives. (Ofshe & Watters, cited in Zerbe Enns, 1996, p. 4)

So bitter is this controversy that, in 1992, the False Memory Syndrome Foundation (FMSF) was founded. Its objective is to work toward the prevention of "false memory syndrome" and to combat the mental health crisis of the 1990s. Generally speaking, there is strong clinical evidence that traumatic memories can be repressed or denied, but the experimental evidence is weak. This controversy will not be resolved easily, as creating experimental conditions that introduce traumatizing events would be unethical. True memories may be distorted by new information.

A therapist who suggests or uses aggressive memory techniques may distort the original memory base. Fabricated or false memories all feel the same. "But it is also the case that imagination, like its cousin, 'guessing,' can lead people to believe that their false memories are real" (Loftus, 1994, p. 443). For example, in a research study Loftus was able to create false memories in adult participants of being lost in a shopping mall during childhood.

The controversy has been felt in courtrooms, licensing boards, and even insurance agencies. Seppa (1996) reported that complaints to licensing boards increased dramatically between 1992 and 1994. According to one insurance company, over 59% of these complaints were initiated by families of clients who maintained that, because of therapist methodology, the family was falsely accused of child abuse.

Falsely accused families are not the only ones who have been hurt by the issue. Mental health professionals have been stalked, threatened, and had demonstrations performed outside their offices. Many therapists now carefully choose their words, and some may be compromising the quality of care their clients receive out of fear of lawsuits. Others will not deal with any situation that smacks of family violence, referring such cases to other mental health professionals.

On the other side of the coin, angry alleged abuse victims have filed grievances because their therapists did not make them feel better. One group called Victims of Child Abuse Laws (VOCAL) actually encourages lawsuits against mental health professionals. Other groups have proposed legislative changes to restrict the substance of what psychologists can talk about with their clients

Legal cases arising from the negligent retrieval of false memories were unheard of until 1992, but now they are common. The increase in "repressed memory" lawsuits may well bankrupt the professional liability insurance programs for mental health professionals (Caudill, 1995). Repressed memory claims

accounted for 16% of all claims filed in 1994 aga
als insured by the American Professional Agency
Expected to Soar," 1995).

Techniques commonly associated with impla
clude high-pressure support groups, "body work,
sion, "reparenting," and the inappropriate use of
(Knapp & Tepper, 1995). Many patients who have
ing false memories also have accused their cour
violations (Knapp & VandeCreek, 1995).

Summary

When counseling clients who remember bein
dren, therapists should be aware that a controvers
which these memories are real. Mental health prof
about what techniques they use and maintain strict

LEARNING FACILITATION AND FOCUS

Divide into groups. Participants in Group A should review the literature
that supports the concept of repressed memory. Participants in Group B should
review the literature that supports the concept of false memory syndrome. Debate the issue and determine if a consensus can be reached regarding these
competing viewpoints.

THE THERAPIST-ABUSED CLIENT

We have already discussed the potential for burnout and stress in the
mental health professional's life. Eventually, this stress may become associated with incompetent patient care. Counselor impairment has received a
great deal of interest lately, and treatment programs are available for mental health professionals.

Because mental health professionals are human and make mistakes, therapists sometimes encounter clients who have experienced ethical or legal transgressions on the part of a previous therapist. Procedures and policies to rectify
such transgressions vary from profession to profession and from state to state.
It is imperative that the conscientious counselor be aware of such procedures in
his or her jurisdiction.

Therapist-Client Sexual Relationships

Studies have estimated that 7% to 10% of male mental health professionals and 1% to 3% of female mental health professionals have sexual interactions with clients (Illingworth, 1995). Dual relationships are the major cause of licensing disciplinary actions in the United States (Pope, 1989). Bouhoutsos reported that 60% to 70% of patients responding to a survey claimed to have had sex with a therapist (cited in Spiller, 1988).

Sexual relationships with patients are clear violations of the ethical mandates of mental health professionals. Such relationships are reported to cause harm 90% of the time (Bouhoutsos, Holroyd, Lerman, Forer, & Greenberg, 1983). The professional codes are quite clear on this issue:

> Psychologists do not engage in sexual intimacies with current patients or clients. (American Psychological Association, 1995, 4.05)

> * * * *

> Social workers should under no circumstances engage in sexual activities or sexual contact with current clients, whether such contact is consensual or forced. (National Association of Social Workers, 1996, 1.09.a)

> * * * *

> Counselors do not have any type of sexual intimacies with clients and do not counsel persons with whom they have had a sexual relationship. (American Counseling Association, 1995, p. A.7.a)

> * * * *

> Marriage and family therapists are aware of their influential position with respect to clients, and they avoid exploiting the trust and dependency of such persons. Therapists, therefore, make every effort to avoid dual relationships with clients that could impair professional judgment or increase the risk of exploitation. When a dual relationship cannot be avoided, therapists take appropriate professional precautions to ensure judgment is not impaired and no exploitation occurs. Examples of such dual relationships include, but are not limited to, business or close personal relationships with clients. Sexual intimacy with clients is prohibited. (American Association for Marriage and Family Therapy, 1991, 1.2)

Borys and Pope (1989) found that 98% of mental health professionals they surveyed believed that sexual contact with clients was unethical, but 32% thought it was ethical to have sex with a former client. Herlihy and Golden (1990) concluded that a sexual relationship after counseling termination was not, in and of itself, unethical.

The professional ethical codes also address the issue of sex with a former client from a temporal dimension:

> Sexual intimacy with former clients for two years following the termination of therapy is prohibited. (American Association for Marriage and Family Therapy, 1991, 1.2)

* * * *

> Counselors do not engage in sexual intimacies with former clients within a minimum of 2 years after terminating the counseling relationship. Counselors who engage in such a relationship after 2 years following termination have the responsibility to examine and document thoroughly that such relations did not have an exploitative nature, based on factors such as duration of counseling, amount of time since counseling, termination circumstances, the client's personal history and mental status, adverse impact on the client, and actions by the counselor suggesting a plan to initiate a sexual relationship with the client after termination. (American Counseling Association, 1995, A.7,b)

* * * *

> Social workers should not engage in sexual activities or sexual contact with former clients because of the potential for harm to the client. If social workers engage in conduct contrary to this prohibition or claim that an exception to this prohibition is warranted because of extraordinary circumstances, it is social workers—not their clients—who assume the full burden of demonstrating that the former client has not been exploited, coerced, or manipulated, intentionally or unintentionally. (National Association of Social Workers, 1996, 1.09.c)

* * * *

> [B]ecause such intimacies undermine public confidence in the psychology profession and thereby deter the public's use of needed services, psychologists do not engage in sexual intimacies with

former therapy patients and clients even after a two-year interval except in the most unusual circumstances. The psychologist who engages in such activity after the two years following cessation or termination of treatment bears the burden of demonstrating that there has been no exploitation, in light of all relevant factors, including (1) the amount of time that has passed since therapy terminated, (2) the nature and duration of the therapy, (3) the circumstances of termination, (4) the patient's or clients' personal history, (5) the patient's or client's current mental status, (6) the likelihood of adverse impact on the patient or client and others, and (7) any statements or actions made by the therapist during the course of therapy suggesting or inviting the possibility of a post-termination sexual or romantic relationship with the patient or client. (American Psychological Association, 1995, 4.07 a, b, c)

Sex with clients is illegal in some states, and consent on the client's part is not a defense that can be employed by the therapist (Smith, 1994). In some states sexual intimacy with clients is a misdemeanor, while in others it is a felony (Coleman & Schaefer, 1986). It has been ruled that sex with a patient creates grounds for negligence (*Walter, Barbara v. Bourhis, R., et al.*,1986) and that licensure boards may revoke a mental health professional's license for having sex with a client (*Morra v. State Board of Examiners*, 1973). Mental health professionals are advised to check their state laws regarding sex with clients.

Characteristics of the Sexually Abusing Therapist

Sexual intimacy in therapy can be defined as any touching, fondling, kissing, or erotic acts (including intercourse) between a patient and a therapist. Nonerotic, supportive, or friendly hugging, greeting, or kissing are not included as sexual intimacies. Thus, a friendly pat on the shoulder does not constitute sexual intimacy (Holroyd, 1983).

Male therapists engage in sexual intimacies with clients more often than female therapists (9.4% versus 2.5%). Male therapists also have more sexual fantasies about clients than do female therapists (27% versus 14%) and consider sexual involvement with clients more often (27% versus .5%). The vast majority of therapists (93.5%) never act out sexual behaviors with clients (Pope, Keith-Spiegel, & Tabachnick, 1986).

Pope and Bouhoutsos (1986) postulated a number of reasons therapists become sexually intimate with their clients. They also commented on the therapists' rationales:

1. Therapists are influenced by their mentors. If students perceive or know of their professor's or supervisor's sexual involvement with subordinates, they may decide this type of behavior is acceptable. Unfortunately, most graduate programs do not deal with the issue of sexual attraction to clients (Holroyd, 1983).

2. Some therapists believe that the only time sexual intimacy with clients is unethical or illegal is when such behavior occurs before therapy is terminated. Sexual intimacy with former clients is unethical and in some states illegal, unless it occurs two years subsequent to therapy. Some feel that even after two years, extenuating circumstances could create an unethical or illegal situation.

3. Some therapists believe that sexual involvement with a client is acceptable if the client initiates it. This rationale, even if raised by attorneys, is not acceptable. The relationship between therapist and client is always in the hands, responsibility, and accountability of the therapist.

4. Some therapists posit that sexual involvement is not unethical if it is consummated outside the therapist's office. This argument holds no weight, because the power of the therapist is always an influencing agent, no matter where the behavior takes place. Most dual relationships are unethical and should be avoided. Of course there are exceptions to this rule. For instance, if a student is in critical need of therapy and a faculty member is the only alternative, therapy should be implemented.

Holroyd and Brodsky (1977) reported that 27% of the therapists they surveyed engaged in erotic kissing, touching, and hugging with their clients occasionally, and 7% frequently performed these behaviors with clients. They also found that 25% of humanistic counselors engaged in erotic activity, but fewer than 5% of therapists whose counseling orientation was described as behavior modification, psychodynamic, or rational-cognitive did so.

Wilson and Masson (1986) concluded that appropriate touching did not lead to further erotic behavior. *Appropriate* was defined as touching that is not meant to meet the therapist's needs. Rather, it is nonsexual contact used to complement a demonstration of empathy. Wilson and Masson also reported that appropriate touching fosters the therapeutic process and meets the needs of the client. They noted that touching may be important in therapeutic communications, and suggested that the training of counselors should include the appropriate use of touching as a means to enhance the value of therapy.

Pope and Bouhoutsos (1986) claimed that one reason therapists sexually abuse clients is because they are almost completely unprepared in graduate school, and in clinical internships, to deal with the phenomenon of sexual attraction to clients. In their survey, over half of the therapists (55%) indicated that they had not received education about such matters; 24% had received very little; and 12% had received some. Only 9% believed the issue of sexual attraction to clients had received adequate attention. Pope and Bouhoutsos believed graduate schools should give more attention to this matter.

Therapists who engage in sexual intimacies with clients tend to be vulnerable, lonely, and frightened of intimacy. Unsatisfying marriages, separations, and divorces also are correlates. The average age of the therapist who engages in sexual contact with clients is 43.5 years (Butler & Zehlen, 1977).

Characteristics of the Sexually Abused Client

Patients who have admitted to sexual intimacies with therapists have a mean age of 22 and typically are unmarried, separated, or divorced. Sexually abused clients generally have low self-regard and low self-actualization, and are mainly other-directed. They tend to be unaccepting of their own aggressive impulses and have difficulty relating to their mothers. Belote found that sexually abused patients were generally sexually dysfunctional, nonorgasmic, and—because of their own feelings of helplessness and dependency—ideal victims (Belote, 1974).

Other studies have shown that sexual intimacy in therapy typically leaves women clients feeling angry, exploited, and distrustful of therapy. Stone (1980) noted that sexually abused clients reported feelings of being used as sexual objects. They also had lower self-esteem than when they began therapy and increased feelings of ambivalence about themselves. Zehlen, Sonne, Meyer, Borys, and Marshall (1985) reported on a group of women who met to discuss their sexually abusive therapy. Three clinical issues repeatedly arose in the group:

1. *Difficulty trusting:* The women in the study described their sexualized therapy experiences as a betrayal of trust. They were told to be assertive outside the group and then encouraged to be dependent in therapy. The effects of the betrayal generalized to the world: They

were reluctant to discuss personal feelings and seemed to mistrust themselves.

2. *Problems with self-concept:* These problems were characterized by low self-esteem, dependency, and a desire for specialness.

3. *Problems expressing anger:* Group members talked of being too fragile to deal with anger. Anger in the group was rarely experienced. If it was expressed, it was manifested in a passive nonverbal way or through dreams.

The birth of sexual behavior with clients is the death of the therapeutic relationship. According to Bouhoutsos et al. (1983), 90% of clients who become sexually involved with their therapists are severely harmed. The harm is manifested by a litany of symptoms: mistrust of opposite relationships, tension, apprehension, hospitalization, dissociation, fatigue, impaired social adjustment, substance abuse, divorce, deterioration of sexual activity with a partner, increased emotional problems, lack of motivation, depression, inability to seek out further therapy, the feeling that one deserves abuse, despair, pessimism, inability to work, self-hatred, and even suicide (Bouhoutos et al., 1983; Pope & Bouhoutous, 1985).

A Training Strategy

Heiden (1993) developed training strategies to prevent counselor-client sexual relationships. The resulting workshop had two goals: (1) to sensitize participants to the ethical issue of counselor-client intimacy, and (2) to enable participants to develop the moral responsibility and ego strength to act morally when confronted with sexual temptation in a professional setting.

In order to sensitize students to the fact that sexual intimacy with clients is morally wrong, Heiden addressed the danger inherent in potential therapist-client sexuality, the law, ethical codes, research, the dynamics of transference and countertransference, and the gender role socialization of men and women.

Heiden also tried to help participants develop a moral resolve to resist sexual temptation. Toward that end, participants broke into small groups and created clinical situations in which intense sexual feelings developed between counselor and client. Students then were asked to respond to these questions: How did this situation happen? How is sexual involvement harmful to the client? What preventative steps could or should you take? What interventions are needed? Who would you turn to for support in this matter?

Counseling the Therapist-Abused Client

> Ms. Carson tells her therapist, Dr. Bennet, that she had sexual intercourse with her former therapist, Dr. Smith, for three months before she discontinued seeing him. Furthermore, Ms. Carson expresses fear, guilt, shame, and ambivalence about the sexual transgression with Dr. Smith. If the allegations are true, Dr. Smith's actions are clearly unethical and in some states illegal, and they may carry a punishment of several years in prison (Coleman & Schaefer 1986).

Dr. Bennet must use his clinical skills to assess the veracity of Ms. Carson. Clients are capable of gross distortions of reality because of paranoia and delusional thinking. If Dr. Bennet believes Ms. Carson's accusations are true, he must decide what to do next.

Dr. Bennet should clearly explain to Ms. Carson that sexual contact with her therapist is ethically wrong and harmful to her. He also should explain to her that it is her right to report the incident to the appropriate agency.

Should Ms. Carson decide to report the incident, Dr. Bennet should help her determine her readiness to do so. Ms. Carson may be in love with Dr. Smith and at the same time angry with him. She may be ambivalent about reporting the incident, fearing others will think it was her fault. Ms. Carson may simply want to leave this sexually abusive situation behind her. She may feel guilty for betraying Dr. Smith. It is Dr. Bennet's responsibility to help Ms. Carson work through all her thoughts and feelings about the sexual transgression. Dr. Bennet must help Ms. Carson come to a resolution of her problem. Dr. Bennet's primary obligation is to his client, and he must respect any decision she makes regarding the matter.

Dr. Bennet also faces an ethical dilemma: He must respect Ms. Carson's decision on whether to report Dr. Smith, but he is also aware that Dr. Smith may be inflicting a great deal of harm on other clients. Professionals who engage in sexual activity with one client often (75% to 80% of the time) engage in sexual activities with other clients (Bouhoutsos et al., 1983). Dr. Bennet must decide if he has any legal obligations in these case. For example, if Ms. Carson was a minor or otherwise incompetent, Dr. Bennet would have no legal alternative but to report Dr. Smith to the proper authorities, regardless of the client's readiness to do so.

Reporting Unethical Conduct

If a therapist has exhausted all avenues to resolve an ethical conflict directly with a colleague, he or she may file an ethics complaint. In fact, therapists are obligated to report unethical behavior. Not doing so may result in their being in violation of the ethical standards. Ethical complaints also can be filed by clients or by someone from the general public.

Complaints can be filed in a number of places. State licensing boards, national certifying boards, national ethics committees, and state certification boards all have structures in place to receive and process ethical complaints against mental health professionals within their jurisdictions. A board may find that the therapist was not in violation of the ethical standards. In that case no action is taken against the therapist and his or her record remains untarnished. If the board finds that the therapist has violated ethical standards, a number of sanctions may be imposed, depending on the severity of the violation and the nature of the board. Sanctions can include such actions as reprimands, probation, mandatory counseling supervision, suspension of certification or license, or loss of license to practice.

Accused of Unethical Conflict

During the time a complaint is being processed by the board, there is a natural emotional reaction on the part of the accused. Chauvin and Remley (1996) reported that ethics complaints sometimes evolve into civil or even criminal lawsuits, and these legal aspects of a complaint must be taken into consideration. The first step a mental health professional should take upon receiving notice of a complaint is to notify his or her professional liability insurance company (Crawford, cited in Chauvin & Remley, 1996). He or she also should promptly retain the services of a lawyer (Anderson & Swanson, cited in Chauvin & Remley, 1996), and follow the attorney's advise precisely (Crawford, cited in Chauvin & Remley, 1966).

Feelings of shock, anger, sorrow, and embarrassment may surface. The therapist probably will want to seek support from friends or family members. However, he or she will need to be discreet about this—and the lawyer will probably advise against it altogether. Sharing emotional reactions to the complaint is probably all right, but divulging details of the incident is not. Disclosing the client's name or the circumstances of the complaint is a violation of confidentiality. As Chauvin and Remley (1996) noted, "Accused counselors are bound under the same counselor/counselee confidentiality toward the accuser as is required with any other client" (p. 565).

Mental health professionals should seek the services of another therapist if they are in emotional turmoil over the ethics complaint. Most often, they continue to see their other clients during the process. Sometimes, emotional problems and associated stress can lead to more encompassing health problems in the future. Feelings of anger, betrayal, and shame should be vented and worked through with another competent professional. Cooper and Payne (1991) reported that obtaining counseling can be the key to a counselor's survival during the ordeal of being accused of unethical or illegal conduct.

Summary

Most of the time, dual relationships are unethical. The therapist who is sexually involved with a client is engaging in unethical (and in some states illegal) behavior. Illingworth (1995) found that 7% to 10% of male therapists have sexual relations with their clients. Sexually abusing therapists tend to be isolated, out of control, compulsive, and self-centered. Bouhoutsos et al. (1983) reported that 90% of sexually abused clients have been seriously harmed by the activity. Sexuality and the counseling process should become a more intricate and intensified part of training for mental health professionals.

LEARNING FACILITATION AND FOCUS

Divide into groups. Each group should pick a different cluster of states for which they are responsible. Members should determine which states have:

1. a law against sexual intimacy between therapist and client,

2. a penalty for sexual transgression between therapist and client,

3. a law in formation regarding sexuality and therapy, and

4. any court cases in progress or previously litigated regarding sexuality and counseling.

You will find this information in a legal encyclopedia. Look under topics such as *sexuality and counseling* or *therapy and sexuality*. Law review journals and computerized legal databases also are excellent sources of information.

THE HOMOSEXUAL CLIENT

For a long time psychiatry, the parent of the helping professions, viewed homosexuality as a mental illness (Klein, 1986). On the basis of mounting research evidence to the contrary, the diagnosis of homosexuality as a mental illness was removed from the revised edition of the *DSM III*. However, gay and lesbian people still are discriminated against on a regular basis.

Marsiglio (1993) found that prejudicial attitudes against homosexuals are associated with older, less-educated individuals from lower socioeconomic backgrounds. Men have been reported to be more prejudiced than women (D'Augelli & Rose, 1990; Grieger & Ponterotto, 1988). Some have found that ethnic and minority groups are more prejudicial toward gay men and lesbians than are Anglo-Americans (Bonilla & Porter, 1990; Ernst, Francis, Nevels, & Lemeh, 1991), but one study failed to support this hypothesis (Alcalay, Sniderman, Mitchell, & Griffin, 1990). According to Simon (1996), people with high self-esteem tend to be less prejudiced toward gay men and lesbians.

Stresses of Gay Men and Lesbians

Many people believe heterosexuality is the only acceptable sexual orientation because it is the only "natural" sexual orientation. Fear, hatred, and prejudice have been consistently directed toward those considered nonheterosexual (Herek, 1991). D'Augelli (1989) reported that 75% of gay men and lesbians in a university community were subjected to verbal insults, and 25% had received threats of physical violence. Rosario, Rotherham-Borus, and Reid (1992) noted that 50% of young ethnic minority gays reported being ridiculed because of their homosexuality.

According to Menola (1980) lesbian women who share their sexual orientation with their parents typically face strong parental disapproval. Additionally, some lesbian women are likely to be in battering relationships with other lesbian women, adding to their stress (Morrow & Hawthurst, 1989).

Significant numbers of gay, lesbian, and bisexual youths have reported being raped, assaulted, or robbed (DeStefano, 1988; Martin & Hetrick, 1988; Rotheram-Borus, Rosario, & Koopman, 1991). Martin and Hetrick (1988) noted that 50% of gay, lesbian, and bisexual youths in their study reported suffering violence at the hands of a family member.

> Despite the increasing public visibility of homosexuality and bisexuality in North American culture, the prevailing assumption among clinicians and researchers is that homoerotic attractions and

desires are the province solely of adulthood and not of childhood and adolescence. This misunderstanding and the ensuing clinical and empirical silence and neglect are particularly consequential because lesbian, gay male, and bisexual youths are disproportionately at risk for stressors that are injurious to themselves and others. In some cases, the threat for youths is not merely their mental health but their very lives. (Savin-Williams, 1994, p. 261)

According to D'Augelli (1991) 70% to 80% of lesbian and gay students hide their sexuality because they fear harassment. They avoid situations in which others might suspect they are gay, and 94% expected harassment in the future. The abuse of lesbian and gay youths may seriously alter their psychological functioning. Gay adolescents are two to three times more likely to attempt suicide than heterosexual youths, and they report high incidences of depression, substance abuse, and psychological distress (D'Augelli, 1993).

Many Christian groups have programs to "convert" homosexuals or to encourage repression of homosexual thoughts or inclinations. "These sacred communities that purport to instill and inspire faith for gay men and lesbians often contribute to the shattering of their faith, the further fragmentation of self and the derailing of their journey toward self-actualization" (Ritter & O'Neil, 1989, p. 11). One major religious group describes same-gender orientation as objectively disordered and inclined toward evil (Ratzinger, 1986).

Representatives and followers of traditional religion have often hurt lesbians and gay men by weaving a moral and historical tapestry of guilt, shame, and repression rather than by providing validation and inspiration for their inherent goodness. Additionally, some mental health professionals, by being ignorant of the pain and unique searchings of the gay or lesbian soul, may miss the opportunity to provide support and healing as well as possibly short-circuit the journey toward identity synthesis and self-actualization. (Ritter & O'Neil, 1989, p. 9)

In spite of all these abuses, Walters and Simon (1993) noted that the acknowledgment of one's sexual orientation is related to greater self-esteem.

Ethnic Minority Lesbians and Gays

Chan (1989) conducted a study with Asian-American gay men and lesbians. Of the 16 men and 19 women in the study, 70% had come out to a family member, but only 9 (26%) had come out to their parents. Participants felt that Asian-Americans denied the existence of lesbians and gay men. One reported,

"There is no frame of reference to understand homosexuality in Asian-American culture" (Chan, 1989, p. 19). The participants also perceived that the lesbian and gay community did not acknowledge their existence either.

> It is a problem to find my support only within the lesbian community, because I feel that, I am either seen as erotic and stereotyped or unaccepted because I am Asian and not like the majority of white lesbians. (Chan, 1989, p. 19)

The majority of men in Chan's study felt they had been discriminated against because they were gay, not because they were Asian. The majority of women perceived they had been discriminated against because they were Asian, not because they were lesbians. Chan concluded that the majority of participants identified more strongly with their lesbian or gay identities than their Asian-American identity, although several insisted on acknowledging their identity as both.

Using six open-ended questions, Loiacano (1989) interviewed six Black-American gay men and lesbians; the interviews lasted between one and two hours. Loicano reported that participants attempted to find validation in the gay and lesbian community. Both men and women experienced the white gay and lesbian community as unaccepting and racist in their attitudes toward them.

> I would go into a bar ... behind young whites who looked a hell of a lot younger than me, and they would have no problems getting in. Whereas, I would be stopped and they would ask for at least two forms of I.D. Also, just the attitudes of the bartenders. They would wait on others before they would wait on me ... and it really saddened me because I thought because we all were gay, we all were fighting for equality. You know, we would pull together. But I found more overt racism among gays than I did among just whites period ... which really upset me. (Loiacano, 1989, p. 23)

Participants also attempted to find validation in the Black community. However, most reported finding a lack of support in the community. One participant worried about being too "out" because of the potential ramifications it could have on her family, who lived in a Black neighborhood. Another spoke of the Black communities as pressuring Black gays to be secretive about their sexual orientation.

> I see more clearly the ways that we perpetuate horizontal violence. I see more clearly that ... those things that we say about white folk can also be true of ourselves. And we indeed can be our greatest oppressor, which is certainly not any effort on my part to blame the

victim, but just a recognition that we have probably taken too many of the attributes of the true oppressor and focused our energies ... within, rather than clearly identifying who the oppressor is and then strategizing cohesively to address the real problem [racism]. (Loicano, 1989, p. 23)

Participants needed to integrate and find simultaneous validation for their various identities. One participant spoke of his struggle for acceptance both as a Black man in the gay community and as a gay man in the Black community.

And that is a real fear that I have ... I fear losing sanity, and so maybe that is the reason why I scrutinize people with such care. Because, I do depend upon others' perceptions of me for validation, and I have been hurt so much by that in the past ... Because, I mean, living in an environment ... where there's been so many things that have told me I was freaky, I was crazy, I was stupid ... And how much I had to fight against that, and struggle ... I had just kind of forgotten how much I fought to remain sane. I lived in a world which wanted to tell me that I wasn't. And that was a real battle. (Loiacano, 1989, p. 23)

Counseling Lesbians and Gay Men

McDermott, Tyndall, and Lichtenberg (1989) surveyed 47 gay men and 36 lesbians from the Midwest. Forty-nine percent of the participants indicated a preference for a gay or lesbian counselor, whereas 39% felt their counselor's sexual orientation did not make a difference. The more homophobic the participants were, the more reluctant they were to discuss concerns central to their sexual identity. The researchers concluded that counselor training should focus on intervention strategies to alleviate internalized homophobia for gay and lesbian clients.

Loiacano (1989) recommended asking the following questions when counseling African-American gays and lesbians:

1. Is there respect for the client's dual identity in the community?

2. Can the client find acceptance and validation from groups in the community specifically organized for the needs of Black-American gays and lesbians?

3. What personal issues must the client confront in developing a gay or lesbian identity while at the same time affirming his or her Black identity?

4. Does the counselor or the client harbor any assumptions about expressing homosexuality that might not be realistic for a Black-American in his or her community?

5. If the community is predominantly White, are there other Black-American gays or lesbians who can be supportive? How are these individuals received in the gay community?

6. What aspect of the client's identity is most central to him or her?

Carballo-Dieguez (1989) recommended counselors ask themselves these questions when counseling gay Hispanic men:

1. Have you taken into account the regional variations of the language used by your client?

2. Do you want to use "bookish" language to add a sense of authority to your message? Or do you prefer the everyday slang of gay groups to make the message more familiar and easy to absorb?

3. If your client chooses one language over the other, what does that choice mean?

4. Do you want to address your client in a formal or a familiar way?

5. Can you benefit from the special emphases that certain words acquire in the mother tongue?

6. Is it possible to use jokes, rhymes, or proverbs in your message?

7. Do you consider the educational level of the client?

Hetherington and Orzek (1989) recommended that counselors prepare themselves to work with lesbian women by:

1. Working to consciously eliminate personal homophobic attitudes,

2. Developing an understanding of the gender issues for women,

3. Learning the model of lesbian identity development,

4. Helping lesbian clients to overcome internalized negative stereotypes,

5. Providing self-exploration assistance in the form of informational interview questions specific to lesbian concerns,

6. Developing a list of job search strategies that lesbian clients may use, and

7. Providing a list of professional associations and resources for lesbian clients. (p. 55)

Mental health professionals who counsel gays and lesbians should be familiar with the model developed by Cass (cited in Chan, 1989). This model can help the counselor understand the six stages an individual passes through in developing an integrated identity as a homosexual person:

1. *Identity Confusion.* The individual realizes that feelings and behaviors can be defined as homosexual, creating conflict about his or her identity which both the individual and environment had previously defined as heterosexual.

2. *Identity Comparison.* The possibility of being homosexual has been acknowledged. The task of this stage is to handle the social alienation that now arises because of feeling different and having a sense of not belonging to subgroups such as peers and family.

3. *Identity Tolerance.* At this stage there is an increased commitment to a homosexual identity, and the process of contacting other homosexuals to counter the isolation and alienation begins. The individual tolerates rather than accepts a homosexual identity.

4. *Identity Acceptance.* There are continued and increasing contacts with other homosexuals to validate and normalize homosexuality as an identity and as a way of life.

5. *Identity Pride.* This stage is characterized by the incongruity that exists between the individual's acceptance of himself/herself as a homosexual while knowing society rejects this concept. The individual takes pride in disclosure of his/her identity as a homosexual.

6. *Identity Synthesis.* The individual is able to integrate his or her homosexual identity with all other aspects of self and no longer sees a clear dichotomy between the heterosexual and homosexual world. (Cass, cited in Chan, 1989, p. 16)

Summary

Until recently homosexuality was viewed as a mental illness, and homosexuals still face a great deal of prejudice from mainstream society. As a result, homosexuals live under a great deal of stress and often are the objects of violent physical attacks—sometime at the hands of family members. Ethnic minority homosexuals often are rejected by their own ethnic groups as well as their homosexual reference groups. Mental health professionals should acquaint themselves with counseling techniques specifically formulated to assist homosexuals who present for therapy.

LEARNING FACILITATION AND FOCUS

Exercise 7.1

Bryan is a well-educated young man who is applying to a therapist-training program. He is open to his own feelings and those of others. He does believe, however, that homosexuals should be counseled to live a "straight" lifestyle. Should Bryan be accepted into the training program given his attitudes about homosexuality? Please include in your answer your thoughts and feelings regarding candidates who harbor a prejudice of any type.

_____

_____

_____

_____

_____

_____

_____

_____

Exercise 7.2

Professor Pure at times stops in at the local pub to have a beer and relax. On one occasion, he hears a student in the social work program in which he teaches speak in a derogatory way about homosexuals. Specifically, the student refers to homosexuals as "faggots." Should Professor Pure engage this student in a dialogue at a future date to ascertain his future in the social work program? Does the fact that the remark was made in a social setting have any bearing on this issue?

_____

_____

_____

_____

_____

_____

_____

_____

Chapter 8

OTHER SPECIAL RELATIONSHIPS

THE SPIRITUAL CLIENT

Today, mental health workers are examining the relationship between spiritual well-being and physical and psychological wellness (Benner, 1988). But, as Ganje-Fling and McCarthy (1996, p. 253) noted, "At present there is no generally agreed on definitions of spirituality." Jung (1958) likened spirituality to an "inner transcendent experience." Frankl ((1978) emphasized the innate human need to find meaning in life. Gilchrist (1992) defined spirituality as "what individuals hold sacred to their lives, what is most important to them at the essence of their being. It is a context for understanding things" (p. 12). Pate and Bondi (1992) likened it to "a view of one's place in the universe" (p. 108).

Until recently, spirituality in counseling did not receive a great deal of emphasis (Berenson, 1990). But two recent books by Moore (1992, 1994) on spirituality have made the *New York Times'* bestseller list and been widely read by therapists. We have also seen an increasing number of workshops devoted to the place of spirituality in counseling (Anderson & Worthen, 1997).

Spirituality often is distinguished from religiosity. *Spirituality* is viewed as a broader concept representing beliefs and values. *Religiosity* is defined as a narrower term that refers to behaviors (Hinterkopf, 1994; Ingersoll,

1994). However, some believe that the definition of spirituality is broad enough to include religious, existential, and unstructured orientations as well, including concepts of God, higher power, and spiritual source (Ganje-Fling & McCarthy, 1996).

The roots of spirituality and well-being are found in the *medical wellness movement*, and its proponents believe that one's spiritual dimension is "an innate component of human functioning that acts to integrate the other components" (West, 1996). Wellness has been defined as the integration of various aspects of human functioning, including social, mental, physical, emotional, spiritual, and occupational dimensions (Bensley, cited in Westgate, 1996; Chandler, Miner-Holden, & Kolander, 1992).

Religious faith has implications for both lifestyle and personal identity (Conroy, 1987). According to Bergin (1989), religious identity is vital in counseling. Prest and Keller (1993) agreed, noting that the spiritual selves of the counselor and the client are always manifested in a therapy session. Counseling and therapy are dependent on presuppositions about human nature. These presuppositions are antecedents to scientific research and theory (May, 1967).

Spirituality and Culture

Christopher (1996) believed that therapists and clients matriculate through the world as "expressions of culture" and that the self is very much influenced by preceding cultural patterns, values, and assumptions. Inherent in these cultural values are moral visions.

> Moral visions operate as interpretive frameworks that implicitly structure and orient our lives by providing an understanding of the good life and the good or ideal person. ... Implicitly or explicitly, moral visions tell us where to go or how to find those things that we deem higher, deeper, or more meaningful—those things that give us strength, integration, wholeness, vitality, dignity, and goodness. They simultaneously define for us what we should avoid, resist, oppose, or even combat, both internally and in the outer world. (Christopher, 1996, p. 18)

Christopher (1996) also reported that moral visions, which are embedded and developed in one's cultural past, are the harbingers of many counseling theories. Western counseling theories presuppose a value for individualism, as demonstrated in several of its manifestations:

- Feminist therapists often encourage behavior that is competent, autonomous, and directed toward self-development. There is a danger in this approach, however, if other important realities of women's lives—such as interdependency and connection—are ignored (Wolszon, cited in Christopher, 1996).

- Family therapy indirectly supports modern individualism by assuming as universal and desirable the modern conception of the nuclear family (Floweres & Richardson, cited in Christopher, 1996).

- Behavioristic, cognitive-behavioral, and reality therapies have a moral vision of utilitarian individualism that stresses instrumental rationality, control over emotions, human liberty, efficiency, and opposition to irrational authority (Richardson, cited in Christopher, 1996).

- Humanistic, client-centered, and gestalt therapies embrace expressive individualism, which is evidenced by a turning inward, making contact with one's inner life, expressing feelings, spontaneity, intimacy, and creativity.

Christopher warned that individualistic counseling practices are problematic for those not raised in an individualistic culture. Individualism is the cultural outlook for only about 30% of the world's population (Triandis, cited in Christopher, 1996). If counseling is a function of cultural and historical embeddedness, then one's assumptions about what a person is and what a person should become are contestable. If mental health professionals think about and behave toward clients from an individualistic framework while their clients think about and behave toward therapists from a collective framework, then the role of ethics in psychological practice is not expansive enough.

Bickhard (1989) expanded the notion of ethics to the quality of the relationship:

> Therapy is not just an activity to which ethical considerations can be applied, nor just an activity which makes use of moral considerations in selecting its instrumental goals. Psychotherapy is a very special kind of intrinsically ethical relating to another person. (p. 163)

Christopher (1996) suggested that mental health professionals should acknowledge their cultural embeddedness, seek to continually clarify and question the moral visions that motivate them, attempt to discern how moral visions affect their work, and regularly engage in public discourse on the nature and appropriateness of their moral visions.

Spirituality as a Fourth Dimension

> Different therapies pay attention to different dimensions of human experience. Three dimensions of experience addressed by most therapies are *time* (events occurring in sequences), *space* (experience organized through the structure of relationships), and *story* (the use of language to shape what has occurred in time and space into structures of meaning). Therapists whose work reflects a spiritual orientation may be influenced by three additional basic assumptions. The first holds to a belief in a fourth dimension of human experience that includes awareness of the existence of a God or Divine Being. The second sees human beings as having an innate yearning for connection with this Divine Being. The third views this Being as taking an active interest in human beings and acting upon their relationships to promote beneficial change. (Anderson & Worthen, 1997, p. 4)

Anderson and Worthen believed that therapists who believe in the fourth dimension will listen to clients from a different perspective than therapists who do not. They will hear their clients expressing symptoms as if they were "voices of the soul" or "unfulfilled spiritual longings." The therapist should also share his or her spiritual self. Disclosure serves as a potential catalyst for people to use spirituality as a positive resource in their relationships with others.

Spirituality and Child Abuse

Ganje-Fling and McCarthy (1996) noted that child sexual abuse creates conflicts about one's spirituality and, that the nature of developmental difficulties often is germane to a sexually traumatized childhood. "In other words, these clients are conflicted about relating to a powerful or determinant force, they struggle with feelings of hopelessness, they lack a sense of purpose, and they are ambivalent about connecting to a community of believers" (p. 254). Ganje-Fling and McCarthy reported that abused clients commonly raise the following spiritual issues in therapy.

1. *Power:* This is a difficult issue for abuse survivors because power was abused repeatedly by their perpetrators. Furthermore, as clients begin connecting with themselves in therapy and feel powerful, they may also feel frightened. Part of this fear is related to spirituality,

because connecting with one's own power often extends into connection with a higher source. Clients can fluctuate between fearing that this spiritual source is another potential abuser and hoping that it is a benevolent power.

2. *Trust:* Trust involves building relationships and dealing with fears of intimacy. Clients frequently benefit from examining and reworking the religious messages and teachings they received as children to define their own beliefs and begin building a personal relationship with a spiritual source. It is important to remember that trust-building within the therapeutic relationship can generalize, allowing clients to seek more intimate spiritual bonds.

3. *Control:* Spiritual growth requires a certain degree of surrendering control. This often is difficult for abuse survivors. They may struggle with the conflict between controlling the spiritual source and yielding to it. Control is related to other issues (e.g., trust). A counselor can help by pointing out the interrelatedness of these concerns.

4. *Transformation:* Therapy involves transformation of oneself and of life. Change can be frightening to sexually traumatized clients, who cling to the safety of predictable experiences. Transformation issues frequently emerge during transitional times: for example, when clients are separating from family or experiencing some type of loss. In searching for reassurance at these times, clients may turn to spiritual sources.

Spirituality and Depression

Westgate (1996) reviewed the literature on spirituality and reported that *spiritual wellness* is a term used by many theorists in an attempt to capture the essence of the spiritual dimension of personality.

> In summary, these theorists believed that the spiritual dimension is an innate component of human functioning that acts to integrate the other components. Spiritual wellness represents the openness to the spiritual dimension that permits the integration of one's spirituality with the other dimensions of life, thus maximizing the potential for growth and self-actualization. (p. 27)

Westgate (1996) also examined the relationship between this spiritual wellness and depression. She first identified four dimensions of spiritual wellness which have been presented in the literature in recent years by several different theorists:

> Nevertheless, four dimensions of spiritual wellness emerge in the literature: meaning in life, intrinsic values, transcendence, and spiritual community. These same dimensions are recurring themes in the clinical and empirical literature on depression, thus supporting the link between spiritual wellness and depression. (p. 28)

Westgate went on to examine the relationship of depression with each of these dimensions by reviewing empirical studies in the area. She found that, in 9 of the 16 studies she reviewed, a significant negative correlation was evidenced between depression and the four dimensions of spiritual wellness. Westgate (1996) concluded:

> The picture of the spiritually well person that emerges from the literature is one who finds meaning and purpose in life and who operates from an intrinsic value system that guides both life and decisions. This person's transcendent perspective allows an appreciation of the sacredness of life and of the mysteries of life and the cosmos. The spiritually well person also lives in the community—praying, chanting, worshipping, or meditating with others. This community not only provides a sense of shared values and identity but also offers mutual support and an avenue for community outreach. In contrast to the spiritually well person, a powerful argument has been made for an association between spiritual void and depression. The depressed person describes symptoms that typically include meaningless, emptiness, and hopelessness, as well as a sense of alienation from values and a narcissistic focus. As the depression deepens, the person often feels detached from others and may withdraw from social contacts. (pp. 33–34)

Summary

Existential theorists have long talked of humankind's striving for meaning in life. Until recently, however, the spiritual aspect of life as it relates to psychology and psychological practice has not been emphasized in the literature. For instance, as recently as 1990, Berenson noted that "the most underutilized resource in family therapy today is God" (p. 50). Today, however, the literature, workshops, and many best-selling books are increasingly drawing attention to the spiritual aspects of counseling.

LEARNING FACILITATION AND FOCUS

Exercise 8.1

Spirituality, as it is outlined in this section, is becoming more popular with mental health professionals. Take some time and think about (1) what part spirituality plays in your life and, (2) how your spirituality or the absence of it affects your counseling practice. Jot down some of your thoughts in the space below.

1. _____

_____

_____

_____

_____

2. _____

_____

_____

_____

_____

THE CLIENT WHO IS A CONSULTEE

The Nature of Consulting

"Consultation is one of the most sought-after services rendered by mental health professionals" (Boylan, Malley, & Scott, 1995, p. 255). Alpert and Meyers (1983) reported that consultation activities are directed at schools, mental health services, and many other organizations. In his classic work *The Theory and Practice of Mental Health Consultation,* Caplan (1970) identified four consulting models:

1. *Client-Centered Case Consultation.* A consultee has difficulty in dealing with the mental health aspects of one of his/her clients and calls in a specialist to investigate and advise on the nature of the difficulties. The consultant makes an assessment of the client's problem and recommends how the consultee should proceed.

2. *Program-Centered Administrative Consultation.* The consultant is invited by an administrator to help with a current problem of program development, with some predicament in the organization of an institution, or with planning and implementation of organizational policies, including personal policies. The consultant is expected to provide feedback to the organization in the form of a written report.

3. *Consultee-Centered Case Consultation.* The consultee's work problem relates to the management of a particular client, and he/she invokes the consultant's help in order to improve handling of the case. The consultant's primary focus is upon clarifying and remedying the shortcomings in the consultee's professional functioning that are responsible for his/her difficulties with the case about which he/she is seeking help.

4. *Consultee-Centered Administrative Consultation.* The consultant helps the administrative staff of an organization deal with current problems in organizational planning, program development, or organizational policies. The focus of attention is the consultee's work difficulties and attempting to help improve his/her problem solving skills. (Caplan, 1970, pp. 109–112)

Brown, Pryzwansky, and Schulte (1987) reviewed and integrated various writers' definitions and listed the following key elements of consultation:

1. The relationship is initiated by either consultee or consultant.

2. The relationship is characterized by authentic communication.

3. The consultees may be professionals or nonprofessionals (e.g., parents).

4. The consultant provides indirect services to third-party clients.

5. The consultant provides direct services to consultees, assisting them to develop coping skills that ultimately make them independent of the consultant.

6. The types of problems considered are work-related when the concept of work is broadly conceived.

7. The consultant's role varies with the consultee's needs.

8. The consultant may be based within the consultee's organization or outside of it.

9. All communication between consultant and consultee is confidential. (Brown et al., 1987, p. 9)

Boylan (cited in Boylan et al.,1995) noted that historically mental health professionals have been involved in providing direct service to clients. Direct service implies that the focus of consultation is on the individual client and the intrapersonal factors affecting him or her. Taking the form of crisis intervention, direct service is thought to consist of psychodiagnosis, and counseling as the primary remedial activities of the mental health professional. The indirect service approach stresses understanding the environment of the client. Interventions are aimed at helping the professional who has responsibility for individuals in the environment. With the development of indirect service approaches, the mental health professional must ensure that role confusion does not hamper the delivery of mental health services.

Kurpius, Fuqua, and Rozecki (1993) asserted that role confusion is best avoided by attending to the stages of consultation. According to Kurpius et al., pre-entry is the initial stage in the consultation process. Consultants form a conceptual foundation from which to work and are able to articulate to themselves and to others who they are and the services they can provide. Consultants should understand their beliefs and values and how families, programs, organizations, and systems cause, solve, and avoid problems. Kurpius et al. (1993) maintained that in the pre-entry stage it is essential for consultants to conceptualize the meaning and operation of consultation to themselves and be ready to do the same with consultees or the consultee system.

Ethical Issues in Consulting

Consulting may involve complex relationships between and among multiple parties, which can create ethical dilemmas unique to the consultation process. As Newman (1993) noted, "Currently, there is little formal guidance available to assist consultants in making the complex ethical judgments encountered in the practice of consultation" (p. 148). Ethical standards are intended to be inspirational in nature and are purposely vague to allow mental health professionals to exercise professional judgment (Austin, Moline, & Williams, 1990).

It is awkward to consider clients of the consultee agency as part of the consulting agreement, since they are not present. They do not have the opportunity to speak of their own priorities and often do not even know a consultation is taking place. However, it is generally agreed that a consultant's responsibility and accountability extend to members of the agency (Brown, Pryzwansky, & Schulte, 1991). The consultant is responsible to society (client system) and only secondarily to the consultee (Fannibanda, 1976).

> Psychologists have a primary obligation and take reasonable precautions to respect the confidentiality rights of those with whom they work or consult, recognizing that confidentiality may be established by law, institutional rules, or professional or scientific relationships. (APA, 1995, 5.02)

* * * *

> Because psychologists' scientific and professional judgments and actions may affect the lives of others, they are alert to and guard against personal, financial, social, organizational, or political factors that might lead to misuse of their influence. (APA, 1995, 1.15)

Assessment and the Consultant

Consultants and therapists often employ tests to make various assessments of their clients. These tests are commonly referred to as *psychometric* or *psychological tests*. Before using any psychological test, the mental health professional is ethically bound to ensure its validity and reliability:

> Counselors recognize the limits of their competence and perform only those testing and assessment services for which they have been trained. They are familiar with reliability, validity, related standardization, error of measurement, and proper application of any technique utilized. Counselors using computer-based test interpretations are trained in the construct being measured and the specific instrument being used prior to using this type of computer application. (ACA, 1995, E.2.a.)

* * * *

> Psychologists who perform interventions or administer, score, interpret, or use assessment techniques are familiar with the reliability, validation, and related standardization or outcome studies of, and proper applications and uses of, the techniques they use. (APA, 1996, 2.04,a)

* * * *

Counselors who provide test scoring and test interpretation services to support the assessment process confirm the validity of such interpretations. They accurately describe the purpose, norms, validity, reliability, and applications of the procedures and any special qualifications applicable to their use. (ACA, 1995, E.5.C)

Validity is the extent to which a test measures what it is said to measure. There are several types of validity:

- *Content validity* is also known as *curricular validity*. A test constructed to determine if a student has mastered the material in a particular course must adequately cover both the content and objectives of the course in order to have content validity.

- Evidence of *predictive validity* is obtained by giving a test and correlating the scores with data collected at a future date.

- The measures used to determine success or failure are the *criterion measures*. Criterion measures for airline pilots, for example, might include number of passenger complaints, supervisory ratings, and the absence of accident.

- *Concurrent validity* is similar to predictive validity except the measures are collected at the time a test is administered.

- *Construct validity* is ascertained by determining what psychological qualities a test actually measures. In other words, the test measures what one wants it to measure.

- *Face validity* means that the test appears to the test-taker to be valid for the purpose he or she is taking it for.

- *Reliability* means that a test consistently measures what it purports to measure. If a student is given an intelligence test, the score he or she receives should be about the same if he or she takes the same test a week later.

When tests are used, those taking them should be informed of their nature and purpose and given an explanation of the results. Lobbying by consumer groups has resulted in laws that guarantee people access to their test results.

Even accused adolescents have the right to review their psychological evaluations (*In re Gault v. U.S. Supreme Court,* 1967, cited in APA, 1995).

> Unless the nature of the relationship is clearly explained to the person being assessed in advance and precludes provision of an explanation of results (such as in some organizational consulting, preemployment or security screening, and forensic evaluations), psychologists ensure that an explanation of the results is provided using language that is reasonably understandable to the person assessed or to another legally authorized person on behalf of the client. Regardless of whether the scoring and interpretation are done by the psychologist, by assistants, or by automated or other outside services, psychologists take reasonable steps to ensure that appropriate explanations of results are given. (APA, 1996, 2.09)

Releasing Raw Data

Consultants and therapists often are asked to provide raw psychological data to other parties. The sharing of raw data, especially with those outside the field of psychology, has been a particularly thorny issue in recent years. Nonetheless, attorneys, judges, and other lay people often request raw data from psychologists. Matarazzo (cited in Tranel, 1994) described raw data this way:

1. *Scores,* which are typically numeric (e.g., the number of items answered correctly on a test) or standardized (e.g., IQ scores, percentile scores);

2. *Test stimuli,* which are the actual items used by the psychologist to elicit responses from the client or patient that form the basis for determining levels of cognitive and behavioral function;

3. *Responses* (i.e., the actual verbal, written or other responses generated by the client/patient to test stimuli); and

4. *Test manuals,* which typically comprise, in addition to the test stimuli information regarding how the test was constructed, its reliability and validity, normative data, appropriate application, and detailed instruction for administration.

Several professional organizations have published guidelines for mental health professionals in this area:

Counselors ordinarily release data (e.g., protocols, counseling or interview notes, or questionnaires) in which the client is identified only with the consent of the client or the client's legal representative. Such data are usually released only to persons recognized by counselors as competent to interpret the data. (ACA, 1995. E.4.6)

* * * *

Psychologists refrain from misuse of assessment techniques, interventions, results, and interpretations and take reasonable steps to prevent others from misusing the information these techniques provide. This includes refraining from releasing raw test data to persons, other than to patients or clients as appropriate, who are not qualified to use such information. (APA, 1995, 2.02.b)

* * * *

A viable course of action if an attorney should request raw data from psychologists (a) would be to advise the attorney to engage the consultation of another psychologist, (b) who is qualified, by virtue of licensure, training, and experience, to receive the data. Psychologist A then could send the raw data to Psychologist B (provided the client or patient has given appropriate consent). Psychologist B could then interpret the data to the attorney. (Tranel, 1994, p. 35)

Interpreting Test Scores

In order to interpret tests accurately, therapists must refer to what the norm is for a score. A score of 100 has no value whatsoever unless one knows the average score of others who have taken the test. Others who have taken the test are considered to be in the *norm group*. If one takes a test and one's particular cultural or ethnic group has not been part of the norm group, a problem may arise with the interpretation of the test results.

A classic example of legal and ethical importance was the case of *Larry P. v. Riles* (1972). Larry P. was an African-American boy who was placed in a class for the educable mentally retarded because of his score on an individual IQ test. His parents objected, noting that the average African-American child scores below the mean on IQ tests and arguing that the tests are unfairly biased. In response, the Ninth Circuit Federal Court of Appeals ruled, among other things, that proof must be established that tests results correlate with classroom measures and that the tests are appropriate for use with minority children. Subsequent to the Court's decision, the law in California (1996) was amended to say that IQ tests cannot be used for special educational placement for African-American children.

Ibrahim and Arredondo (1986) contended that conducting psychological assessments without first clarifying a client's world is unethical. Many collective cultures regard what are considered to be manifestations of mental health in America as marks of immaturity. For instance, Japanese people believe that one should be modest and avoid those things which draw attention to oneself. As Markus and Kitayama (1991) noted, "The nail that sticks out gets pounded down" (p. 6).

> Many of the most commonly used concepts are problematic, especially when extended to people who are not raised in an individualistic culture. Individualism is most likely the cultural outlook for only 30% of the world's population. ... If this is true and we as counselors fail to address how individualism as a moral vision influences counseling, then we run the risk that counseling theories and concepts are at best representative of 30% of humanity and they are being extended in potentially harmful ways to the other 70%. The potential for distorting the experiences of ethnic minorities, women, and those from non-Western cultures is clear if we fail to realize that all of our counseling theories and concepts presuppose moral visions. (Christopher, 1996, pp. 21-22)

* * * *

> Counselors recognize that culture affects the manner in which clients' problems are defined. Clients' socioeconomic and cultural experience is considered when diagnosing mental disorders. (ACA, 1995, E.5.b.)

* * * *

> Psychologists attempt to identify situations in which particular interventions or assessment techniques or norms may not be applicable or may require adjustment in administration or interpretation because of factors such as individuals' gender, age, race, ethnicity, national origin, religion, sexual orientation, disability, language, or socioeconomic status. (APA, 1995, 2.04.C)

* * * *

> Certified counselors must proceed with caution when attempting to evaluate and interpret performances of any person who cannot be

appropriately compared to the norms of the instrument. (National
Board of Certified Counselors, 1996, C.8)

Summary

Consultation activities are directed at schools, mental health services, and
many other organizations. The consultant may focus his or her services toward
the consultee (a direct service) or toward the consultee's employees (an indirect service). It is important that consultants determine the meaning and operation of consultation to themselves and to consultees. Also, consultants must
determine who they are ethically responsible and accountable to.

LEARNING FACILITATION AND FOCUS

Exercise 8.2

Dr. Pfile—a psychologist who has conducted training programs in
communication, supervision, and group dynamics—has been contacted
by Mr. Guthrie—the chief administrator for the Brine Company, which
manufactures and processes materials to be used in water purification
plants. Dr. Pfile and Mr. Guthrie are good friends.

Mr. Guthrie explains to Dr. Pfile that company profits are down; he
believes there are a number of reasons for this, including a lack of communication between the maintenance and production departments and a
lack of supervisory skills on the part of members of both department. He
asks Dr. Pfile to construct a training model for members of the two departments. Dr. Pfile constructs an idiosyncratic model that consists of
supervision and organizational development. He contracts with Mr.
Guthrie to work with the Brine Company formally and to present a final
written report with recommendations.

During the course of the training Dr. Pfile hears repeatedly from
workers that they think Mr. Guthrie is incompetent. He doesn't listen to
their legitimate complaints and he is dogmatic and autocratic in his decision making. Members of the maintenance and production departments
also inform Dr. Pfile that they have no intention of communicating with
one another; basically, they dislike one another.

A trainee requests a private audience with Dr. Pfile and tells him
about two workers who are stealing carbon materials from the plant. Dr.

Pfile also observes that two workers at the plant are incapacitated almost daily because of substance abuse.

Taking into consideration the information from the literature and the ethical codes, develop an informed consent form for this consultation. This form should include the consultant's philosophical and ethical principles regarding:

1. who the client is and who is the consultant's primary responsibility;

2. the meaning of confidentially in consulting;

3. possible uses of information;

4. who should define the problem(s);

5. what the consultant might do about potential conflicts of interests;

6. if the consultant is obligated to report certain behaviors; and

7. the consultant's statement regarding dual relationships.

THE CLIENT WHO IS A MINOR

In most states parents or guardians determine their children's access to medical, dental, and mental health services.

- *Children* refers to those who have not reached the age of maturity—18 years old in most states. There are exceptions to the rule, however. Alaska and Colorado define minors as those who have not yet reached the age of 19 or 21, respectively (Freed & Walker, 1988).

- A *guardian* is appointed by a family's will or by a court. A guardian can make the same choices for minors as a parent can.

- Typically, an *emancipated minor* is a minor who is no longer living at home and who has been providing for his or his own welfare for some period of time. A minor becomes emancipated by going to court and obtaining a court order for emancipation. The emancipated minor, for the most part, is treated as an adult in the eyes of the law.

Traditionally parents have had a right to act on behalf of their children. In *Bellotti v. Baird* (1979), the U.S. Supreme Court reinforced the idea that parents are in control of and act as representatives of their children. "The peculiar vulnerability of children; their inability to make critical decisions in an informed, mature manner; and the importance of the parental role necessitate a control on the child's decisions" (*Bellotti v. Baird*, 1979, p. 643).

Many minors suffer emotional trauma and are in need of therapy (Tuma, 1989), yet fear of legal entrapment sometimes interferes with parents' seeking therapy for their children (Kazdin, 1989). Recognizing that minors who need therapy may not have assess to it, the laws in this country are changing. They differ from state to state and from situation to situation. For example, some states have laws that permit minors to make valid and competent contracts. Others have laws that relate specifically to emancipated minors, mature minors in limited cases (Myers, 1982), minors in emergency situations, and minors under court order.

While these laws differ from state to state, they also sometimes conflict within the same state. For example, Pennsylvania law permits involuntary treatment for minors between 14 and 17 years old without parental consent. This treatment can be on an inpatient or outpatient basis. It also allows, without parental consent, voluntary inpatient treatment. However, the law explicitly omits coverage of voluntary outpatients. Consequently, minors who are seen on an outpatient voluntary basis—in either a mental health clinic or private practice—are not covered by the law, and parental consent is required before they can receive therapeutic services.

Another section of the same law says it is the duty of staff members to notify parents that a minor is being treated on an inpatient basis.

In addition to the issues of consent, the law deals with the issue of release of records, stating that an inpatient minor may consent to the release of his or her records without parental consent. Treatment plans for outpatient minors must be approved by the parent (or guardian), but outpatient minors control release of their records. As Elwork (1993) noted:

> These regulations appear to be inconsistent. That is, it is arguable that it is illogical to give adolescents the right to consent to the release of their records and not give them the right to consent to their own treatment. (Elwork, 1993, p. 2)

As a general rule, minors cannot make legally binding contracts for therapy. However, the laws are different in different states. Mental health professionals should know the laws of their state before they conduct therapy with minor patients. "The consensus is growing that older minors are competent to partici- pate in at least some form of treatment decision and the competence and desire to do so increases with age" (Swenson, 1997, p. 390).

Counseling Pregnant Minors

> A pregnant woman's constitutional right to choose between child- birth and abortion was established in 1973 by the Supreme Court's landmark ruling in *Roe v. Wade*. All woman, including those under 18, are entitled to a safe, legal abortion. But in many states, a young woman may have a very difficult time exercising that right because laws require that she first notify her parents or obtain their consent. (American Civil Liberties Union, 1996, p. 1)

The Supreme Court recognized that minors do have a constitutionally pro- tected interest in privacy in abortion decisions. At the same time, the court worried about possible dangers inherent in minors making such decisions. The court assumed that (a) minors might be vulnerable to serious psychological after-effects of the decision, (b) minors might not have the ability to make reasoned decisions, and (c) minors may benefit from consulting with their par- ents (Melton, 1987).

The Supreme Court held that states cannot impose an absolute parental veto of abortion. The state must provide an alternative decision maker (some- one who could veto or approve a minor's decision to have an abortion) without requiring the minor to first seek approval from her parents. States who use this option set up procedures for bypassing parents and going to a judge (Melton, 1987). In 1988, 13 states required parental consent for a minor having an abortion, and 10 states required parental notification (Rust, cited in Swenson, 1997). "Most states requiring parental notification or consent allow a pregnant minor to go to court and request permission for a confidential abortion (that is, without parental involvement)" (American Civil Liberties Union, 1996, p. 3).

Available research indicates that judicial bypass is merely a formality. Mnookin, Pliner, and Yates (cited in Melton, 1987) reported that 90% of preg- nant minors in Massachusetts who do not seek parental consent and go to court are found mature. Yet, the American Civil Liberties Union (1996) contended, "This procedure ... is costly and humiliating and traumatizing. Teenagers must reveal detailed personal information to as many as 20 or more strangers on staff in the court system" (p. 3).

The United States has one of the highest teenage pregnancy rates in the world, and it is growing every year (Guttmacher, cited in Marecek, 1987). In 1981, 42% of American teenagers reported having sexual intercourse. By 1986, 80% of American teenage males and 70% of females reported having had sexual intercourse (Brody, cited in Marecek, 1987). Russo reported that 40% of 20-year-old women had at least one pregnancy in their teens (cited in Marecek, 1987). Thus, Marecek contended, any counselor who works with female clients should be prepared to deal with problems related to pregnancies.

Broken, Klerman, and Brochen (cited in Marecek, 1987) outlined a four-stage decision model for counseling teenagers with problem pregnancies: (a) confirming and acknowledging the pregnancy, (b) exploring and weighing the alternatives, (c) deciding among the alternatives, and (d) making a commitment to the decision. The goals in counseling a teenager with a problem pregnancy are these:

1. To mobilize the teenager's coping skills

2. To provide the information, referrals, and emotional support needed for the teenager to reach and implement an informed decision about the pregnancy

3. To help the teenager make a final, fully integrated decision with the least amount of regret

4. Insofar as possible, to aid the teenager in using the crisis as an opportunity for personal growth and self-reflection (Marecek, 1987, p. 90)

Counselors also must examine their own values and attitudes toward abortion. At times counselors may experience a dissonance between their own values and the choice a client is making. Joffe explained that counselors sometimes are uncomfortable upholding a client's rights and are torn between letting the client make her own decision and confronting her on the wrong decision she is making (cited in Marecek, 1987). Kahn-Edrington (1981) believed counselors must examine their own values toward birth and adoption and uphold the belief that each person has the right and responsibility to make a decision about abortion. Counselors also must be knowledgeable of myths and risks and be sensitive to values of other cultures.

Summary

In most states children are considered minors until they reach the age of 18. Traditionally, parents have had the right to act on behalf of their minor children. However, there is a growing consensus that children should have the right to participate in decisions germane to their mental health.

Some believe that minors have the right to obtain an abortion if they so wish. Still, many states have passed laws requiring either parental consent or notification. However, since the Supreme Court held that states cannot impose an absolute parental veto on abortion, these states also have judicial bypass procedures that allow pregnant minors to go to court without parental involvement.

LEARNING FACILITATION AND FOCUS

Exercise 8.3

Answer these questions, pertinent to a minor's right to abortion.

1. I think that, no matter what, a minor   YES ( )   NO ( )   NOT SURE ( )
   has the right to choose to have an
   abortion or not to have an abortion.

2. I think that, no matter what, a minor   YES ( )   NO ( )   NOT SURE ( )
   has the right to choose not to have
   an abortion and keep her baby.

3. I think that a mildly retarded minor   YES ( )   NO ( )   NOT SURE ( )
   has the right to choose to have an
   abortion or not to have an abortion.

4. I think that a minor who is indigent   YES ( )   NO ( )   NOT SURE ( )
   and addicted to cocaine and alcohol
   has the right to choose not to have
   an abortion and keep her baby.

5. I think that a minor with a border-   YES ( )   NO ( )   NOT SURE ( )
   line personality disorder has the
   right to choose to have an abortion
   or not have an abortion.

6. I think that a minor with a border-   YES ( )   NO ( )   NOT SURE ( )
   line personality disorder has the
   right to choose not to have an
   abortion and to keep her baby.

Exercise 8.4

If you think, for any reason, that a minor's right to keep or abort her fetus should be limited, please explicate what structures and procedures should be used to arrive at the decision.

_____

_____

_____

_____

_____

_____

THE CLIENT IN MANAGED CARE

The report issued by the Council on Ethical and Judicial Affairs of the American Medical Association (1994) noted that a theory of adequate medical care probably will never maintain a universal definition. However, the council did outline some of the ethical issues involved in grappling with such a theory.

1. *The degree of benefit.* This refers to the difference in outcome when treatment is compared to no treatment. For example, maximum benefit is present when the treatment prevents the development of a condition that would be fatal without treatment.

2. *Likelihood of benefit.* This may be relevant in a number of ways. For example, to use a diagnostic test such as mammography, the desirability of usage depends on the likelihood that an abnormal finding will result. As a result, such tests are basic for only certain high-risk people. A treatment desirability depends on its efficacy. Thus, if empirical data do not demonstrate that a treatment is effective, there is insufficient justification for its use.

3. *Duration of benefit.* Treatments that permanently eliminate an illness provide greater benefits than treatments that have only a temporary effect.

4. *Number of people benefiting.* A treatment can benefit not only the patient but also those with whom he or she comes into contact. Vaccinations and antibiotics are examples of treatments that benefit a large number of people. Also, a treatment may treat a medical condition that is relatively common, and its inclusion in a package therefore benefits a great many people.

5. *Cost alone.* Cost is relative to effectiveness. For example, some treatments may achieve the same benefit but at a lower cost.

In reality, however, the council noted that economic decisions may determine what is adequate. They specifically mentioned the Oregon State Legislature which, after prioritizing the comparative health benefits, placed a line between covered and uncovered benefits. Consequently, an economic cap determined adequacy of health care in Oregon.

The delivery of health care services today involves a wide variety of behaviors that are designed to impose regulations on health care (Dorwart, 1990). The corporations managing these behaviors and regulations for the health care system are commonly known as *entities of managed care*. Reducing the cost of health care is the guiding principle for managed care entities (Institute of Medicine, 1989); and mental health care is the most likely aspect to be regulated by managed care systems (Falik, 1991).

To address this issue, Congress created the Agency for Heath Care Policy and Research (AHCPR) in 1989. The sole purpose of this agency was to determine the cost effectiveness of intervention modalities for specific health disorders and to publish clinical practice guidelines. Thus, optimal strategies for intervention have been articulated in some areas, such as major depressive disorders (Barlow, 1996). Once they are incorporated into the evolving mental health system, the clinical intervention guidelines published by the AHCPR and other government agencies will limit the range of services offered by managed care companies (VandenBos, 1993). These companies already have been accused of rationing psychiatric and medical treatment to the detriment of patients (Borenstein, 1990).

Most of the cases listed below are examples of medical care malpractice claims. Medical malpractice cases are found more often than psychiatric malpractice cases, because there are more of them. However, the legal basis for medical negligence is similar in most psychiatric or mental health cases.

In one case already litigated in California, a patient named Wickline had postoperative complications after vascular surgery. Consequently, at the end of her insurance-approved stay, her surgeon recommended that she stay longer in the hospital. Medi-Cal, Ms. Wickline's state Medicaid plan, which also performed its own managed care function, disagreed with the doctor's recommendation. The doctor requested eight additional days, but Medi-Cal said four days was the maximum time allowed. The surgeon thought he had no choice in the matter, and Ms. Wickline was discharged from the hospital. Within a few days, her leg began to turn blue. By the time she saw a physician, her leg had to be amputated (*Wickline v. State*, 1986).

* * * *

Carley Christie was diagnosed with Wilms' tumor, a rare yet life-threatening form of kidney cancer. Carley was treated by Palo Alto Medical Clinic, a medical provider group that had contracted with TakeCare to administer medical services. The medical group referred Carley to a urologist who did not have experience in removing a Wilms' tumor or any other malignant kidney cancers from children. Carley's parents were repeatedly denied their request to have their daughter referred to pediatric surgeon. Finally, Carley's parents chose to have surgery performed by a qualified pediatric surgeon. TakeCare refused to pay for even the hospital expenses associated with the operation.

Consequently, the California Commissioner of Corporations filed an accusation against TakeCare, which then requested a hearing before an administrative law judge. On October 11, 1996, the judge found that cause existed for TakeCare because they failed (a) to provide ready referrals for Carley Christie, (b) to make certain services available to her, and (c) to demonstrate to the Department of Corporations that it had rendered a medical decision unhindered by fiscal and management considerations. TakeCare was fined $500,000, the largest fine imposed by the department on a managed care organization in California (*Commissioner of Corporation of California v. TakeCare Health Plan*, 1996).

* * * *

On October 1, 1996, one of the first claims to go to a jury trial against a health maintenance organization (HMO) was decided. The plaintiff was unsuccessful in proving that doctors employed by the HMO had discouraged needed medical care. The plaintiff's strategy was directed at the HMO industry in general. One of the plaintiff's expert witnesses described all HMOs as "monsters" (*Gross v. Prudential Health Care Plan*, 1996).

Unless one has firsthand experience in mental health care, one may not recognize just how expensive many current "cost-saving" measures actually are. The loss of family stability, productivity, physical health, and psychological functioning caused by inadequate treatment play out over many years. Thus, the devastating price the patient and society pay often are obscured by lapse of time and other intervening variables (Welch, 1996, p. 1).

In short, the managed care system may change the long-recognized historical standard of care. As Applebaum (1993) noted, "Managed care in its present form is a relatively new phenomenon on the mental health scene. ... At this point, definitive answers are not possible" (p. 252). Applebaum also reported that new duties may arise for both clinicians and managed care reviewers and entities. These may include the duty to appeal adverse decisions, disclose, continue treatment, and review with reasonable care.

These new duties raise some perplexing questions. For example, if a clinician feels a decision made by a reviewer is antithetical to a client's well-being, is he or she obligated to protest the decision? And if payment is stopped before the therapist or client feels therapy should be terminated, what duty does the therapist have to continue treatment?

On the other side of the coin, what are the legal duties of managed care companies and their reviewers? In *Huges v. Blue Cross of Northern California*, Blue Cross refused to pay for several episodes of inpatient care for a client who kept decompensating after he left the hospital. The client's father sued, and the company was found to be liable for compensatory and punitive damages for failing to meet a standard of medical necessity (cited in Applebaum, 1993).

Concern over the implications of managed care activities has lead several major health-related organizations to articulate a Bill of Rights to protect individuals seeking treatment for mental, psychological, and substance abuse disorders. This bill—titled *Principles for the Provision of Mental Health and Substance Abuse Treatment*—was developed by the American Counseling Association, the American Association for Marriage and Family Therapy, the American Family Therapy Academy, the American Nurses' Association, the American Psychiatric Association, the American Psychiatric Nurses' Association, the American Psychological Association, the National Association of Social Workers, and the National Federation of Societies for Clinical Social Work.

Other groups that have supported the Bill of Rights include the National Mental Health Association, the American Group Psychotherapy Association, the American Psychoanalytic Association, and the National Association of Drug and Alcohol Abuse Counselors. The Bill of Rights is an attempt to shift the focus in managed care from controlling costs to quality of care.

Principles for the Provision of Mental Health and Substance Abuse Treatment focuses on issues of central importance to mental health professionals and their constituents:

1. *The Right to Know.* Individuals have the right to be provided information from their insurance companies about the nature and extent of their coverage, the qualifications of treating professionals, and other optional treatment modalities. Patients also should be informed of any contractual limitations that could interfere with or influence treatment recommendations, such as information that may be disclosed for the purpose of paying benefits.

2. *Confidentiality.* Individuals have the right to be guaranteed the protection of confidentiality except when laws or ethics dictate otherwise. Entities who receive information for the purpose of benefit determination must protect such clinical information with the same regard for confidentiality as the provider of care or be penalized accordingly for violations.

3. *Parity.* Individuals have the right to receive benefits for mental health and substance abuse counseling in the same way that they do for any other illness.

4. *Discrimination.* Individuals have the right not to penalized for receiving mental health or substance abuse treatment, by later being refused health or disability insurance.

5. *Benefit Usage and Design.* Individuals have the right to the entire scope of benefits within a given benefit plan, and providers shall provide whatever affords the individual the greatest level of protection.

6. *Treatment Review.* Individuals have the right to expect that any reviewer have the appropriate qualifications to make treatment judgments and have no financial interest in the decision.

7. *Accountability.* Individuals have the right to hold the treating professional accountable for any gross incompetence or negligence. Treating professionals shall act as advocates documenting the necessity of care if third-party payment is denied. Pay-

ers may be held accountable and liable to individuals for any
injury caused by negligence or incompetence by clinically un-
justified decisions. (Morrissey, 1997, p. 1)

Summary

The United States today is struggling with the concept of adequate medical
care. Federal agencies are developing guidelines as to what intervention strategies are most appropriate for selected disorders. Managed care companies have
proliferated in this era. The code word for managed care systems is *cost-effectiveness*. The emphasis on cost-effectiveness may create situations in which
new legal duties are imposed on both mental health professionals and those
who manage the care of others.

LEARNING FACILITATION AND FOCUS

Exercise 8.5

Harry Rittenauer works for a large company. His mental health plan
at one time paid for 80% of his therapy. For about 12 years, Harry was
under the care of various and sundry therapists—13 in all. His symptoms
never seemed to change. He was depressed, sad, and isolated from support groups. Most of his therapists diagnosed Harry as having a narcissistic personality disorder. Harry now belongs to an HMO that does not
allow him to be in constant therapy, and his living expenses are such that
he cannot afford to pay for his own counseling.

1. Comment on your values regarding people like Harry who seem to be in
   therapy forever._____

   _____

   _____

2. Is it right for an insurance company to severely limit the therapeutic help
   Harry can receive?_____

   _____

   _____

3.   What should be done to facilitate the mental health of people like Harry?

_____

_____

_____

_____

THE SUBSTANCE-ABUSING CLIENT

Clients with psychoactive substance use disorders are among the most complex and difficult to treat. Addictive disorders constitute a serious national health threat, with the lifetime incidence of psychoactive substance abuse approaching 20% of the population. Fewer than 10% of individuals with addictive disorders receive professional treatment or belong to self-help groups (Frances & Miller, 1991).

Considerable controversy exists over the etiology of psychoactive substance use disorders. Biologically based models emphasize genetic predisposition (Goodwin & Warnock, 1991), while psychoanalytic and psychodynamic perspectives suggest that chemical dependency is symptomatic of underlying psychopathology or personality dysfunction (Cox, 1987; Forrest, 1985). Leigh (1985) suggested that substance abuse and dependence are the products of a combination of variables, including personality traits, environmental factors, and the immediate self-reinforcing properties of the desired substance.

Marlatt, Baer, & Larimer (1995) suggested that substance abuse may be an impulse/behavioral (acquired habit pattern) disorder that results in disease states (e.g., cirrhosis). Beck and Emery (1977) and Ellis, McInerney, DiGiuseppe, and Yeager (1988) identified substance-dependent cognitions (belief systems and thinking styles) as critical factors precipitating substance dependence. Wallace (1991) described the biopsychosocial model in discussing crack cocaine dependence. This model considers genetic predisposition, the pharmacological reinforcing properties of substances, psychological/personality factors, and the social/environmental component (learning and reinforcement).

Psychoactive substance-disordered individuals are a heterogeneous and highly complex population. Because of the high frequency of coexisting additional forms of psychopathology, including significant characterologic features, addictive-disordered populations are extremely challenging to work with, and success rates with particular clinical subtypes may be modest at best.

Trends and approaches in the treatment of psychoactive substance disorders are changing, partly out of necessity because of shifting reimbursement patterns of third-party providers and also because of continuing advances in biological, psychological, and psychiatric research. In addition, as more researchers come to view psychoactive substance use disorders as biopsychosocial in nature, greater emphasis is being placed on combining multiple interventions, including detoxification, intense individual and group psychotherapy, social skills training and psychoeducation, psychopharmacological trials, and community-based self-help networks.

Assessment Instruments

Mental health professionals who counsel clients for psychoactive substance pathology may find it useful to acquaint themselves with standardized assessment instruments as an adjunct to clinical interviews and observation. Two instruments that have good reliability and validity and that can be scored and interpreted quickly are the *Drug Abuse Screening Test-20* (*DAST-20*; Skinner, 1982) and the *Addiction Severity Index* (*ASI*; McClellan, Luborksy, & Cacciola, 1985; Orvaschel, 1993).

The *DAST-20* is a 20-item self-report inventory that provides a quantitative index of the degree of consequences and severity of drug abuse. The *DAST-20* yields a total cumulative score with severity intervals (i.e., none, low, moderate, substantial, and severe).

The *ASI* is a structured interview instrument that provides a multidimensional assessment of degree of impairment due to substance use in various areas (medical, employment, severity of chemical use, family/social relationships, and legal and psychiatric status).

The *ASI* requires both administration and interviewer severity rating skills; therefore, counselors must have adequate training to use this instrument. The *DAST-20*, on the other hand, requires only a tabulation of item scores, and the interpretation is objective. Although neither instrument is independently adequate to provide an accurate diagnosis, both are valuable tools for gleaning additional information as well as for identifying specific areas for treatment focus.

Counseling Recommendations

It is important for counselors who work with substance abusing/dependent clients to adopt an objective and factual approach to assessment interviews. As many clients enter treatment for substance-related problems because of external pressures (i.e., family, employers, the legal system), the counselor must convey an impression that he or she is an ally to the client in addressing his or her problems. In asking assessment questions, the counselor should use the objective criteria as a guideline and proceed in a nonjudgmental and matter-of-fact way. He or she should avoid asking leading questions such as, "You don't abuse drugs or alcohol, do you?" (Bukstein, 1990).

Initial interviewing goals include establishing a flow of information and disclosure about the client's level of motivation for treatment, and obtaining the necessary information to formulate an objective impression.

The mental health professional must realize that the substance-abusing client frequently enters treatment with a strong sense of ambivalence, which affects treatment motivation. The key to working through ambivalence is to foster *engagement and trust* as early as possible, which can be done by discussing treatment ambivalence and emphasizing the client's presenting negative consequences from substance use.

The counselor should relay the results of the assessment interview to the client in the same objective fashion and emphasize that the assessment is based on the information the client provided and from data from assessment instruments. This process may help the client work though treatment resistance as well as reinforce the therapeutic alliance. Below are some general guidelines for working with substance-abusing clients.

1. *Understand the emotional role the substance of choice plays for the client.* A central challenge for the counselor is to identify the client's rationale for using a mood-altering substance. Almost invariably that rationale has an affective base (i.e., substance use to avoid or escape negative situations or to acquire a desired affective state). Once the affective motivation is established, the counselor can undertake treatment to develop adaptive coping responses. As depth-psychology-oriented treatment may be difficult with substance-dependent clients because of relapse risk, therapists should be cautious in immediately addressing traumatic issues if the client has had only a brief period of abstinence or if affect tolerance/modulation appears tenuous.

2. *Identify the internal and external triggering events for substance cravings and impulses.* Substance-using impulses often are precipitated by events that may or may not be evident to the client. The counselor needs to detect the internal (i.e., thoughts, feelings, memories, attitudes) and external (i.e., interpersonal conflicts, social isolation, interpersonal/existential losses) antecedents for the client's substance use impulses and cravings. Helping the client identify these triggers when they occur allows him or her to implement substance-avoidance behaviors. Once substance triggers are identified, specific operationalized behavior plans for coping with them can be constructed.

3. *Confront internal versus external locus of control regarding substance-using behaviors.* Many substance-abusing clients rationalize their substance use by either relinquishing responsibility for control ("I can't help it") or externalizing control over their behavior ("My boss makes me use—he's so demanding"). The counselor must confront the client by reflecting that he or she ultimately chooses to use a substance regardless of the circumstances. Once clients accept this reality, controlling the impulses to use becomes a treatment focus.

4. *Challenge substance-dependence reinforcing cognitions* (i.e., beliefs and thinking styles). Many substance-abusing clients present belief systems that reinforce chemical dependency ("Without my crack, I can't deal with life" or "I need a drink to control myself"). The counselor should challenge such maladaptive cognitions.

5. *Help the client learn and apply abstaining behaviors.* Coping with cravings and impulses is a vital therapeutic goal. A useful resistance skill is for the client to focus on previous negative consequences of substance use when he or she experiences cravings or impulses. This technique shifts the psychological focus from the desired and expected immediate mood-altering effect to associating the substance with emotionally negative events. This technique of "thinking the craving through" can divert clients from impulsiveness and make them aware of adaptive options. Counselors should review with clients the distinctions between thinking, feeling, and physical action (doing). Clients need to realize that they can have substance-oriented cravings and impulses and not carry them out.

6. *Practice therapeutic rather than antagonistic confrontation.* As treatment engagement on the part of the client is critical, the coun-

selor must be careful not to confuse confrontation with intoler-ance. Therapeutic confrontation occurs when the counselor pre-sents the client with concrete examples of clinical material repre-sentative of the disorder. Therapeutic confrontation is based on objective data or behavior that the client presents—not upon a conflict of personal values. Attempts to impose guilt or shame on the client increases the potential for treatment dropout. Reflect-ing clinical observations back to the client in a nonthreatening and constructive way increases the probability that the client will accept and work with the intervention.

7. *Establish healthy developmental goals.* An important part of coun-seling substance-abusing clients is addressing the frequent develop-mental disturbances that accompany maladaptive patterns of sub-stance use (dropping out of school, getting fired from jobs, family disruptions, etc.). Part of the treatment plan should include a return (perhaps gradually) to normal and productive functioning. Frustra-tion and anxiety tolerance may be a central focus, depending on the severity and duration of psychosocial disturbances.

Preventing Relapse

Relapse prevention is defined as "a self-management program designed to enhance the maintenance stage of the habit-change process" (Marlatt, 1985a, 1985b). Behaviorally, relapse prevention can be seen as one set of operationalized target behaviors implemented and practiced consistently over time that results in another set of targeted undesired behaviors being discontin-ued. Below are some general framework suggestions for an operationalized psychoactive substance relapse prevention program.

1. *Help the client identify high-risk situations.* High-risk situations may include attending social events where substance use is prominent or spending time at places where substances are readily available. Be-ing aware of high-risk situations alerts the client to consider avoid-ance or to apply specific behavior plans for increasing controls to maintain abstinence.

2. *Help the client make necessary lifestyles changes and relationship modifications.* The client must gain awareness of specific lifestyle behaviors (theft, prostitution, drug sales, etc.) that are specifically related to the substance-using pattern. Often the client must change those behavior patterns in order to maximize the prognosis for absti-

nence. Likewise, specific relationships that reinforce substance use must be confronted, modified, or even discontinued until the client has gained sufficient behavioral and impulse controls to withstand the influence of others who advocate substance use.

3. *Reduce access to psychoactive substances.* A strategic component of relapse prevention is reducing access to psychoactive substances. This may occur by removing psychoactive substances from the client's residence, eliminating routine purchases of substances (alcohol), or identifying specific places (high-risk situations) where substances are readily available or promoted.

4. *Address any underlying psychopathology.* Untreated psychiatric disorders (or psychopathology) constitute one of the most common reasons for psychoactive substance relapse (McClellan, 1986). Mood, anxiety, or personality disorders or other forms of psychopathology that persist into the abstinence period should be formally evaluated and treated. Using simultaneous combination treatments (psychotherapy, pharmacotherapy, family therapy, and self-help groups) may be most advantageous.

5. *Help the client rebound from a relapse.* Relapses happen; in specific patient subtypes (i.e., severe personality disorders, untreated mood or anxiety disorders), they may be common. The counselor must be clinically prepared for relapse and assure the client that a relapse should not be viewed fatalistically but rather as a mistake with the current treatment focus. The client should be encouraged to resume abstinence and to gain an understanding of the dynamics of the relapse. Relapses can be used as restarting points in treatment if therapeutic engagement is maintained.

Summary

The etiology of psychoactive substance abuse disorders is not clear. Genetic disposition, underlying pathology, personality and environmental factors, impulse/behavior disorders, and other biopsychosocial factors are some of the reasons given for substance abuse. Mental health professionals should strive to understand the emotional role the substance of choice plays for the client, identify internal and external triggering events, and help the client learn and apply abstaining behaviors.

LEARNING FACILITATION AND FOCUS

Exercise 8.6

Your client John has been recovering from alcohol abuse for some time. Lately he has stopped attending his support group, stopped his exercise program, and started associating with people who use alcohol. What tactics should you employ to address these changes in behavior?

_____

_____

_____

_____

_____

_____

Exercise 8.7

Use the following questions in a role-play situation or with an actual client to help you practice gathering appropriate information about substance abuse.

1. What do you or have you used?

2. How long have you used (beginning with experimentation)?

3. How often are you high in a week?

4. How many of your friends use?

5. Are you on medication?

6. Do you owe money for chemicals? How much?

7. How much do you spend for chemicals in a month (if you were to pay for all the chemicals you use)?

8. Who provides if you are broke?

9. Have you ever been busted (by police, at school, at home, or through DWIs)?

10. Have you lost a job because of your use?

11. What time of day do you use?

12. Do you use on the job or in school?

13. Does it take more, less, or about the same amount to get you high as it did a year ago?

14. Have you ever shot up? What? Where on your body?

15. Do you sneak using? How do you do it?

16. Do you hide drugs or alcohol?

17. Do you have rules for using? What are they? How did they come about?

18. Do you use alone?

19. Have you ever tried to quit?

20. Have you had any withdrawal symptoms?

21. Have you lost your "good time highs"?

22. Have you ever thought about suicide?

23. Do you mix your chemicals when using?

24. Do you ever shift from one chemical to another? What happened that made you decide to shift?

25. Do you avoid people who don't use?

26. Do you avoid talking about chemical dependency?

27. Have you done things when using you are ashamed of? What happened?

28. Who is the most important person in your life, including yourself?

29. How are you taking care of him or her?

30. On a scale of 1 (low) to 10 (can't use 10), how is your life going?
    ____ Explain

31. Are there any harmful consequences you are aware of in your chemical use other than those touched upon?

32. Do you think your chemical is harmful to you? Do you think you have a chemical problem?

Part E

CONSIDERATIONS IN SCHOOLS, GROUPS, MARRIAGES, AND FAMILIES

Chapter 9

THE MENTAL HEALTH PROFESSIONAL IN THE SCHOOL

THE SCHOOL COUNSELOR

Increasingly, counseling psychologists and social workers are found in schools. School psychologists have long been involved with diagnostic and consulting activities. For the most part, however, school counselors have provided whatever services were available in school systems. In this section, we will refer to all mental health professionals functioning in schools as *counselors* or *school counselors*.

Typically, school counselors must be licensed or certified, or both. A Nationally Certified School Counselor (NCSC) must take the National Counselor Exam (NCE), which is administered by the National Board of Certified Counselors (NBCC), and work the equivalent of two years as a school counselor. School counselors are advised of their ethical obligations through the *Ethical Standards for Schools Counselors*, a publication of the American School Counselor Association (ASCA, 1992).

Competence

> School counselors are exposed to every psychological problem that
> exists in school-age populations. When a student is referred or seeks
> the help of a counselor, that counselor feels a strong obligation to
> do whatever he or she can to help that student. Nevertheless, school
> counselors must be cognizant of the limits of their training and abili-
> ties and know when to refer students to more capable helpers. Fail-
> ure to do so may result in legal culpability. (Davis & Richie, 1993,
> p. 23)

According to the American School Counselor Association, the school
counselor:

> is responsible for keeping abreast of laws relating to students and
> strives to ensure that the rights of students are adequately provided
> for and protected. … The school counselor also makes appropriate
> referrals when professional assistance can no longer be adequately
> provided to the counselee. Appropriate referral necessitates knowl-
> edge of available resources. (1992, pp. 5, 7)

According to Keith-Spiegel and Koocher (1985), if the school counselor
attempts to provide therapy he or she is not qualified to provide, he or she may
face a lawsuit. School counselors have been found negligent for not having the
competencies they should have (*Kelson v. City of Springfield*, 1985; *Eisel v.
Board of Education*, 1991).

Confidentiality and Privileged Communication

> School counselors respect student clients' rights to confidenti-
> ality. Each person has the right to privacy and thereby the right
> to expect the counselor-client relationship to comply with all
> laws, policies, and ethical standards pertaining to confidential-
> ity. (ASCA, 1992, p. 4)

School counselors function in a different context than other mental health
professionals. They are subjected to community standards or what is and is not
tolerated. School personnel also work *in loco parentis* (in place of the parent),
acting as a parent with respect to care, supervision, and discipline. As a result,
a school counselor "informs appropriate officials of conditions that may be
potentially disruptive or damaging to the school's mission, personnel and property" (ASCA, 1992, D.2). Of course, student clients must be informed if there
are any limits to confidentiality. A school counselor:

> informs the counselee of the purposes, goals, techniques, and rules of procedure under which she/he may receive counseling assistance at or before the time when the counseling relationship is entered. Prior notice includes confidentiality issues such as the possible necessity for consulting with other professionals, privileged communication, and legal or authoritative restraints. The meaning and limits of confidentiality are clearly defined to counselees. (ASCA, 1992, p. A.3)

A written informed consent disclosure document should be signed by the student and the parent or the student's legal representative. When counselor communications with students are about curriculum or career issues and require minimum contact with the student, oral or written consent may not be necessary. However, when counseling involves personal or social issues not clearly related to curriculum, a written consent form should be used (Davis & Richie, 1993).

A survey of counselors in Ohio revealed that only 10% routinely secured written consent from parents or children they were counseling (Richie & Porten, cited in Davis and Richie, 1993). In some states, information shared in a school counseling session is considered privileged communication, while in others it is not. Counselors should be knowledgeable of privilege statutes in their states.

Accountability

Counselors should collect accountability data both to become more responsible in the services they provide and to ensure their professional survival (Fairchild & Zins, 1986; Keene & Stewart, 1989; Wiggins, 1985). Models for collecting accountability data are readily available (Burck & Peterson, 1975; Crabbs, 1984: Pulvino & Sanborn, 1972).

Fairchild (1993) surveyed a random sample of school counselors who were members of the ASCA, using the following categories:

- *enumerative data* (time spent in various services)

- *process data* (personal characteristics of counselors)

- *outcome data* (behavior changes as a result of counselor intervention)

Of the counselors who reported, 93.5% collected enumerative data, 56.5% collected process data, and 51.4% collected outcome data. Accountability data were requested by supervisors 30.4% of the time; by the central office, 35.5% of the time; and by the state department of education, 23.2% of the time. Fairchild (1993) recommended that counselors understand the potential benefits accruing from accountability efforts and become more involved in the methods used to collect such data.

SPECIAL ISSUES

Student Records

The Family Educational Rights and Privacy Act (FERPA), also known as the Buckley Amendment, was enacted in 1974. FERPA guarantees to parents and students 18 years old or older certain rights with regard to the inspection of educational records and their dissemination. It applies to all schools and school districts that receive federal financial assistance through the U.S. Department of Education. The only records not subject to inspection by parents, if the student is under 18, are those that remain in the sole possession of the maker thereof and that are not accessible or revealed to any other individual except a substitute. Personal files of psychologists, counselors, or other professionals that are entirely private and not available to other individuals are not considered education records.

Child Abuse

School counselors are legally obligated to report their suspicions of child abuse immediately to the appropriate child protection agency. Failure to report child abuse may result in fines ranging from $500 to $1,000, prison terms, or both. What constitutes suspected child abuse sometimes is not clear, as the definition varies from state to state. And not all suspicions of child abuse cause a duty to report, but only those based on a reasonable cause to suspect that the abuse has occurred (Besharov, 1988).

In all states, counselors are immune from retaliatory lawsuits for reporting child abuse. Malicious reporting is illegal in all states (Besharov, 1988). Courts have rejected defamation suits brought against educators when the actual abuse was not established (*Kirkorian v. Barry*, 1987; *McDonald v. State of Oregon*, 1985).

Educators have been charged with failure to report suspected child abuse by school employees. Whether the abuse took place on school grounds is not a factor (*Pesce v. J. Sterling Morton High School District*, 1987; *Sowers v. Bradford Area School District*, 1988; *State v. Freitag*, 1986).

Counselors also may serve as a consultants to teachers in regard to child abuse. If a child reports abuse to a teacher, it is crucial that the teacher react in a calm and supportive manner (Hillman & Solek-Tefft, 1988) rather than with horror and disbelief (Allsopp & Prosen, 1988).

Sometimes counselors are called upon to discuss sexuality issues with parents. Issues of sexuality may be difficult for parents to address (Brandt, 1989; Kempe & Kempe, 1978), but knowledgeable parents are more readily able to help children who become victims of sexual abuse.

Substance Abuse

Schools today incorporate primary and secondary alcohol and drug prevention programs in their curricula (Bradley, 1988; Erickson & Newman, 1984). Primary prevention programs involve teaching about the dangers of alcohol and drugs, their effects, and how students can resist peer pressure to use them. Techniques for coping with stress are also taught. Secondary substance abuse prevention programs are sometimes called *student assistance programs* (*SAPs*). These programs set up teams to identify students at-risk and attempt to rectify the situation. SAP teams typically, although not always, are made up of teachers, the school principal, counselors, and the school nurse.

Palmer and Paisley (cited in Cole, 1995) asserted that, if a school-based secondary prevention program is to be successful, "Adults within the school setting need to be proactive in identifying and providing assistance to students with substance abuse problems" (p. 288). They strongly recommended that secondary prevention programming at all school levels include formalized procedures for early identification, in which teachers play a key role; assessment, to determine the nature and severity of the student's problems (performed by a school counselor with special training in substance abuse); referral to in-school prevention groups or to an outside treatment agency; and follow-up procedures, including in-school after-care groups (cited in Cole, 1995).

In a survey of school counselors, Cole (1995) reported that 46% indicated their schools did not have formalized procedures for identifying students at-risk. When these counselors were asked about the effectiveness of their prevention programs, 38% reported their programs were ineffective in identifying students at-risk; 20.2% were unsure; and 41.8% thought their programs were effective. Almost 70% of respondents said they were part of the identification process.

Huey and Remley (cited in Cole, 1995) noted that lack of formal guidelines and procedures, especially for confidentiality and record keeping, is a major ethical and legal problem for schools and school counselors. This is especially problematic when counselors are engaged in secondary prevention programming.

Peer Sexual Harassment

Sexual harassment is any type of unwelcome conduct, verbal or nonverbal, directed at an individual because of his or her gender. It often is more an expression of power than of sexual interest, and it is considered a form of sex discrimination under the law (Seigel, Hallgarth, & Capek, 1992).

The problem of sexual harassment in schools is reaching epidemic proportions. School administrators are being inundated by a new wave of lawsuits, which are proving costly to school districts. For example, Tianna Ugarte was awarded $500,000 by a jury in California for enduring sexual taunting and threats from a sixth-grade classmate.

A set of federal guidelines was sent to all school districts in 1996. These guidelines indicated that schools must take adequate steps to stop sexual harassment or they will be in violation of the law that prohibits sexual discrimination in schools that receive federal funding.

This issue presents a new dilemma for school counselors, who report that one of their most problematic issues is knowing what to do when a student reports being sexually harassed. Secondary school counselors, in particular, have noted an increase in the number of students coming to them to talk about being harassed. These counselors have expressed a variety of issues around the topic of peer harassment, including questions of how to investigate and follow through with allegations of harassment, how to prevent it, how to help students assert themselves, and how best to work with administrators and parents regarding peer sexual harassment (Rowell, McBride, & Leaf, 1996, p. 196).

School counselors who are engaged in developing policies and programs to prevent sexual harassment and discrimination in the schools should include the elements listed below. These elements (from Scott, 1995) were adapted from a policy statement by the National Council for Research on Women (1994).

Scott's elements included:

1. representatives from each of the constituents in the school (including students),

2. a clear statement that sexual harassment will not be tolerated,

3. a definition of sexual harassment,

4. complaint procedures,

5. sanctions,

6. a statement on confidentiality,

7. protection against retaliation,

8. a provision for neutral, well-trained investigators,

9. education and training for students, teachers, and staff,

10. identification of support services, and

11. mechanisms for feedback.

Preventing Violence

Koop and Lunberg (1992) expressed concern about violence among youths, noting that this issue poses a serious public health problem in the United States. The U.S. Department of Health and Human Services (1990) recommended that schools teach conflict resolution skills as one way of diffusing the problem.

Orpinas et al. (1990) implemented a three-year violence prevention program for middle-school students in a large urban school district in Texas. School counselors can benefit from their experience implementing such programs. Specifically, Orpinas et al. noted that counselors implementing a program should:

- ensure support from the district's administration,

- make sure teachers get involved early in the program,

- phase in program components,

- use peer mediation,

- create a school health promotion council,

- develop district policy for required training of teachers, and

- get parents involved.

School counselors should be aware that prevention programs share one salient philosophy: Such programs are most effective when they are comprehensive and systematic. A commitment on the part of all constituents is imperative. Administrators, teachers, staff, students, parents, school, and board members must all be involved.

STUDENT REFERRAL

Whiteside (1993) divided the referral process for school counselors into three distinct areas:

1. Referrals with maximum cooperation

2. Referrals with intermediate cooperation

3. Referrals with minimum cooperation

When family members are aware there is a problem and are amenable to solving it with the counselor, the counselor's task is rather simple. He or she should listen carefully to the family, while being empathetic to their pain. He or she also should try to find the appropriate intervention, which may include recommending a self-help book or family therapy. "The counselor's job is to spend most of the time guiding the family to a certain type of therapist rather than 'selling' the parents on the idea of therapy" (Whiteside, 1993, p. 275).

In referrals with intermediate cooperation, the family is clearly interested in helping the child, but the counselor is not sure if they would be happy being identified as part of the problem. Family members may know they need therapy but are reluctant to expose their own problems. In this case, the counselor should stress the seriousness of the problem—not allowing the family to minimize the situation—while emphasizing how other families have benefited from therapy. Talk about the referral should be based on the child's needs at first; gradually, the counselor can move the scope of the treatment to include the whole family.

In situations where there is minimum cooperation, the counselor should inform family members that they need outside help for their child and should consult a therapist. The tension level in these cases often runs high, with the parents blaming the school for the problem. Quite often, a confrontation between school officials and parents develops over what decision should be made for the student.

In this case, the counselor's function is to lower the emotional intensity of everyone involved. The focus should be kept on the student's problem, as any suggestions that the issues may be associated with family dynamics probably will be inflammatory. If the family refuses to seek therapy, the counselor should continue to employ the principal and school psychologist to support the decision for the child to receive therapy.

SUMMARY

School counselors must be careful to counsel students only in their area of competence. In order to be more responsive to the services they provide, and to ensure their professional survival, counselors should collect accountability data. Counselors are expected to design, implement, and evaluate substance abuse, child abuse, violent abuse, and sexual harassment programs. The ethical and legal implications of these programs are myriad. Therefore, school counselors are advised to seek training and education in all of these areas.

LEARNING FACILITATION AND FOCUS

Exercise 9.1

A fellow counselor has come to you throughout the school year to discuss his extremely bitter divorce proceedings. Although he rarely discusses his situation with other staff members, he has been quite open with you about his negative feelings toward marriage and women in general. Later in the year he informs you that he will be conducting a counseling group for adolescents experiencing divorce in their families. The group has been approved by school administrators.

1. What are the ethical and legal implications in this case?_____

_____

_____

2. What should you do? _____

_____

_____

_____

Exercise 9.2

A family new to the United States recently moved into your district. After a short time, it becomes clear that their second-grade son is having serious difficulty in school. A referral is made and the parents agree to an assessment. The assessment reveals that the boy qualifies for special services in several areas. At the meeting called to discuss the results, it becomes apparent that, despite the family's reasonable understanding of English, they may not understand the implications of the decision to be made. Even after several meetings the parents deny placement, insisting that their son remain in the regular classroom, where he is falling further and further behind.

1. What are the ethical and legal implications in this case? _____

_____

_____

2. What should you do? _____

_____

_____

_____

Exercise 9.3

A referral has been made to you for an adolescent boy who has been acting out in school. The boy is suspected of stealing money from his teacher and setting fires in the school bathroom, although neither charge can be proved. In order to better understand the boy, you make a home visit and find a chaotic environment in which the father is gone most of the time and the mother is unable to control her five children.

When you meet with the parents to discuss the problem, they seem genuinely interested and listen attentively to your advice that they seek outside intervention. Several months later, however, the boy is still exhibiting difficulty, so you call the family again. The mother explains that they have sought outside intervention through prayer, and that this is the way such matters are handled in their household. She also says that the boy may not receive any more counseling.

1. What are the ethical and legal implications in this case?_____

_____

_____

_____

2. What should you do? _____

_____

_____

_____

Exercise 9.4

You have been working with a group of four girls from the middle school. One morning you are made aware that one of the girls in the group did not come home the night before and is not present in school. The other three girls confide in you that they know where she is, although they do not want to tell you anything more specific. The principal informs you that the police are searching for the girl and may visit your office shortly. Your rapport with the group is excellent, and they believe what they tell you is confidential.

1. What are the ethical and legal implications in this case?_____

_____

_____

_____

2. What should you do? _____

_____

_____

_____

Exercise 9.5

You are working with a seventh-grade boy. As he begins to trust you, he reveals more and more about himself through his poetry and artwork. You confide in the school psychologist. Both of you believe the child is deeply troubled and potentially suicidal. Both of you are of the opinion that the suicide is not imminent, but you feel that, unless the boy gets professional help, he will definitely be suicidal in the future. The boy's parents will not permit him to undergo treatment. They say the psychological treatment is for "crazy people."

1.   What are the ethical and legal implications in this case? _____

_____

_____

_____

2.   What should you do? _____

_____

_____

_____

Chapter 10

IN A GROUP CONTEXT

GROUP COUNSELING

The antecedents to therapy groups—or counseling groups, as they are known today—were born in the early part of the twentieth century under the guise of vocational or group guidance. Group guidance activities still are emulated and employed today, especially in elementary and middle schools. Units of activity are planned, developed, and implemented for subjects such as career choice and human sexuality.

Between 1950 and 1970, the impetus for group counseling and group psychotherapy accelerated. Influenced by the advance of the study of group dynamics, various group process entities began to manifest, including these:

- Sensitivity and encounter groups that emphasize experiential-based learning processes and activities.

- Social skills training groups.

- Structured groups, in which individuals are taught to be more assertive and increase their communication skills.

- Psychotherapy groups. According to Moreno (1962, p. 26), "group psychotherapy simply means to treat people in groups."

- Organizational development groups.

- Self-help groups.

These groups combined and integrated many of the concepts of group dynamics, social interaction correlates, and communication patterns and were similar in nature, content, and expression. However, there were also differences in objectives and architectural structure. As a result, different behaviors were manifested in the groups by both leaders and participants. For example:

> *Encounter groups* as we define the term, refers to intensive small group experiences in which the emphasis is upon personal growth through expanding awareness, exploration of intrapsychic as well as interpersonal issues, and release of dysfunctional inhibitions. There is relatively little focus on the group as a learning instrument; the trainer takes a more active and directive role; and physical interaction is utilized. Other modes of expression and sensory exploration such as dance, art, massage, and nudity are currently being tried as part of the encounter experience. (Eddy & Lubin, 1971, p. 626)

Social skills groups allow participants to practice a variety of skills necessary to achieve a desired social or organizational goal. This approach assumes that many responses to social situations should be developed, nurtured, and stored to compliment and enhance the myriad social interactions of today's society. Group leaders respond to the social implications of a member's behavior. For example, if a member expresses to the group leader with noticeable hostility that he or she is dissatisfied with the direction the group is taking, the leader's response will be social in nature rather than interpersonal. Ignoring the hostile affect, the leader might respond, "Is there some way you can help the group get more focused? I'm sure your ideas would be appreciated."

Notice that the leader does not respond to the affect expressed by the member in a social group. In an experientially based and interpersonal process group, the leader might respond, "I notice that you seem angry with the direction the group is taking. Would you like to talk more about how you feel?"

In the counseling and therapy groups that are common today, the leader's competency, qualifications, and training are crucial. Psychological risks and members' rights are two common concerns. Group counseling tends to focus on developmental issues, while group therapy tends to focus on pathological issues. The behavior of the leader, however, and the dynamics exemplified by various group members may be similar.

The particular techniques of the leader sometimes are salient factors in determining the direction of a group's process. At the same time, conducting group sessions designed to help members nurture their human potential (rather than address major psychic reconstruction of intrapsychic processes) usually involves obvious and discernible differences in the conduct of group members, the content expressed, and the process evidenced. With the advent of recent federal and mental health guidelines and their implications for the economic realities of treatment, the differentiation between group therapy and group counseling is becoming more evident. Note the statement formulated by the task force of the American Association for Marriage and Family Therapy.

> Practice of marital and family therapy means the diagnosis and treatment of nervous and mental disorders, whether cognitive, affective, or behavioral, within the context of marital and family systems. Marital and family therapy involves the professional application of psychotherapeutic and family systems theories and techniques in the delivery of services to individuals, marital pairs, and families for the purpose of treating such diagnosed nervous and mental disorders. Marital and family counseling is that specialized part of marital and family therapy that focuses on marital adjustment, preparation for marriage, and parent-child and other family relationships in which there is no diagnosed nervous or mental disorder. (cited in Shields, Wynne, McDaniel, & Gawinski, 1994, p. 125)

GROUP THEORIES

Adlerian Theory

Many group leaders today use techniques derived from theoretical constructs proposed by Alfred Adler. Breaking with Freud, Adler contended that people are driven by conscious factors to master their environment rather than by unconscious factors. For example, people perceiving their inferiority in early childhood (especially as compared to their older siblings) often develop inferiority complexes. These complexes are antithetical to human nature, which is to achieve significance and mastery of one's environment. Thus, people can develop mistaken assumptions about themselves, which they have learned in their first social context—the family. These mistaken assumptions are variables that impede one's journey toward fulfillment in life. Fulfillment may be described as being socially connected with the rest of society, working toward belonging, and establishing meaningful relationships. People should strive toward perfection without being perfectionistic. Perfectionism implies a static lifestyle that impedes moving forward because of mistaken basic assumptions.

Since mistaken assumptions were learned in a social environment, the group context was and is a natural environment for counseling and therapy. "Since man's problems and conflicts are recognized in their social nature, the group is ideally suited not only to highlight and reveal the nature of a person's conflicts and maladjustments but to offer corrective influences" (Dreukers, 1969, p. 43). Adlerian counseling has four goals, which closely parallel the stages an Adlerian group would take:

1. Establishing an empathetic relationship based on mutual respect

2. Understanding beliefs, feelings, motives, and goals

3. Developing insight into mistaken goals and self-defeating behaviors

4. Seeing alternatives and making new choices

Humanistic and Existential Groups

Humanistic and existential groups are predicated on the assumption that the individual is a totality and capable of making choices. There are philosophical differences between the two and, as a result, different therapeutic approaches to group leadership, but the flavor and texture of therapeutic response is often more similar than different.

Existentialists focus more on choices and their meaning, while *humanists* focus on the inherent tendency in the organism to move toward becoming all it can be. Existentialists differentiate between neurotic anxiety and anxiety that is extant merely because the person exists; that is, the freedom of choice may be anxiety-producing. Thus, anxiety may impede the acquisition of freedom; the loss of freedom does not result from being victim of circumstance, but because one makes the choice to lose it. Humanists, on the other hand, focus on one's need to actualize the very nature of the organism in the world. This actualization process may be impeded because the appropriate nutrient elements in the environment were not evident in childhood.

Humanist group leaders strive to create environments that allow an individual to *become*. "Individuals have within themselves vast resources for self-understanding and for altering their self-concepts, basic attitudes, and well-directed behavior; these resources can be tapped if a definable climate of facilitative attitudes can be provided" (Rogers, 1980, p. 115). The stance of the humanist therapist is characterized by genuineness, unconditional positive regard, and empathy.

Existential group leaders use similar techniques to develop group participants' awareness of themselves in the world. Extension of one's awareness is equated to the extension of one's choice. Practically, the styles of existential and humanistic therapists may be captured in the following scenario.

The client in a humanistic group recounts: "My husband is awful; he puts me down and belittles me all the time, it's awful, but I can't leave him." The therapist might respond, "Now let me see, on the one hand, your husband's behavior makes you feel bad—or is *insignificant* the right word?—but, on the other hand, something else keeps you in the position you have found yourself."

Given the same client statement, an existential group leader might respond: "It sounds like you have a number of choices. One choice is to stay with your husband, one is to leave him. Can you talk about what it means to you to stay, and what it would mean to leave?"

Note that the humanist approach emphasizes what the client is feeling, whereas the existential approach emphasizes what the client's meaning and awareness systems are. Volition is to existentialism what nurturance is to humanism.

Transactional Groups

Transactional analysis (TA) groups emphasize the cognitive, rational, and behavioral notations of personality. Those who conduct TA groups believe that personality is composed of three dynamic ego states: parent, adult, and child. These ego states are introjections of parental modeling and behavior. *Parent ego states* are composed of shoulds and oughts. *Adult ego states* are functional and unemotional. The energy in the adult ego state is necessary for things like mathematical calculations and reading road maps. *Child ego states* employ impulses and feelings.

Obviously these ego states resemble Freud's superego, ego, and id. The main differences between Freud's concepts and those of TA groups is that Freud's ego states become fixated and can only be attended by the therapist's proper employment of the transference phenomenon. TA ego states can be realized by the observation and analysis of one's own behavior. Once awareness is achieved, one can change the behavior.

Behavioral Groups

Behavioral group therapy, which is becoming increasingly popular today, is based on various experimental approaches to psychology that are grounded in theories of how things are learned. The basic premise of behavioral therapy is that certain problematic cognitive functioning behaviors and emotions are learned. These functions, and their potentially resultant pathological or neurotic correlates, are in themselves the problems and not merely symptoms of underlying unconscious and unresolved childhood problems. Relaxation exercises, cognitive restructuring, desensitization, and reinforcement are forms of behavioral therapy.

Group participants in behavioral therapy first take an inventory of their current identifiable problems as they are manifested in their behavior. The focus of their therapy is specific to these behaviors and unequivocal in its prescription. Kuehnel and Leberman (1986) scripted the process of behavioral assessment this way:

1.   Identify maladaptive behaviors along with a description of their intensity, frequency, and length of time experienced.

2.   Determine the client's strength.

3.   Identify the context in which the problematic behavior manifests itself.

4.   Determine a strategy to measure lack of the problematic behaviors.

5.   Identify potential reinforcers—people and activities that may provide motivation for treatment.

6.   Form treatment goals.

The summary of various groups in this chapter is certainly not all-inclusive. Psychodrama, gestalt, reality therapy, and many others are potential contexts for therapeutic practice.

CHARACTERISTICS OF GROUP LEADERS

Corey (1995) did not attribute the success or failure of groups to either participant personalities or the technique used. Rather, he asserted, the use of group techniques cannot be separated from the leader's personal characteristics and behaviors. Corey (1995) articulated the following personal characteristics of group leaders as vitally related to the group process.

1. *Presence.* In order to be effective, group leaders must be able to give expression to their own emotions; consequently, they can be moved to compassion and empathy with others in the group.

2. *Personal power.* Group leaders must not deny the influence they have on others. They should feel a sense of power in their own lives and feel they have the capacity to control their own destinies. This power is not equated with domination, but with the feeling that the leader will offer encouragement to members to use and develop their own strengths.

3. *Courage.* Leaders must be capable of risk-taking and vulnerability.

4. *Willingness to confront oneself.* Group leaders must experience an on-going and never-ending process to analysis and question their motivations, expressions, and behaviors in a group. As Corey (1995) noted,

   > This essential characteristic of effective leadership includes awareness not only of one's needs and motivations but also of personal conflicts and problems, of defenses and weak spots, of areas of unfinished business, and of the potential influence of all of these on the group process. (p. 55)

5. *Sincerity and authenticity.* Group leaders at times must be direct, which involves telling group members what they don't want to hear.

6. *Sense of identity.* Group leaders must have a clear sense of their own identity, their strengths and weaknesses, what they want from life, and how they are going to achieve it.

7. *Belief in the group process and enthusiasm.* Group leaders must enjoy the work they do. Group members' lack of enthusiasm may reflect a lack of enthusiasm in the group leader.

8. *Inventiveness and creativity.* Group leaders should not get trapped in orthodox techniques that can become neutralized.

COMPETENCY AND THE GROUP LEADER

One of our purposes for summarizing various groups here was to highlight the differences in the theoretical orientations of mental health professionals. All group counselors, however, are ethically and legally bound to make sure their behavior in groups is competent. It is difficult to see how, in this age of specialization, group counselors could be competent administering group therapy under the rubric of all the possible orientations and techniques available.

The situation is compounded when mental health professionals specialize not only with respect to specific orientation but also often in the context of a special population such as children, adults, delinquents, or geriatrics. Group counselors should declare their area of specialization and make sure they have the appropriate training and experience to provide competent therapy for the clientele they intend to serve. Reading how to run a group or relying on one's past experience as a group member may not be sufficient to satisfy the ethical and legal criteria for being a group leader.

> Counselors practice only within the boundaries of their competence, based on their education, training, supervised experience, state and national professional credentials, and appropriate professional experience.
>
> Counselors will demonstrate a commitment to gain knowledge, personal awareness, sensitivity, and skills pertinent to working with a diverse client population. (ACA, 1995, 3A)

* * * *

> Counselors practice in specialty areas new to them only after appropriate education, training, and supervised experience. While developing skills in new specialty areas, counselors take steps to ensure the competence of their work and to protect others from possible harm. (ACA, 1995, 3b)

* * * *

> Social workers should accept responsibility or employment only on the basis of existing competence or the intention to acquire the necessary competence. (NASW, 1997, 4.01a)

* * * *

> Social workers should strive to become and remain proficient in professional practice and the performance of professional functions. Social workers should critically examine, and keep current with, emerging knowledge relevant to social work. Social workers should routinely review professional literature and participate in continuing education relevant to social work practice and social work ethics. (NASW, 1997, 4.01b)

* * * *

Social workers should base practice on recognized knowledge, including empirically based knowledge, relevant to social work and social work ethics. (NASW, 1997, 4.01c)

* * * *

Psychologists provide services, teach, and conduct research only within the boundaries of their competence, based on their education, training, supervised experience, or appropriate professional experience. (APA, 1995, 1.04a)

* * * *

Psychologists provide services, teach, or conduct research in new areas or involving new techniques only after first undertaking appropriate study, training, supervision, and consultation from persons who are competent in those areas or techniques. (APA, 1995, 1.04a)

* * * *

Psychologists who engage in assessment, therapy, teaching, research, organizational consulting, or other professional activities maintain a reasonable level of awareness of current scientific and professional information in their fields of activity, and undertake ongoing efforts to maintain competence in the skills they pursue. (APA, 1995, 1.05)

Mental health professionals should attend workshops and conferences whose content is germane to their expertise and should subscribe to and read journals that publish research and articles opposite to their theoretical orientation. Remember, counselors present themselves as those who have much more knowledge and expertise than the average lay person. It is imperative that they continually update their area of expertise and theoretical orientation and know their limitations. They must not try to perform therapeutic functions beyond their area of expertise.

Hall (1988) cautioned mental health professionals not to practice beyond their competence, reminding them that other professionals are available for consultation. Without timely consultation, the possibility of endangering client welfare always exists, and those in private practice are wise to create a formal or informal network of colleagues to whom they can turn when they need help.

Corey (1995) noted that whether competence to lead a specific type of group is an ongoing question all mental health professionals face. Regarding specific groups, Corey urged therapists to question themselves about such issues as qualifications, how to upgrade their skills, what kinds of clients they work best with, and when they should refer clients.

CONFIDENTIALITY

Group leaders should stress at the beginning of the group and at several points during the group's life the importance and necessity of confidentiality. Confidentiality is a foundation for effective and authentic process. The group should discuss confidentiality at great length because it is much better for participants to integrate the importance of the concept than for the group leader to legislate it.

Participants may ask if they can talk about the group at home without mentioning any names, or if they can include the material in research case studies and disguise the names of members. The group leader should have a policy on such matters and respond accordingly. Group members usually will take the lead of the group leader; and if they know, understand, and sense that the leader takes confidentiality seriously, there is a better chance they also will.

> In group work, counselors clearly define confidentiality and the parameters for the specific group being entered, explain its importance, and discuss the difficulties related to confidentiality involved in group work. The fact that confidentiality cannot be guaranteed is clearly communicated to group members. (ACA, 1995, B2a)

> * * * *

> When social workers provide counseling services to families, couples, or groups, social workers should seek agreement among the parties involved concerning each individual's right to confidentiality and obligation to preserve the confidentiality of information shared by others. Social workers should inform participants in family, couples, or group counseling that social workers cannot guarantee that all participants will honor such agreements. (NASW, 1997, 107F)

PRIVILEGED COMMUNICATION

Privileged communication is a legal term, and the legal system usually does not honor the endowment of privileged information on communication expressed in the presence of a third-party. This is called the *third-party rule*, and it states that it is not reasonable to expect or to assume that information will necessarily remain private once disclosure of the information is made in the presence of a third party. Although a few states have created a group-therapy privilege (Myers, 1991), most laws regarding privilege follow the tradition of a mental health professional doing therapy with individual clients. Exceptions to the third-party rule are rare because courts see this type of exception as one that keeps appropriate evidence from the public (Schwitzgebel & Schwitzgebel, 1980).

ETHICAL GUIDELINES FOR GROUP COUNSELORS

Before conducting group counseling activities, group counselors should be familiar with the ethical guidelines for group leaders. These guidelines, revised in 1989 by the Association for Specialists in Group Work, are presented below.

Preamble

One characteristic of any professional group is the possession of a body of knowledge, skills, and voluntarily, self-professed standards for ethical practice. A code of ethics consists of those standards that have been formally and publicly acknowledged by the members of a profession to serve as the guidelines for professional conduct, discharge of duties, and the resolution of moral dilemmas. By this document, the Association for Specialists in Group Work (ASGW) has identified the standards of conduct appropriate for ethical behavior among its members.

The Association for Specialists in Group Work recognizes the basic commitment of its members to the Ethical Standards of its parent organization, the American Association for Counseling and Development (AACD) [Now the American Counseling Association, ACA] and nothing in this document shall be construed to supplant that code. These standards are intended to complement the AACD [ACA] standards in the area of group work by clarifying the nature of ethical responsibility of the counselor in the group setting and by stimulating a greater concern for competent group leadership.

The group counselor is expected to be a professional agent and to take the processes of ethical responsibility seriously. ASGW views "ethical process" as being integral to group work and views group counselors as "ethical agents." Group counselors, by their very nature in being responsible and responsive to their group members, necessarily embrace a certain potential for ethical vulnerability. It is incumbent upon group counselors to give considerable attention to the intent and context of their actions because the attempts of counselors to influence human behavior through group work always have ethical implications.

The following ethical guidelines have been developed to encourage ethical behavior of group counselors. These guidelines are written for students and practitioners, and are meant to stimulate reflection, self-examination, and discussion of issues and practices. They address the group counselor's responsibility for providing information about group work to clients and the group counselor's responsibility for providing group counseling services to clients. A final section discusses the group counselor's responsibility for safeguarding ethical practice and procedures for reporting unethical behavior. Group counselors are expected to make known these standards to group members.

Ethical Guidelines

1. *Orientation and Providing Information:* Group counselors adequately prepare prospective or new group members by providing as much information about the existing or proposed group as necessary.

    Minimally, information related to each of the following areas should be provided.

    a. Entrance procedures, time parameters of the group experience, group participation expectations, methods of payment (where appropriate), and termination procedures are explained by the group counselor as appropriate to the level of maturity of group members and the nature and purpose(s) of the group.

    b. Group counselors have available for distribution a professional disclosure statement that includes information on the group counselor's qualifications and group services that can be provided, particularly as related to the nature and purpose(s) of the specific group.

    c. Group counselors communicate the role expectations, rights, and responsibilities of group members and group counselor(s).

d. The group goals are stated as concisely as possible by the group counselor including "whose" goal it is (the group counselor's, the institution's, the parent's, the law's, society's, etc.) and the role of group members in influencing or determining the group's goal(s).

e. Group counselors explore with group members the risks of potential life changes that may occur because of the group experience and help members explore their readiness to face these possibilities.

f. Group members are informed by the group counselor of unusual or experimental procedures that might be expected in their group experience.

g. Group counselors explain, as realistically as possible, what services can and cannot be provided within the particular group structure offered.

h. Group counselors emphasize the need to promote full psychological functioning and presence among group members. They inquire from prospective group members whether they are using any kind of drug or medication that may affect functioning in the group. They do not permit any use of alcohol and/or illegal drugs during group sessions and they discourage the use of alcohol and/or drugs (legal or illegal) prior to group meetings which may affect the physical or emotional presence of the member or other group members.

i. Group counselors inquire from prospective group members whether they have ever been a client in counseling or psychotherapy. If a prospective group member is already in a counseling relationship with another professional person, the group counselor advises the prospective group member to notify the other professional of their participation in the group.

j. Group counselors clearly inform group members about the policies pertaining to the group counselor's willingness to consult with them between group sessions.

k. In establishing fees for group counseling services, group counselors consider the financial status and the locality of prospective group members. Group members are not charged fees for group sessions where the group counselor is not present and the policy of charging for sessions missed by a group member is clearly communicated. Fees for participating as a group member are contracted between group counselor and group member for a specified period of time. Group counselors do not increase fees for group counseling services until the existing contracted fee structure has expired. In the event that the established fee structure is inappropriate for a prospective member, group counselors assist in finding comparable services of acceptable cost.

2. *Screening of Members:* The group counselor screens prospective group members (when appropriate to their theoretical orientation). Insofar as possible, the counselor selects group members whose needs and goals are compatible with the goals of the group, who will not impede the group process, and whose well-being will not be jeopardized by the group experience. An orientation to the group (i.e., ASGW Ethical Guideline #1) is included during the screening process.

Screening may be accomplished in one or more ways, such as the following:

a. Individual interview,

b. Group interview of prospective group members,

c. Interview as part of a team staffing, and,

d. Completion of a written questionnaire by prospective group members.

3. *Confidentiality:* Group counselors protect members by defining clearly what confidentiality means, why it is important, and the difficulties involved in enforcement.

a. Group counselors take steps to protect members by defining confidentiality and the limits of confidentiality (i.e., when a group member's condition indicates that there is clear and imminent danger to the member, others, or physical property, the group counselor takes reasonable personal action and/or informs responsible authorities).

b. Group counselors stress the importance of confidentiality and set a norm of confidentiality regarding all group participants' disclosures. The importance of maintaining confidentiality is emphasized before the group begins and at various times in the group. The fact that confidentiality cannot be guaranteed is clearly stated.

c. Members are made aware of the difficulties involved in enforcing and ensuring confidentiality in a group setting. The counselor provides examples of how confidentiality can nonmaliciously be broken to increase members' awareness, and help to lessen the likelihood that this breach of confidence will occur. Group counselors inform group members about the potential consequences of intentionally breaching confidentiality.

d. Group counselors can only ensure confidentiality on their part and not on the part of the members.

e. Group counselors video or audio tape a group session only with the prior consent, and the members' knowledge of how the tape will be used.

f. When working with minors, the group counselor specifies the limits of confidentiality.

g. Participants in a mandatory group are made aware of any reporting procedures required of the group counselor.

h. Group counselors store or dispose of group member records (written, audio, video, etc.) in ways that maintain confidentiality.

i. Instructors of group counseling courses maintain the anonymity of group members whenever discussing group counseling cases.

4. *Voluntary/Involuntary Participation:* Group counselors inform members whether participation is voluntary or involuntary.

a. Group counselors take steps to ensure informed consent procedures in both voluntary and involuntary groups.

b. When working with minors in a group, counselors are expected to follow the procedures specified by the institution in which they are practicing.

    c.   With involuntary groups, every attempt is made to enlist the cooperation of the members and their continuance in the group on a voluntary basis.

    d.   Group counselors do not certify that group treatment has been received by members who merely attend sessions, but did not meet the defined group expectations. Group members are informed about the consequences for failing to participate in a group.

5.   *Leaving a Group:* Provisions are made to assist a group member to terminate in an effective way.

    a.   Procedures to be followed for a group member who chooses to exit a group prematurely are discussed by the counselor with all group members either before the group begins, during a prescreening interview, or during the initial group session.

    b.   In the case of legally mandated group counseling, group counselors inform members of the possible consequences for premature self-termination.

    c.   Ideally, both the group counselor and the member can work cooperatively to determine the degree to which a group experience is productive or counter-productive for that individual.

    d.   Members ultimately have a right to discontinue membership in the group, at a designated time, if the predetermined trial period proves to be unsatisfactory.

    e.   Members have the right to exit a group, but it is important that they be made aware of the importance of informing the counselor and the group members prior to deciding to leave. The counselor discusses the possible risks of leaving the group prematurely with a member who is considering this option.

    f.   Before leaving a group, the group counselor encourages members (if appropriate) to discuss their reasons for wanting to discontinue membership in the group. Counselors intervene if other members use undue pressure to force a member to remain in the group.

6. *Coercion and Pressure:* Group counselors protect member rights against physical threats, intimidation, coercion, and undue peer pressure insofar as is reasonably possible.

   a. It is essential to differentiate between "therapeutic pressure" that is part of any group and "undue pressure" which is not therapeutic.

   b. The purpose of a group is to help participants find their own answer, not to pressure them into doing what the group thinks is appropriate.

   c. Counselors exert care not to coerce participants to change in directions which they clearly state they do not choose.

   d. Counselors have a responsibility to intervene when others use undue pressure or attempt to persuade members against their will.

   e. Counselors intervene when any member attempts to act out aggression in a physical way that might harm another member or themselves.

   f. Counselors intervene when a member is verbally abusive or inappropriately confrontive to another member.

7. *Imposing Counselor Values:* Group counselors develop an awareness of their own values and needs and the potential impact they have on the interventions likely to be made.

   a. Although group counselors take care to avoid imposing their values on members, it is appropriate that they expose their own beliefs, decisions, needs, and values, when concealing them would create problems for the members.

   b. There are values implicit in any group, and these are made clear to potential members before they join the group. (Examples of certain values include expressing feelings, being direct and honest, sharing personal material with others, learning how to trust, improving interpersonal communication, and deciding for oneself.)

c.   Personal and professional needs of group counselors are not met at the members' expense.

d.   Group counselors avoid using the group for their own therapy.

e.   Group counselors are aware of their own values and assumptions and how these apply in a context.

f.   Group counselors take steps to increase their awareness of ways that their personal reactions to members might inhibit the group process and they monitor their countertransference. Through an awareness of the impact of stereotyping and discrimination (i.e., biases based on age, disability, ethnicity, gender, race, religion, or sexual preference), group counselors guard the individual rights and personal dignity of all group members.

8.   *Equitable Treatment:* Group counselors make every reasonable effort to treat each member individually and equally.

a.   Group counselors recognize and respect differences (e.g., cultural, racial, religious, lifestyle, age, disability, gender) among group members.

b.   Group counselors maintain an awareness of their behavior toward individual group members and are alert to the potential detrimental effects of favoritism or partiality toward any particular group member to the exclusion or detriment of any other member(s). It is likely that group counselors will favor some members over others, yet all group members deserve to be treated equally.

c.   Group counselors ensure equitable use of group time for each member by inviting silent members to become involved, acknowledging nonverbal attempts to communicate, and discouraging rambling and monopolizing of time by members.

d.   If a large group is planned, counselors consider enlisting another qualified professional to serve as a coleader for the group sessions.

9.   *Dual Relationships:* Group counselors avoid dual relationships with group members that might impair their objectivity and professional

judgment, as well as those which are likely to compromise a group member's ability to participate fully in the group.

a.   Group counselors do not misuse their professional role and power as group leader to advance personal or social contacts with members throughout the duration of the group.

b.   Group counselors do not use their professional relationship with group members to further their own interest either during the group or after the termination of the group.

c.   Sexual intimacies between group counselors and members are unethical.

d.   Group counselors do not barter (exchange) professional services with group members for services.

e.   Group counselors do not admit their own family members, relatives, employees, or personal friends as members to their groups.

f.   Group counselors discuss with group members the potential detrimental effects of group members engaging in intimate intermember relationships outside of the group.

g.   Students who participate in a group as a partial course requirement for a group course requirement for a group course are not evaluated for an academic grade based upon their degree of participation as a member in a group. Instructors of group counseling courses take steps to minimize the possible negative impact on students when they participate in a group course by separating course grades from participation in the group and by allowing students to decide what issues to explore and when to stop.

h.   It is inappropriate to solicit members from a class (or institutional affiliation) for one's private counseling or therapeutic groups.

10.   *Use of Techniques:* Group counselors do not attempt any technique unless trained in its use or under supervision by a counselor familiar with the intervention.

    a.   Group counselors are able to articulate a theoretical orientation that guides their practice, and they are able to provide a rationale for their interventions.

    b.   Depending upon the type of an intervention, group counselors have training commensurate with the potential impact of a technique.

    c.   Group counselors are aware of the necessity to modify their techniques to fit the unique needs of various cultural and ethnic groups.

    d.   Group counselors assist members in translating in-group learning to daily life.

11. *Goal Development:* Group counselors make every effort to assist members in developing their personal goals.

    a.   Group counselors use their skills to assist members in making their goals specific so that others present in the group will understand the nature of the goals.

    b.   Throughout the course of a group, group counselors assist members in assessing the degree to which personal goals are being met, and assist in revising any goals when it is appropriate.

    c.   Group counselors help members clarify the degree to which the goals can be met within the context of a particular group.

12. *Consultation:* Group counselors develop and explain policies about between-session consultation to group members.

    a.   Group counselors take care to make certain that members do not use between-session consultations to avoid dealing with issues pertaining to the group that would be dealt with best in the group.

    b.   Group counselors urge members to bring the issues discussed during between-session consultations into the group if they pertain to the group.

    c.   Group counselors seek out consultation and/or supervision regarding ethical concerns or when encountering difficulties which interfere with effective functioning as group leaders.

    d.   Group counselors seek appropriate professional assistance for their own personal problems or conflicts that are likely to impair their professional judgment and work performance.

    e.   Group counselors discuss their group cases only for professional consultation and educational purposes.

    f.   Group counselors inform members about policies regarding whether consultation will be held confidential.

13. *Termination from the Group:* Depending upon the purpose of participation in the group, counselors promote termination of members from the group in the most efficient period of time.

    a.   Group counselors maintain a constant awareness of the progress made by each group member and periodically invite the group members to explore and reevaluate their experiences in the group. It is the responsibility of group counselors to help promote the independence of members from the group in a timely manner.

14. *Evaluation and Follow-Up:* Group counselors make every attempt to engage in ongoing assessment and to design follow-up procedures for their groups.

    a.   Group counselors recognize the importance of ongoing assessment of a group, and they assist members in evaluating their own progress.

    b.   Group counselors conduct evaluation of the total group experience at the final meeting (or before termination), as well as ongoing evaluation.

    c.   Group counselors monitor their own behavior and become aware of what they are modeling in the group.

    d.   Follow-up procedures might take the form of personal contact, telephone contact, or written contact.

    e.   Follow-up meetings might be with individuals, or groups, or both to determine the degree to which: (i) members have reached their goals, (ii) the group had a positive or negative effect on the participants, (iii) members could profit from some type of referral, and (iv) as information for possible modification of future groups. If there is no follow-up meeting, provisions are made available for individual follow-up meetings to any member who needs or requests such a contact.

15. *Referrals:* If the needs of a particular member cannot be met within the type of group being offered, the group counselor suggests other appropriate professional referrals.

 a. Group counselors are knowledgeable of local community resources for assisting group members regarding professional referrals.

 b. Group counselors help members seek further professional assistance, if needed.

16. *Professional Development:* Group counselors recognize that professional growth is a continuous, ongoing, developmental process throughout their career.

 a. Group counselors maintain and upgrade their knowledge and skill competencies through educational activities, clinical experiences, and participation in professional development activities.

 b. Group counselors keep abreast of research findings and new developments as applied to groups.

Source: Association for Specialists in Group Work. (1989). *Ethical Guidelines for Group Leaders*. Alexandria, VA: Author. Reprinted with permission.

SUMMARY

Group leaders may employ many theoretical orientations when they conduct group sessions. However, all group leaders are ethically and legally bound to make sure their behavior in groups is competent, and it is important that leaders do not practice beyond their expertise. Group leaders must make sure that group members are aware that their communications in the group cannot be guaranteed as confidential. Group leaders should be familiar with the ethical guidelines for group counselors before they begin conducting group sessions.

LEARNING FACILITATION AND FOCUS

Exercise 10.1

In individual counseling, the therapist may use some psychological theory and principle to determine his or her response to the client. For example, a Rogerian therapist may choose empathetic responses, while an existential therapist may choose more confronting responses. All are responding within a context of some psychological framework to determine their responses. Naturally, they choose responses they feel will best benefit the client, and the responses are systematic. One may say the mental health professional is implementing an art (his or her response) based on some scientific psychological principle.

In group counseling the members often respond to one another based on how they feel. In short, their responses are based on their feelings as opposed to any scientific principles. These responses may not be in the best interests of other clients. For example, a woman who was abused as a child by her father may be traumatized when confronted by a vociferous and angry man. Conversely, a strong-willed group member who is manipulative may receive empathetic as opposed to confrontive responses.

Thus, responses to clients from mental health professionals are calculated using some theoretical base. The theoretical or scientific base informs the counselor on how to respond to best enhance the well-being of the client. On the other hand, group members may respond to other members (clients) based on their feelings about them. These responses may be destructive to the well-being of other group members.

1. Please explicate your answer to this seemingly ethical and legal dilemma. _____

_____

_____

_____

_____

_____

_____

_____

_____

Chapter 11

IN A MARRIAGE AND FAMILY CONTEXT

MARRIAGE AND FAMILY THERAPY

Although marriage and family therapists do not subscribe to any one theory, their techniques typically are grounded in systems theory. *Systems theory* is a therapeutic approach that focuses on the individuals and the marriage, family, or community of which they are a part. For instance, the family may involve the couple and other important family members (Huber & Baruth, 1987). As Shields, Wynne, McDaniel, and Gawinski (1994) noted,

> It is not systems theory that makes family therapy a distinctive mental health discipline; more crucially, the difference is that family therapy examines interpersonal relationships first—rather than biological, intrapsychic, or societal processes—when attempting to understand human distress. (p. 118)

Generally, the initial work for a family therapist involves having family members express themselves to one another. The therapist facilitates this process. This facilitation may include the therapeutic techniques of empathy, interpretation, advanced accurate empathy, clarification, and summarization. The therapist ensures that each family member gets a chance to speak and points out who speaks for another and who does not speak for him- or herself. Most importantly, the family therapist demonstrates and educates family members about how they can more effectively talk about difficult family issues.

Family therapy is different from individual therapy, in that the individual therapist deals primarily with *intrapsychic conflict*, whereas the family therapist deals with *interpsychic issues*. The general goal of the family therapist is to help the family move toward a more effective form of accommodation or to become more collaborative (Jacobson & Margolin, 1979) or rejunctive (Boszormenyi-Nagy & Ulrich, 1981).

Obviously by increasing the collaborative aspects of family interaction, a number of ethical issues are raised. What if one family member is mentally healthy but the system is pathological? The only path available to a healthy individual to maintain his or her sanity may be to separate from the system. Can the same therapy techniques be used with mildly dysfunctional systems and pathological system? What if the therapist believes that the only way for one member to become mentally healthy is to separate and differentiate from the system, but the family's orientation is more communal? Frome (1996) spoke to the obligation of therapists to create an ethical position in family therapy, and Olson and Doherty (1996) asserted that psychotherapy must promote moral responsibility regarding difficult issues in therapy.

DETERMINING WHO THE CLIENT IS

"Because the phenomena of concern in family therapy are the interactions among family members, family therapists—much more than individual therapists—found a greater need for recording the rapid, complex flow of the therapeutic process" (Shields et al., 1994, p. 121). As a result of this systematic approach, authors have raised ethical concerns over who the client is in family therapy (Whitaker & Miller, 1969).

One question often posed is this: "Is the family or is the individual in the family the primary concern of the therapist?" Margolin (cited in Swenson, 1997) related that counterproductivity for family integration may result when an intervention serves only one member. According to Margolin, counselors must ensure that interventions that improve the status of one family member do not occur at the expense of another. In other words, counselors must balance concern for the family with concerns for individuals in the family. Counselors also must be aware of their own ethical positions on the systems effects of the interventions they make. In summary, Margolin (1982) noted:

Attempting to balance one's therapeutic responsibilities toward individual family members and toward the family as a whole involves intricate judgments. Since neither of these responsibilities cancels out the importance of the other, the family therapist cannot afford blind pursuit of either extreme, that is, always doing what is in each individual's best interest or always maintaining the stance as family advocate. (p. 790)

BIASES

Goldberg and Goldberg (1985) contended that middle-class values and morals predominate the inclinations of marriage and family therapists. These inclinations include:

- respect for the institutional value of marriage,

- the use of child-rearing modalities that fit the needs of each child,

- a desire to pass on the cultural values of the family to the next generation, and

- a belief that maintaining a family is a prerequisite of mental health.

As the authors noted, "Most family therapists—deliberately or unwillingly, consciously or unconsciously—proselytize for maintaining a family way of life" (Goldberg & Goldberg, 1985, p. 249).

Mental health professionals who have been trained in structural intervention (Fieldsteel, 1982) also may assume too much responsibility for change in family systems. One result of this phenomenon is that family clients may not use their own powers of perception and analysis, instead deferring to the therapist and putting more trust in him or her than in themselves. If this happens, clients' concerns may be directed more to the therapist's response than to effecting change in their situation.

The APA Task Force on Sex Bias and Sex-Role Stereotyping (cited in Margolin, 1982) reported that family therapists are particularly vulnerable to:

1. assuming that remaining in a marriage would result in better adjustment for a woman,

2. demonstrating less interest in or sensitivity to a woman's career than to a man's career,

3.   perpetuating the belief that child rearing and thus the child's problems are solely the responsibility of the mother,

4.   exhibiting a double standard for a wife's versus a husband's affair, and

5.   deferring to the husband's needs over those of the wife.

Hare-Mustin (1980) reported that mental health professionals routinely involve family members in therapy even when they have successfully differentiated from an enmeshed family. They also noted that family therapists are consistently drawn to entertaining attitudes about the "ideal family." According to Hare-Mustin (1980), maintaining a family may be the ultimate value of family therapists, regardless of the cost to individuals.

Leigh, Loewen, and Lester (1986) agreed, reporting that the therapist's personal values often find expression in the style and methodology of intervention. The therapist's approach to individual or family therapy, confidentiality, and termination often is colored by certain biases such as preserving marriages and supporting traditional family roles.

CONFIDENTIALITY

In chapter 4 we discussed the limits of confidentiality. In general, these limits apply to both family and marital counselors. The informed consent procedures for confidentiality used in individual therapy also are applicable in family and marital therapy. There is, however, one important difference: Because family and marital therapy involves more than one person in the same session at the same time, confidentiality becomes much more complicated. A single family member may entrust information to the therapist during an individual session, in a telephone call, or through the mail. Because the therapist has access to information considered private or delicate, complicated questions of confidentiality can arise.

Revealing or not revealing confidential information to other members of the family is a strategic decision. Some therapists would keep the information confidential, asserting that the secret(s) might help them better understand the family system, or that they can help the client reveal the secret to the family at an appropriate time. Other therapists maintain that secrets should not be kept, because the possession of privileged information could give the appearance of a special alliance with an individual and thus be counterproductive to the therapeutic process for the group.

Of course, there are gradations between no disclosure and full disclosure of confidential information. The therapist may tell clients that he or she will not keep secrets unless the client specifically requests that private information be kept confidential. Or the therapist may inform the family that individual confidences will be revealed if the therapist decides that the disclosure will benefit the family system. Individual family members must then determine what secrets they will reveal ànd which, if any, they will not. Whatever policy the therapist chooses, Hare-Mustin (1980) noted, he or she must make it explicit at the beginning of family sessions.

Baruth and Huber (1984) agreed, noting:

> [T]he bottom line in how the issue of confidentiality should be handled is that a therapist must determine a policy that is compatible with his or her approach to conducting therapy, and this policy must be explained to the couple. (p. 284)

Finally, the therapist must not reveal communications made in individual sessions to others in group sessions without permission. He or she must make agreements pertinent to such disclosure with each client before therapy begins (Huber & Baruth, 1987).

PRIVILEGED COMMUNICATION AND INFORMED CONSENT

Sugarman (cited in Margolin, 1982) reported that a wife's or husband's confidentiality is not always protected in regard to information revealed in joint marital sessions. However, therapists should find out if a marital communication privilege applies in the state where they practice (Freed & Walker, 1988). Family therapists should take care to implement informed consent procedures.

THERAPISTS AND THE LAW

Family counselors and therapists must have some knowledge of the law *before* they consult with lawyers about issues and family affairs (Brown & Christensen, 1986). Therapists should be able, on an informed basis, to consult with and refer to lawyers as needed (Huber & Baruth, 1987). The AAMFT (1991) advised mental health professionals to understand particularly the anticipated emotional and legal implications of divorce. According to Swenson (1997), "The family therapist with some knowledge of divorce procedures and family law will provide more realistic and more helpful counseling services for divorcing clients" (p. 265). Diamond and Simbovg (1985) noted that most family therapists do not have adequate knowledge of the legal system, and so should seek competent legal advice.

Family and marital therapists may function as mediators or evaluators in disputes between parents. Mediation focuses on cooperation rather than adversarial competition. A primary goal of mediation is to arrive at a fair agreement between parties (Emery & Wyer, 1987). The typical mediation team is composed of a lawyer and a mental health professional. The process may be jointly shared, or there may be sequential sessions, with the therapist handling parenting problems and the lawyer dealing with financial matters (Kelly, 1992).

In a family dispute, either party may use an evaluator to support his or her claims for custody. In any custody battle, the same question arises: Should the child be evaluated as separate from or as part of a family system? Brown and Christensen (1986) asserted that an evaluation conducted independently of the family system can be misleading because it does not take into account power struggles, triangles, and coalitions within the family. Levy (1987) reported that most judges believe evaluation reports are the best guides to determining what is best for children.

TRAINING ISSUES

Most therapists believe that life experience—that is, experiencing a variety of life events—enhances self-understanding and is a necessary ingredient in competent and effective family therapy. In their review of the literature, Lyman, Storm, and York (1995) found the following assumptions regarding the effectiveness of family therapy and its correlation with life experiences:

1. Many young therapists lack the life experiences they need to understand the problems their clients face. Ideally, their caseloads should include only those clients in development stages they have experienced themselves.

2. It is important for trainees to have integrated their own identity.

3. Therapists should learn about children by having their own.

4. Trainees should have previous employment experience.

5. The aging and maturing process contributes to therapeutic effectiveness. With age, people learn behaviors that allow them to use more varied therapeutic approaches (Stanton, 1991).

6. Families should have the option of disqualifying any therapist who has not experienced their present state of life.

7. Personal maturity is a critical requirement for admission to training as a family and marital therapist.

8. AAMFT programs should require previous professional employment as an admission requirement.

Lyman, Storm, and York (1995) also conducted a study to determine if these assumptions were related to trainee effectiveness. They concluded, "Overall, there was a significant relationship between life experience and clients' ratings of effectiveness. *Trainees with less life experience were rated as more effective by their clients* [emphasis ours]" (p. 200). The authors concluded that the results of their study were antithetical to a belief that permeates the field, and that more research is needed regarding life experience as it relates to effective therapy. However, they added, "We should be careful not to assume that more is better in trainees" (p. 201).

Shields et al. (1994) noted some primary concerns about AAMFT training. Specifically, they noted that family therapy is "marginalized" relative to the broader fields of mental and physical health care, and that family therapy needs to develop new models of interchange and selective integration with other healthcare professions.

For example, Shields et al. (1994) reported that the quality of outcome for family therapy is clearly superior than that for treatment using medication or individual therapy alone. But no studies have convincingly documented that family therapy alone is effective in the treatment of major psychopathology. Therefore, the authors contended, trainees must understand that family therapy can be effective if "integrated into broader treatment programs for major mental illness" (p. 132).

Shields et al. (1994) also drew an analogy between family therapy and medical treatment, arguing that marital discord and divorce pose health risks as real as those posed by hypertension, for example. The problem is that not enough time has been spent documenting therapy's efficacy at reducing these risks. If research conclusively demonstrated that the relief of family discord prevents subsequent problems, more health-care plans would make such treatment reimbursable. As Shields et al. (1994) noted, "During the last 20 to 25 years, the lack of research data on the efficacy of psychoanalytic treatment, in contrast to research on pharmacotherapy and brief psychotherapy, has contributed to the near demise of psychoanalysis" (p. 121).

Supervision

When White and Russell (1995) reviewed the literature on supervision of family therapists, they found two interesting facts:

- First, while there has been an increase in the number of journal articles and annual conventions devoted to the topic, little consensus or empirical data exist to support the myriad models of supervision.

- Second, since a comprehensive model of supervision does not exist, most supervisors employ their own unique models.

Using a modified Delphi study, White and Russell (1995) collected data on 800 unique essential elements participants identified as influencing the outcomes of supervision. The researchers asserted that the large number of elements identified attests to the complexity of the supervisory process for marriage and family therapists.

Aris and Sparenkle (cited in White & Russell, 1995) voiced concern that this complexity has vitiated the progress of research on family therapy outcomes. White and Russell (1995) concluded that the relationship between supervisor and supervisee and the sheer number of activities and interactions in supervision contribute to differences in conceptualization and actual behavior.

Genograms

Students of family and marital therapy often are asked to construct genograms. *Genograms* are systematic diagrams that reflect facts and figures about which conclusions can be drawn regarding relationship patterns over several generations (Bradley & Mims, 1992). The construction of a genogram allows the student to think about themselves and other members of their generational heritage. Graphic presentations permit the presence of the now and the beyond in both spatial and temporal dimensions. Students can see form for exposition or classification of the various parts of their journey through life.

Many instructors believe genograms offer students an opportunity to investigate their families of origin and to determine the nature and relations of their constituents through such commonly taught variables as triangles, roles, myths, and rituals. The assumption is that the process will embellish the students' therapeutic skills (Kramer, 1985), help them learn family systems concepts (Green & Saegar, 1982), and enhance the process of supervision (Getz & Protinsky, 1994).

The objective of the genogram is to illustrate and clarify family system concepts and to allow trainees to focus, attend to, and explore their own emotional issues with their families of origin. A genogram's use as a training tool differs from its use as a clinical tool. "The personal component of the therapy relationship viscerally relates the therapist to the client's life" (Aponte, 1994).

Genograms can emphasize and focus a cultural awareness of one's background. Current efforts by educators have focused on creating a cultural awareness in trainees. Cultural awareness is achieved through the inculcation of content about various cultures. Unfortunately, this didactic process does not always promote cultural sensitivity. For the most part, awareness is a cognitive function, while sensitivity is an affective function (Hardy & Laszloffy, 1995).

Regarding multicultural training, Hardy and Laszloffy (1995, p. 227) noted that focusing on content allows trainers to avoid being affectively challenged about their own cultural backgrounds. As a result, students are not taught how their cultural identities influence their acceptance and understanding of both different and similar cultures.

Hardy and Laszloffy believed cultural genograms could help develop this sensitivity by doing several things:

- Illustrating and clarifying the influence culture has on the family system

- Helping trainees identify the groups that contributed to their own cultural identity

- Encouraging candid discussions that reveal and challenge culturally based assumptions and stereotypes

- Helping trainees discover their culturally based emotional triggers

- Helping them explore how their unique cultural identities affect their therapeutic style and effectiveness

Ethical Considerations and Genograms.   "By its very nature, the process of counselor education invites discussion of dual relationships" (Goodman & Carpenter-White, 1996, p. 232). Dual relationships and their problematic aspects have been discussed in more than one counselor-training context. Training groups (Forester-Miller & Duncan, 1990), supervision (Tarvydas, 1995), and students being used as laboratory clients (Patrick, 1989) are some examples of training activities that invite potential dual-relationship problems. The code of ethics of the AAMFT provides guidance for educators and therapist trainers regarding dual relationships:

> Marriage and family therapists should be aware of their position with respect to students, employees, and supervisees, and should avoid exploiting the trust and dependency of such persons. Therapists, therefore, should make every effort to avoid dual relationships that could impair professional judgment or increase the risk of exploitation. When a dual relationship cannot be avoided, therapists should take appropriate professional precautions to ensure judgment is not impaired and no exploitation occurs. Examples of such dual relationships include, but are not limited to, business or close personal relationships with students, employees, or supervisees. Providing therapy to students, employees, or supervisees is prohibited. Sexual intimacy with students or supervisees is also prohibited. (AAMFT, 1991, 4.1)

Goodman and Carpenter-White (1996) listed two of the potential ethical problems inherent in using genograms in training:

1. *Students may disclose material about family members.* Through this process, family members become participants without ever being informed or consenting to such. These family members may be exposed to public disclosure of their homosexuality, sexual violence, alcoholism, or other sensitive issues.

2. *Students may choose to protect their roles and feelings about their family membership.* The feelings they have could motivate them to talk to family members and thereby confront highly charged issues that were never resolved. If these issues are brought out in class, the student may experience confusion about the role the instructor is playing or should be playing.

Based on their review of the literature, Goodman and Carpenter-White (1996) concluded that when unresolved issues surface in class, the trainer should not attempt to resolve them for students.

If students or supervisees request counseling, supervisors or counselor educators should provide them with acceptable referrals. Supervisors or counselor educators do not serve as counselors to students or supervisees over whom they have administrative, teaching,
or evaluative roles unless this is a brief role associated with a training experience. (American Counseling Association, 1995, F.3.c)

SUMMARY

Many family therapists use systems theory, a technique that focuses on
interpersonal relationships, in order to understand the pain and suffering of
individuals in the family system. As a result, a potential ethical conflict exists
as the therapist attempts to balance his or her responsibilities toward individual
family members and the family as a whole. Therapeutic interventions directed
toward an individual may be at the expense of another member of the family.
Consequently, family therapists must be aware of their own ethical positions
before they begin intervention strategies in family therapy.

The literature reveals that middle-class values and morals color the ethical
inclinations of family therapists.

The therapist's attitude and values about confidentiality are especially important in family therapy. The literature reveals that individual family members or spouses invariably find a way to communicate private thoughts to the
therapist. It is imperative that the therapist's policy on confidentiality be revealed prior to therapy.

Since so many training programs use the genogram, duel relationships became a particular problem in the training of family therapists. The genogram,
by its very nature, forces students to evaluate family relationships and highly
charged family issues. The student may experience confusion about what role
the teacher or trainer is playing.

LEARNING FACILITATION AND FOCUS

Exercise 11.1

You have been working with the Gist family for a month. The problem presented is 14-year-old Rebecca's anger, which is manifested in school and at home by defiant gestures and language. Rebecca has begun to lose weight, as well, and her parents believe she is purging. Rebecca is the third and youngest child in the family.

After examining the family system, your analysis is that the father is an overbearing dictator and his wife, who was once passive and complementary to his dominant personality, is beginning to assert herself. This process has short-circuited a family system held in homeostases by dominant and passive personalities. As a result, the arguments between husband and wife have intensified greatly. Your clinical judgment is that Rebecca's behavior is an attempt to hold the system together so that her mother and father will not separate.

1.   What intervention strategy should you employ?_____

_____

_____

_____

2.   What ethical considerations are germane to this problem?_____

_____

_____

_____

3.   Should Rebecca's interests be held above those of the family?_____

_____

_____

_____

Exercise 11.2

You are an instructor in a marriage and family training class that employs genograms as a training method. You have instructed your students to complete an assignment with the following directions: *Using crayons, draw a portrait of your family. You may use stick figures or any other symbolic representation for your portrait. Be prepared to show your drawing in class and to talk about various family members and your feelings about them.* One of the class members, upon presentation, begins to sob uncontrollably.

1. Is it ethical for you to request that this information be publicly revealed?_____

   _____

   _____

2. Should genograms be used?_____

   _____

   _____

3. Should cultural issues revealed by the genogram be discussed in the classroom?_____

   _____

   _____

Part F

CONSIDERATIONS
IN TRAINING

Chapter 12

IN A TRAINING CONTEXT

TRAINING AND ETHICS

Bernard and Carmen (1986) conducted a study with 170 graduate students in 25 APA-approved clinical training programs. They asked the students what they *should* do in a hypothetical situation in which a friend violated an ethical principle. When the same students were asked what they *would* do, approximately half said they would do less than they knew they should. Bernard and Carmen concluded that the participants understood the behavior was in ethical violation, but they chose not to behave in an ethical manner. The problem was not one of misunderstanding (ignorance of the ethical mandate), but of motivation. The authors concluded, "Psychologists need to carefully examine this question and to arrive at ways to reorder priorities so that their responsibility to monitor their own practice is taken more seriously" (p. 315).

Harris (1995) analyzed syllabi from ethics courses of accredited marriage and family training programs and concluded that students are taught the basics of ethics and professional issues, but that only a few programs put much emphasis "on diversity of course activities and projects to help stimulate critical thinking about ethical and professional issues ... what students get is the clinical and academic self of the professor" (pp. 45–46).

More training in ethics is greatly needed in professional education and practice (Welfel, 1992). Lindsay (1985) demonstrated this when he prompted graduate students to listen to taped scripts involving ethical dilemmas in client-therapist interactions. Nearly 50% of the students failed to recognize the ethical issues. Training to develop appropriate boundaries when professional relationships are established is especially crucial (O'Connor-Slimp & Burian, 1994).

SUPERVISION

"Individual psychotherapy supervision is the principle vehicle for preparing mental health specialists for the practice of psychotherapy" (Guest & Beutler, 1988, p. 653). It is possible, however, that supervisors are working beyond their areas of competence (Harrar, VandeCreek, & Knapp, 1990) and that most supervisors do not meet specified criteria to perform competently (Borders & Leddick, 1988).

APA guidelines specifically warned against such practice: "Psychologists recognize the boundaries of their particular competencies and the limitations of their expertise. They provide only those services and only use the techniques for which they are qualified by education training and experience" (APA, 1995, 1.04,a).

Harrar et al. (1990) agreed, noting, "This principle suggests that psychologists must have received training in how to supervise or must in some ways demonstrate competence as supervisors before they can supervise others" (p. 37).

Minimal standards for supervisory practice have been proposed by the Association for Counselor Education and Supervision (1993); however, the literature suggests that many mental health professionals are conducting supervision with little knowledge of the legal and ethical implications.

McCarthy, Julakowski, and Kenfield (1994) reported that 72% of the experienced licensed psychologists they surveyed were not sure whether their supervisors had been trained to supervise them. The authors recommended that a written supervision contract be part of clinical supervision. The supervisor should be aware that he or she operates under the doctrine of *respondiat superior* (let the master respond). This doctrine says that supervisors may be held responsible and accountable for the actions of their supervisees.

According to Borders and Leddick (1988), supervision contracts should include (a) what supervisory method the supervisor will employ, (b) what the supervisor requires, (c) supervisor-supervisee responsibilities, and (d) any due process procedures. The supervisor's qualifications and limits to confidentiality also should be articulated (Bernard & Goodyear, 1992).

A written supervision contract can provide security for both supervisor and supervisee (Bernard & Goodyear, 1992). McCarthy, Sugden, Koker, Lamendola, Maurer, and Renninger (1995) grouped the information that should be included in a written contract into seven categories.

1. *Purpose:* The contract should inform the supervisee of the structure of the supervisory experience.

2. *Professional disclosure statement:* The contract should inform the supervisee of the supervisor's credentials, qualifications, and theoretical orientation to supervision.

3. *Practical issues:* The contract should inform the supervisee of the pragmatic aspects of supervision. For example, it should say whether the supervision is to be individual or group and how to contact the supervisor in an emergency situation.

4. *Supervision process:* The contract should inform the supervisee of the methods to be used during supervision.

5. *Evaluation and due process:* The contract should inform the supervisee of the frequency of formal and informal evaluations and of due process procedures.

6. *Ethical and legal issues:* The contract should inform the supervisee of the ethical and legal parameters of the supervisory relationship, including the limits of confidentiality and issues pertaining to dual relationships.

7. *Statement of agreement:* This statement, at the end of the contract, should be signed by supervisor and supervisee. It assures that both parties understand, agree, and will adhere to the information in the informed consent document.

Harrar et al. (1990) reported that the ethical and clinical aspects of supervision should prompt one to consider several things:

1. The duties and responsibilities of the supervisor must be clear. These responsibilities include not supervising more trainees than one can responsibly manage.

2. Supervisors must have sufficient knowledge of each client, develop policies for feedback, and document their supervisory work.

3. Supervisors must be aware of the problems of dual relationships.

4. Issues of direct liability—for example, assigning a task beyond the competence of a trainee—must be considered.

5. The program must include a standard of care for supervisors.

6. Supervisors must think about the limits of confidentiality.

Quality of supervision can be measured by the supervisee's disposition to disclose information about the client, the therapeutic interaction, the supervisory interaction, and self-disclosure. Ladnay, Hill, Corbett, and Nutt (1996) surveyed the nature and importance of what trainees *do not* disclose to their supervisors. Their results suggested that most trainees withhold information from their supervisors. This is a disturbing finding because, "Individual psychotherapy supervision is the principle vehicle for preparing mental health specialists for the practice of psychotherapy" (Guest & Beutler, 1988, p. 653).

To be open (Fitzgerald & O'Leary, 1990), cooperative (Orlinsky & Howard, 1986), able to accept personal responsibility (Corey, 1986), and able to express feelings effectively (Ridgeway & Sharpley, 1990) are the hallmarks of competent counselors (cited in Wiggins-Frame & Stevens-Smith, 1995). According to Ladnay et al. (1996), the most frequently cited reason for nondisclosure was a negative reaction to the supervisor. They also found that the nature of the nondisclosed material was mostly passive, and that the issues that were not disclosed were usually talked about with someone else.

Guest and Beutler (1988) found that therapeutic skills are developed in different ways, depending on the trainee's experience. In the early stage of training, supervisees benefit most from supportive techniques. In the latter stages, they seek more technical guidance. Early training also may have a long-lasting influence on the supervisee's theoretical orientation.

In a survey conducted by Hamilton-Usher and Borders (1993), the authors found that a sample of National Certified Counselors (NCCs) preferred collegial and relationship-oriented supervisors rather than ones who were task-oriented. The respondents also preferred supervisors who emphasized process skills rather than professional behaviors. Worthington (1984) reported that supervisee satisfaction was related to the supervisor's acceptance and support rather than his or her instruction in technical skills. And Cherniss and Egnatios (1977) reported that *laissez faire* supervision was negatively related to trainee satisfaction, while authoritarian supervision was negatively related to the supervisee's developing confidence.

We have already discussed dual relationships and their potential effects on the counseling relationship (see chapter 7). Dual relationships with students are also a problem for the mental health profession. It sometimes is impossible to avoid dual relationships with interns (Bernard & Goodyear, 1992). All of these relationships can be problematic, but some are more benign than others.

Unfortunately, it appears that the most pervasive dual relationship is of a sexual nature. Glaser and Thorpe (1986) found that 17% of female psychologists reported sexual contact with faculty members or supervisors while they were in training, and 31% said they had received sexual advances from faculty. The respondents also thought these interactions were damaging to their professional lives. Some of the respondents reported threats and harassment from spurned faculty admirers, withdrawal from the program, and feelings of isolation and embarrassment.

Pope and Bouhoutsos (1986) suggested that, just as the psychiatrist in *Zipkin v. Freeman* (1968) was found liable for mishandling transference with a client, a supervisor could be found liable for mishandling the transference phenomenon in supervision.

DISMISSAL PROCESSES IN TRAINING

When a student in training is found to be impaired, three major concerns arise (Wiggins-Frame & Stevens-Smith, 1995).

1. The first concern is for the student's well-being. Faculty involved in a student impairment issue must be careful to safeguard the student's confidentiality and also to protect the student's due process rights (Knoff & Prout, cited in Wiggins-Frame & Stevens-Smith, 1995).

2. The second concern arises when there is a hesitancy on the part of the faculty to make a judgment about the student, because of a discrepancy between clinical skills and high scores on written examinations. Some faculty feel that written exams are more objective than clinical observations (Scoll & Hank, cited in Wiggins-Frame & Stevens-Smith, 1995).

3. The third area of concern is ethical and potential legal responsibility to the student counselor's clients (Custer, cited in Wiggins-Frame & Stevens-Smith, 1995).

Wiggins-Frame and Stevens-Smith (1995) concluded that the first priority of counselor educators and supervisors is to ensure that clients are protected from incompetent counselors. When a student counselor is considered for dismissal, it is imperative to use explicitly and clearly defined monitoring and dismissal procedures that include due process.

CREDENTIALS OF THE MENTAL HEALTH PROFESSIONAL

All states require mental health professionals to obtain credentials in order to preserve public safety (Bednar et al., 1991). There are several different levels of certification:

*   Registration requires the professional to complete minimum educational requirements and allows him or her to perform limited clinical functions, usually under supervision.

*   In some states, certification requires the professional to meet minimum educational requirements and have a stipulated number of supervised hours.

*   Professional certification requires the mental health professional to meet or exceed the requirements for state certification and to take a written test.

*   Mental health professionals who obtain a license must have specific educational experiences, verify requisite supervised hours, and pass a written test. By restricting entry into the profession, licensing maximizes prestige and reduces competition (Schwitzgebel & Schwitzgebel, 1980).

State governments grant broad powers to licensing boards, allowing them to issue credentials and to regulate professional practice. For the most part, two types of licensing laws exist. *Title protection laws* determine which professionals can use a particular occupational title, such as *psychologist* or *counselor*. *Practice acts laws* define what services a professional may deliver to the general public.

All 50 states have licensure laws pertinent to the practice of psychology and regulations as to who can call themselves a psychologist. Forty-one states have licensing laws for counselors with statutory power to confer credentials, determine the definition of ethical practice, and impose sanctions. Licensure may be defined as "The salutary process by which an agency of government, usually a state, grants permission to a person meeting predetermined qualifications to engage in a given occupation and/or use a particular title, and to perform specified functions" (Fritz & Mills, 1980, p. 7).

One rationale for licensing mental health professionals is that licensed professionals tend to be more competent those not licensed. However, there is no research evidence that licensure directly affects the competence of mental health professionals (Cottingham, 1980). In fact, most studies have found no relationship between academic knowledge and competence in therapy (Bednar et al., 1991).

When a group becomes licensed, the group's status, privilege, and income tend to increase. The group's services generally become more expensive, thus affording less attention and service to the poor and to minority groups (Hogan, 1979). And Rogers (1980) contended that there are as many certified charlatans as there are uncertified practitioners.

Davis and Yzak (1996) asked 124 licensing board members to rate the actual and ideal goals and tasks of counseling licensing boards. The ideal goals were (a) to protect the public from unprofessional practice, (b) to improve counseling in the state, and (c) to improve the human condition. However, when asked which tasks received the most time and attention, they rated them this way:

1. Determining appropriate disciplinary actions

2. Investigating ethics complaints

3. Reviewing applications for licensure

RESEARCH WITH HUMAN SUBJECTS

The science of psychology is dedicated to advancing knowledge and to providing techniques to ensure the well-being and survival of society's members. Often the research conducted by mental health professionals to advance the science of psychology is done with human subjects. Participants in research projects have the same rights as participants in therapy, and they must be informed of any implications the research may have for them.

Using language that is reasonably understandable to participants, psychologists inform participants of the nature of the research; they inform participants that they are free to participate or to decline to participate or to withdraw from the research; they explain the foreseeable consequences of declining or withdrawing; they inform participants of significant factors that may be expected to influence their willingness to participate (such as risks, discomfort, adverse effects, or limitations on confidentiality, except as provided in Standard 6.15, Deception in Research); and they explain other aspects about which the prospective participants inquire. (APA, 1995, G.11,b)

* * * *

In obtaining informed consent for research, counselors use language that is understandable to research participants and that (1) accurately explains the purpose and procedures to be followed; (2) identifies any procedures that are experimental or relatively untried; (3) describes the attendant discomforts and risks; (4) describes the benefits or changes in individuals or organizations that might be reasonably expected; (5) discloses appropriate alternative procedures that would be advantageous for subjects; (6) offers to answer any inquiries concerning the procedures; (7) describes any limitations on confidentiality; and (8) instructs that subjects are free to withdraw their consent and to discontinue participation in the project at any time. (ACA, 1995)

Deceiving research participants is acceptable only when three criteria are met:

1. When the advancement of knowledge or scientific value from the study would be significant and no other acceptable alternative is available

2. When there are no physical risks, discomforts, or unpleasant emotional experiences

3. When the investigator explains to the participants, as soon as possible, the reasons for the deception

Research projects should be planned carefully. Any ambiguity that may compromise ethical guidelines must be dealt with in a stringent fashion. Most states and the federal government have rules concerning human participants in research. Failure to follow ethical guidelines, state or federal rules, and moral principles could result in sanctions or lawsuits. Consequently, researchers should always consult with their institution's Human Subjects' Committee (usually organized at the department or school level) or the Institutional Review Board (committees that serve entire institutions).

Reporting of research results also should follow exacting criteria:

- Reports should never include fabrication.

- Reports should include an explanation of all the variables and conditions that may have influenced the outcomes or interpretations of a study.

- Researchers should never withhold results that reflect unfavorably on institutions, programs, or other vested interests.

- Researchers must acknowledge the contributions others have made in the research.

- Researchers must disguise the identity of participants.

- Researchers must allow the research data to be used for replication.

- Researchers should correct any errors they find in their data.

SUMMARY

Scholars investigating the internalization of strict ethical behavior by students in mental health profession training programs generally have not been satisfied with their findings. Several areas of mental health training need some improvement, including these:

- More training in ethics is greatly needed.

- Written informed consent forms should be used in supervisory practices.

- Sexual relationships between supervisors and trainees are embarrassingly widespread and must be eliminated.

- Finally, dismissal processes for impaired students in training should include due process procedures.

LEARNING FACILITATION AND FOCUS

Exercise 12.1

You have earned 60 credits in counseling and a college has hired you to coordinate and administer its internships. One of your students—Ms. Harris—consistently receives excellent written reports from the field from her supervisor—Dr. Kelsey. After six months, Dr. Kelsey retires and Ms. Harris is assigned a new supervisor—Dr. Woods. Dr. Woods does not give you an evaluation of Ms. Harris for two months.

Eight days before Ms. Harris is to receive her master's degree, Dr. Woods calls you and says Ms. Harris should not be graduated. Dr. Woods says she believes Ms. Harris would be harmful to her clients, and she tells you about some strange behavior on the part of Ms. Harris. You have not yet filled out Ms. Harris's grade, but she has a 3.8 average in her other courses.

For this reason, Dr. Woods says she has no alternative but to give Ms. Harris a failing grade. Grades are assigned based on the field supervisor's report and the campus supervisor's recommendation. Upon questioning, Ms. Harris's campus supervisor reports that he also thought Ms. Harris to be a questionable candidate, but he did not have any hard data to support his opinion. He feels he must give her a satisfactory performance rating.

1. What is the most ethical thing to do in this situation?_____

   _____

   _____

   _____

2. What procedures should be implemented to arbitrate this type of situation in the future?_____

   _____

   _____

   _____

   _____

Exercise 12.2

Professor Harmen has just been hired to direct a training program for mental health professionals. After years of training counseling professionals, Professor Harmen has made some observations about the training process. He has noted that some students can create an instant rapport with clients. Their clients feel they are genuine and trustworthy. Yet, some of these same students find it difficult to label, conceptualize, and articulate the *what* and *why* of their behavior.

Dr. Harmen also has observed that some students are very articulate, well-read, and readily able to rationalize many counseling theories. However, some of them are not very good in their interactions with other people. Professor Harmen characterizes these two groups of students as those who can move well with the music but don't know the words and those who know the words but don't dance very well.

Professor Harmen has proposed that the two groups of students receive different experiences in a counseling theory course. In course A, students would be required to interact with one another using accepted theoretical frameworks. For example, they would review a case study and analyze how Carl Rogers or Alfred Adler would view the client dynamics. In class B, students would be required to interact with one another without using any theoretical context. For example, they would review the same case study and analyze how they themselves would view the client dynamics.

1.   Comment on the merits of Professor Harmen's proposal._____

   _____

   _____

   _____

2.   Comment on the ethical implications of Professor Harmen's proposal.

   _____

   _____

   _____

Exercise 12.3

Harris (1995) asserted that diversity and stimulation of critical thinking about the teaching of ethical and professional issues could be vastly improved.

1. How do you think the teaching of ethics and professional issues should be accomplished? Should ethical issues be considered in every course, should they be taught in one course, or should there be some combination? Also, to what extent should the teaching be experiential or didactic?_____

_____

_____

_____

_____

_____

Exercise 12.4

Professor Voorhees and Professor Jonkton disagree on the content and structure of a course in ethical and professional issues. Professor Voorhees believes that the course should include legal problems. Professor Jonkton disagrees, asserting that the introduction of legal issues would cause students to focus on their own survival rather than on the more heuristic process of learning how to think in a critical moral manner.

1. Comment on the merits of Professor Voorhees's and Professor Jonkton's positions. _____

_____

_____

_____

_____

_____

REFERENCES

Alcalay, R., Sniderman, P. M., Mitchell, J., & Griffin, R. (1990). Ethnic differences in knowledge of AIDS transmission and attitudes toward gays and people with AIDS. *International Quarterly of Community Health Education, 10,* 213–222.

Alexander, P. C., & Lupfer, S. L. (1987). Family characteristics and long-term consequences associated with sexual abuse. *Archives of Sexual Behavior, 16,* 235–245.

Allsopp, A., & Prosen, S. (1988). Teacher reactions to a child sexual abuse training program. *Elementary School Guidance Counseling, 22,* 299–305.

Alpert, J. L., & Meyers, J. (1983). *Training in consultation.* Springfield, IL: Charles C. Thomas.

American Association for Marriage and Family Therapy. (1991). *Code of ethical principles for marriage and family therapists.* Washington DC: Author.

American Civil Liberties Union. (1996). *American Civil Liberties Union briefing paper number 7.* New York: Author.

American Counseling Association. (1988). *Ethical standards.* Alexandria, VA: Author.

American Counseling Association. (1995). *Code of ethics and standards of practice*. Alexandria, VA: Author.

American Medical Association. (1988). *LLL progress on the prevention and control of AIDS* (Reference Committee E, pp. 204–222, 473). Washington, DC: Author.

American Psychiatric Association. (1987). *Diagnostic and statistical manual of mental disorders* (3rd ed.). Washington, DC: Author.

American Psychiatric Association, Ad Hoc Committee on AIDS Policy. (1988). AIDS policy: Confidentiality and disclosure. *American Journal of Psychiatry, 145*, 541–542.

American Psychological Association. (1981). Ethical principals of psychologists. *American Psychologist, 36*, 633–638.

American Psychological Association. (1991a). APA Council of Representatives adopts new AIDS policies. *Psychology & AIDS Exchange, 7*, 1.

American Psychological Association. (1991b). *Legal liability related to confidentiality and the prevention of HIV transmission*. Washington, DC: Author.

American Psychological Association. (1995). *Ethical principles of psychologists and code of conduct*. Washington, DC: Author.

American School Counselor Association. (1992). *Ethical standards for school counselors*. Alexandria, VA: Author.

Anderson, D. A., & Worthen, D. (1997). Exploring a fourth dimension: Spirituality as a resource for the couple therapist. *Journal of Marital and Family Therapy, 23*, 3–12.

Annell, A. L. (Ed.). (1971). *Depressive states in childhood and adolescence*. New York: Halstead.

Aponte, H. J. (1994). How personal can training get? *Journal of Marital and Family Counseling, 20*(1), 3–15.

Aponte, J. F., Rivers, R. Y., & Wohl, T. (1995). *Psychological interventions and cultural diversity*. Boston: Allyn & Bacon.

Applebaum, P. S. (1985). *Tarasoff* and the clinician: Problems in fulfilling the duty to protect. *American Journal of Psychiatry, 142*(4), 425–429.

Applebaum, P. S. (1993). Legal liability and managed care. *American Psychologist, 48*(3), 251–257.

Applebaum, P. S., & Meisel, M. A. (1986). Therapists' obligations to report their patients' criminal acts. *Bulletin of the American Academy of Psychiatry and the Law, 14*(3), 221–229.

Association for Counselor Education and Supervision. (1993, Summer). Ethical standards for counselor supervisors. *ACES Spectrum, 53*(4), 5–8.

Association for Specialists in Group Work. (1989). *Ethical guidelines for group leaders*. Alexandria, VA: Author.

Atcherson, E. (1993, Fall). Ethics and information: How vulnerable is your campus to computer crime? *CUPA Journal, 4,* 35–38.

Ausdale, D. V., & Feagin, J. R. (1996). Using social and ethnic concepts: The critical case of young children. *American Sociological Review, 61*, 779–793.

Austin, K. M., Moline, M. E., & Williams, G. T. (1990). *Confronting malpractice*. Thousand Oaks, CA: Sage.

Axelson, J. A. (1985). *Counseling and development in a multicultural society*. Pacific Grove, CA: Brooks/Cole.

Banning, A. (1989). Mother-son incest: Confronting as prejudice. *Child Abuse and Neglect, 13*, 563–570.

Barlow, D. (1996). Health care policy, psychotherapy research, on the future of psychotherapy. *American Psychology, 51*(10), 1050–1058.

Barrett, T. (1985). Does suicide prevention in the school have to be such a "terrifying" concept? *Newslink, 11*(1), 3.

Barron, F. (1987). Clinical psychology: Racing into the future with old dreams and visions. *Clinical Psychologist, 40*(4), 93–96.

Barth, F. (1969). *Ethnic groups and boundaries*. Boston: Little, Brown.

Baruth, L. G., & Huber, C. H. (1984). *An introduction to marital theory and therapy.* Pacific Grove, CA: Brooks/Cole.

Baxter, A. (1986). *Techniques for dealing with child sexual abuse.* Springfield, IL: Charles C. Thomas.

Beauchamp, T. L. (1985). Suicide: Matters of life and death. *Suicide and Life-Threatening Behavior, 24*(2), 190–195.

Beauchamp, T. L., & Childress, J. F. (1979). *Principles of biomedical ethics.* New York: Oxford University Press.

Beauchamp, T. L., & Childress, J. F. (1994). *Principles of biomedical ethics* (4th ed.). New York: Oxford University Press.

Beck, A., & Emery, G. D. (1977). *Cognitive therapy of substance abuse.* Philadelphia: Center for Cognitive Therapy.

Bednar, R. L., Bednar, S. C., Lambert, M. J., & Waite, D. R. (1991). *Psychology with high-risk clients: Legal and professional standards.* Pacific Grove, CA: Brooks/Cole.

Bellotti v. Baird, 11, 443 U.S. 634 (1979).

Belote, B. (1974). *Sexual intimacy between female clients and male psychotherapists: Masochistic sabotage.* Unpublished doctoral dissertation, California School of Professional Psychology, San Francisco.

Benner, D. G. (1988). *Psychotherapy and the spiritual quest.* Grand Rapids, MI: Baker.

Berenson, D. (1990). A systemic view of spirituality: God and twelve-step programs as resources in family therapy. *Journal of Strategic and Systemic Therapies, 9,* 50–70.

Bergin, A. E. (1989). Religious faith and counseling: A commentary on Worthington. *Counseling Psychologist, 17,* 621–623.

Berman, A. (1986). A critical look at our adolescence: Notes on training. *Suicide and Life-Threatening Behavior 16*(1), 1–12.

Berman, A. L., & Cohen-Sandler, R. (1982). Suicide and the standard care: Optimal vs. acceptance. *Suicide and Life-Threatening Behavior 12*(2), 114–122.

Bernard, J. L., & Carmen, S. J. (1986). The failure of clinical psychology graduate students to apply understood ethical principles. *Professional Psychology Research and Practice, 17*(4), 313–315.

Bernard, J. M., & Goodyear, R. K. (1992). *Fundamentals of clinical supervision.* Boston: Allyn & Bacon.

Bersoff, D. H. (1996). The virtue of principle ethics. *Counseling Psychologist, 24*(1), 86–91.

Besharov, D. J. (1988). Child abuse and neglect reporting and investigation: Policy guidelines for decision making. *Family Law Quarterly 22*(1), 1–16.

Bickhard, M. H. (1989). Ethical psychotherapy and psychotherapy as ethics. *New Ideas in Psychology, 7,* 159–164.

Bongar, B., & Harmatz, M. (1989). Graduate training in clinical psychology and the study of suicide. *Professional Psychology: Research and Practice, 20*(4), 209–213.

Bonilla, L., & Porter, J. (1990). A comparison of Latino, Black, and non-Hispanic White attitudes toward homosexuality. *Hispanic Journal of Behavioral Sciences, 12,* 437–452.

Borders, I. D., & Leddick, G. R. (1988). A nationwide survey of supervision training. *Counselor Education and Supervision, 27,* 271–283.

Borenstein, D. B. (1990). Managed care: A means of rationing psychiatric treatment. *Hospital and Community Psychiatry, 41,* 1095–1098.

Borys, D. S., & Pope, K. S. (1989). Dual relationships between therapist and client: A national study of psychologists, psychiatrists, and social workers. *Professional Psychology: Research and Practice, 20*(5), 283–293.

Boszormenyi-Nagy, I., & Ulrich, D. N. (1981). Contextual family therapy. In A. S. Gurman & D. P. Kniskern (Eds.), *Handbook of family therapy.* New York: Brunner/Mazel.

Bouhoutsos, J. C., Holroyd, J., Lerman, H., Forer, B. R., & Greenberg, M. (1983). Sexual intimacy between psychotherapists and patients. *Professional Psychology: Research and Practice. 14*(2), 185–196.

Boylan, J. C., Malley, P. B., & Scott, J. (1995). *Practicum and internship textbook for counseling and psychotherapy*. Muncie, IN: Accelerated Development.

Boynton v. Burglass, No. 89–1409 , Fla. Ct. App., 3d Dist. (September 24, 1991).

Bradley, D. F. (1988). Alcohol and drug education in the elementary school. *Elementary School Guidance and Counseling, 23,* 99–105.

Bradley, R., & Mims, G. (1992). Using family systems and birth order dynamics as the basis for a college career decision-making course. *Journal of Counseling and Development, 70,* 445–448.

Brainer, C. J., Reyna, C. F., & Brandse, E. (1996). Are children's false memories more persistent than their true memories? *Psychological Science 6*(6), 359–364.

Brammer, L. M., & MacDonald, G. (1996). *The helping relationship: Process and skills.* Boston: Allyn & Bacon.

Brandt, L. M. (1989). A short-term group therapy model for treatment of adult female survivors of childhood incest. *Group, 13,* 74–82.

Brassard, M. R., Germain, R., & Hart, S. N. (1987). *Psychological maltreatment of children and youth.* New York: Pergamon.

Briere, J. (1989). *Therapy for adults molested as children: Beyond survival.* New York: Springer.

Bromberg, W. (1975). *From shaman to psychologist.* Chicago: Henry Regnery.

Bross, A. (1991, July 7). A touch of evil. *The Boston Globe Magazine,* 12–25.

Bross, D. C. (1984). When children are battered by the law. *Barrister, 11*(4), 8–11.

Brown, D., Pryzwansky, W. B., & Schulte, A. C. (1991). *Psychological consultation: Introduction to theory and practice.* Boston: Allyn & Bacon.

Brown, J. H., & Christensen, D. N. (1986). *Family therapy: Theory and practice.* Pacific Grove, CA: Brooks/Cole.

Buckley, J. (1988). Legal proceedings, reforms, and emergency issues in child sexual abuse cases. *Behavioral Science and the Law, 6*(2), 153–180.

Buckner, S. (1978). *Conspiracy of silence.* San Francisco: New Glide.

Bukstein, O. G. (1990). *A primer on psychoactive substance use disorders in DSM-I-R.* Unpublished paper, Western Psychiatric Institute and Clinic.

Burck, H. D., & Peterson, G. W. (1975). Need more evaluation, not research. *Personnel Guidance Journal, 53,* 563–569.

Butler, S. (1978). *Conspiracy of silence.* San Francisco: New Glide.

Butler, S., & Zehlen, S. L. (1977). Sexual intimacies between therapists and patients. *Psychotherapy: Theory, Research, and Practice, 14,* 139–145.

Caplan, G. (1970). *The theory and practice of mental health consultation.* New York: Basic Books.

Capuzzi, D., & Golden, L. (1988). *Preventing adolescent suicide.* Muncie, IN: Accelerated Development.

Carballo-Dieguez, A. (1989). Hispanic culture, gay male culture, and AIDS: Counseling implications. *Journal of Counseling and Development, 68,* 26–30.

Carlino v. State, 294 N.Y.S. 2d 30 (1968).

Caudill, B. (1995, February). *The repressed memory war.* Presentation at the Annual Convention of the California Psychological Association, La Jolla.

Celotta, B., Golden, J., Keys, S. S., & Cannon, G. (1988). A model prevention program. In D. Capuzzi & L. Golden (Eds.), *Preventing adolescent suicide* (pp. 269–296). Muncie, IN: Accelerated Development.

Chaffin, M., & Milner, J. (1993). Psychometric issues for practitioners in child maltreatment. *APSAC Advisor, 6*(1), 9–13.

Chan, C. S. (1989). Issues of identity development among Asian-American lesbians and gay men. *Journal of Counseling and Development, 68,* 16–20.

Chandler, C. K., Miner-Holden, J., & Kolander, C. A. (1992). Counseling for spiritual wellness: Theory and practice. *Journal of Counseling and Development, 71,* 168–174.

Chauvin, J. C., & Remley, T. P., Jr. (1996). Responding to allegations of unethical conduct. *Journal of Counseling and Development, 74,* 563–567.

Cheatham, H. E. (1994). A response to multicultural training. *Counseling Psychologist, 22*, 290–295.

Chemtob, C. M., Hamada, R. S., Bauer, G. B., Kinney, B., & Torigoe, R. Y. (1988). Patient suicide: Frequency and impact on psychiatrists. *American Journal of Psychiatry, 145*, 224–228.

Cherniss, C., & Egnatios, E. (1977). Styles of clinical supervision in community mental health programs. *Journal of Consulting and Clinical Psychology, 45*, 115–196.

Child Protective Services Law Act of 1975. P.L. 438. No. 124. Act of 1982. No. 136. Act of 1983. No. 42.

Christopher, J. C. (1996). Counseling's inescapable moral visions. *Journal of Counseling and Development, 75,* 17–25.

Closen, M. L., & Isaacman, S. H. (1988). The duty to notify private third parties of the risks of HIV infection. *Journal of Health and Hospital Law, 21,* 295.

Cohen, E. D. (1990). Confidentiality, counseling, and clients who have AIDS: Ethical foundations of a model rule. *Journal of Counseling and Development, 68*(3), 282–286.

Cole, K. M. (1995). Legal challenges in secondary prevention programming for students with substance abuse problems. *The School Counselor, 43*, 35–41.

Cole, S. S. (1984–1986). Facing the challenges of sexual abuse in persons with disabilities. *Sexuality and Disability, 7,* 71–88.

Coleman, E., & Schaefer, S. (1986). Boundaries of sex and intimacy between client and counselor. *Journal of Counseling and Development, 64*(5), 341–344.

Comiskey v. State of New York, 418 N.Y.S. 2d 233 (1979).

Commissioner of Corporation of California v. TakeCare Health Plan, Inc. No. 933– 0290 (California Department of Corporations October 11, 1996).

Connell, H. M. (1972). Depression in childhood. *Child Psychiatry and Human Development, 4,* 71–85.

Conroy, M. (1987). *Growing in love and freedom: Personal experiences of counseling and spiritual direction.* Denville, NJ: Dimension Books.

Cook, D. A., & Helms, J. E. (1988). Visible racial/ethnic group supervisees' satisfaction with cross-cultural supervision as predicted by relationship characteristics. *Journal of Counseling Psychology, 35*, 268–274.

Cooper, C. L., & Payne, R. (1991). *Personality and stress: Individual differences in the stress process*. New York: Wiley.

Corey, G. (1986). *Theory and practice of counseling and psychotherapy* (3rd ed.). Pacific Grove, CA: Brooks/Cole.

Corey, G. (1995). *Theory and practice of group counseling* (4th ed.). Pacific Grove, CA: Brooks/Cole.

Corey, G., Corey, M. S., & Callanan, P. (1988). *Issues and ethics in the helping professions* (3rd ed.). Pacific Grove, CA: Brooks/Cole.

Cormier, L. S. & Hackney, H. C. (1993). *Professional counselor: A process guide to helping*. Boston: Allyn & Bacon.

Cottingham, H. F. (1980). Some broader perspectives on credentialing counseling psychologists. *Counseling Psychologist, 9*(1), 19–22.

Council on Ethical and Judicial Affairs. American Medical Association. (1994). *JAMA, 272*, 1056–1060.

Cox, M. (1987). Personality theory and research. In H. T. Blane & K. E. Leonard (Eds.), *Psychological theories of drinking and alcoholism* (pp. 55–84). New York: Guilford.

Crabbs, M. A. (1984). Reduction in force and accountability: Stemming the tide. *Elementary School Guidance and Counseling, 18*(3), 167–175.

D'Augelli, A. R. (1989). Lesbians' and gay men's experiences of discrimination in a university community. *American Journal of Community Psychology, 17*, 317–321.

D'Augelli, A. R. (1991). Gay men in college: Identity processes and adaptations. *Journal of College Student Development, 32*, 140–146.

D'Augelli, A. R. (1993). Preventing mental health problems among lesbian and gay college students. *Journal of Primary Prevention, 13*, 245–261.

D'Augelli, A. R., & Rose, M. L. (1990). Homophobia in a university community: Attitudes and experiences of heterosexual freshmen. *Journal of College Student Development, 31,* 484–491.

Dalton v. State, 308 N.Y.S. 2d 441 (Sup, CF. N.Y. App. 1970).

Darton, N., Springer, K., Wright, L., & Keene-Osborn, S. (1991, October 7). The pain of the last taboo. *Newsweek,* 70–72.

Davis, A., & Yzak, D. (1996). Professional issues: Goals and tasks of licensing boards. *Counselor Education and Supervision, 35,* 308–317.

Davis, J. M. (1985). Suicidal crisis in schools. *School Psychology Review, 14*(3), 117–123.

Davis, T., & Richie, M. (1993). Confidentiality and the school counselor: A challenge for the 1990s. *The School Counselor, 41,* 23–40.

Delarosa, R. (1987). Viability of negligence actions for sexual transmission of the acquired immune deficiency syndrome virus. *Capital University Law Review, 17,* 101–195.

DeStefano, A. M. (1988, October 7). New York teens antigay, poll finds. *Newsday,* 7, 21.

Deutsch, C. J. (1984). Self-reported stresses among psychotherapist. *Professional Psychology: Research and Practice, 15*(6), 833–845.

Deutsch, P. M., & Parker, E. C. (1985). *Rehabilitation testimony: Maintaining a professional perspective.* New York: Matthew Bender.

Diamond, A. L., & Simbovg, M. (1985). CEB forum: Psychological aspects on marital dissolutions. *California Lawyer, 5*(5), 14–18.

Dickens, B. M. (1990). Confidentiality and the duty to warn. In L. O Gostin (Ed.), *AIDS and the health care system* (pp. 98–112). New Haven, CT: Yale University Press.

Dixon, W. A., Heppner, P. P., & Rudd, H. D. (1994). Problem-solving appraisal, hopelessness, and suicide ideation: Evidence for a mediational model. *Journal of Counseling Psychology, 41*(1), 91–98.

Dorland, D. (1974). *Dorland's medical dictionary.* New York: Macmillan.

Dorn, F. (1984). The counselor goes to court. *Journal of Counseling and Development, 63*(3), 62–63.

Dorwart, R. A. (1990). Managed mental health care: Myths and realities in the 1990s. *Hospital and Community Psychiatry, 41,* 1087–1091.

Dreukers, R. (1969). Group psychotherapy from the point of view of Adlerian psychology. In H. M. Ruitenbeck (Ed.), *Group therapy today: Styles, methods, and techniques.* Chicago: Adline/Atherton.

Eddy, W. B., & Lubin, B. (1971). Laboratory training and encounter groups. *Personnel and Guidance Journal, 49,* 625–735.

Edel, A., Flower, E., & O'Connor, F. W. (1994). *Critique of applied ethics: Reflections and recommendations.* Philadelphia: Temple University Press.

Ehrenwald, J. (1976). *The history of psychotherapy.* New York: Jason Aronson.

Eisel v. Board of Education, 597 A.2d 447 (Md. 1991).

Eisenberg, L. (1984). The epidemiology of suicide in adolescents. *Pediatric Annuals, 13*(1), 47–53.

Ellenberger, H. F. (1970). *The discovery of the unconscious.* New York: Basic Books.

Ellis., A., McInerney, J., DiGiuseppe, R., & Yeager, R. (1988). *Rational-emotive therapy with alcoholics and substance abusers.* New York: Pergamon.

Elwork, A. E. (1993, April). Adolescents and information consent: Facts and fictions. *Pennsylvania Psychologist, 14,* 1–3.

Emery, R. E., & Wyer, M. M. (1987). Child custody mediation and litigation: An experimental evaluation of the experience of parents. *Journal of Consulting and Clinical Psychology, 55*(2), 179–186.

Erickson, E. L., McEnvoy, A., & Colucci, N. D. (1984). *Child abuse and neglect: A guidebook for educators and community leaders* (2nd ed.). Holmes Beach, FL: Learning Publications.

Erickson, L., & Newman, I. M. (1984). Developing support for alcohol and drug education: A case study of a counselor's role. *Personnel and Guidance Journal, 62,* 289–291.

Ernst, P. A., Francis, R. A., Nevels, H., & Lemeh, C. A. (1991). Condemnation of homosexuality in the Black community: A gender–specific phenomenon? *Archives of Sexual Behavior, 20,* 579–585.

Essandoh, P. K. (1996). Multicultural counseling as a "fourth force": A call to arms. *Counseling Psychologist, 24*(1), 126–137.

Etherington, K. (1995). Adult male survivors of childhood sexual abuse. *Counseling Psychology Quarterly, 8*(3), 233–241.

Evans, S., & Schaefer, S. (1987). Incest and chemically dependent women: Treatment implications. *Journal of Chemical Dependency Treatment, 1,* 141–173.

Fairchild, T. (1993). Accountability procedures of school counselors: 1990 national survey. *The School Counselor, 40,* 363–373.

Fairchild, T. N., & Zins, J. E. (1986). Accountability practices of school counselors: A national survey. *Journal of Counseling and Development, 65,* 196–199.

Falik, M. (1991, January). Harnessing the potential of managed care. *Policy in Perspective, 1,* 3–5, 7.

Fannibanda, D. K. (1976). Ethical issues of mental health consultation. *Professional Psychology: Research and Practice, 7,* 547–552.

Farber, B. A. (1983). Psychotherapists' perceptions of stressful patients' behavior. *Professional Psychology: Research and Practice, 14*(5), 697–705.

Farrow v. Health Service Corp., 604 p. 2d 474 (Utah Supreme Ct., 1979).

Fieldsteel. N. (1982). Ethical issues in family therapy. In M. Rosenbaum (Ed.). *Ethics and values in psychotherapy: A guidebook.* New York: Free Press

Finkelhor, D. (1979). *Sexually victimized children.* New York: Free Press.

Finkelhor, D. (1984, September). The prevention of child sexual abuse: An overview of needs and problems. *Seicus Report,* 1–5.

Fitzgerald, K., & O'Leary, E. (1990). Cross-cultural counseling: Counselors' views on barriers, benefits, personal qualities, and necessary preparation. *Irish Journal of Psychology, 11*(3), 238–248.

Forester-Miller, H., & Duncan, J. (1990). The ethic of dual relationships in the training group. *Journal for Specialists in Group Work, 15*, 88–93.

Forge, J. L., & Henderson, P. (1990). Counselor competency in the courtroom. *Journal of Counseling and Development, 68*, 456–459.

Forrest, G. G. (1985). Psychodynamically oriented treatment of alcoholism and substance abuse. In T. E. Bratter & G. G. Forrest (Eds.), *Alcoholism and substance abuse* (pp. 307–336). New York: Free Press.

Frances, R. J., & Miller, S. I. (Eds.). (1991). *Clinical textbook of addictive disorders.* New York: Guilford.

Frankl, V. (1978). *The unheard cry for meaning.* New York: Simon & Schuster.

Freed, D. L., & Walker, T. B. (1988). Family law in the fifty states: An overview. *Family Law Quarterly 21*(4), 417–572.

Freeman, L., & Roy, J. (1976). *Betrayal.* New York: Stein & Day.

Fremouw, W., Callahan, T., & Kashden, J. (1993). Adolescent suicidal risk: Psychological, problem solving, and environmental factors. *Suicide and Life-Threatening Behavior, 23*(1).

Friedman, J. T. (1985). Questions to trap the experts. *Family Law Quarterly, 24*(4), 309–406.

Fritz, B. R., & Mills, D. H. (1980). *Licensing and certification of psychologists and counselors.* San Francisco: Jossey-Bass.

Frome, M. W. (1996). Creating an ethical position in family therapy. *Journal of Marital and Family Therapy, 22*(2), 276–277.

Fromuth, M. E. (1986). The relationship of childhood sexual abuse with later psychological and sexual adjustment in a sample of college women. *Child Abuse and Neglect, 10*, 5–15.

Fujimura, L. E., Weis, D. M., & Cochran, F. R. (1985). Suicide: Dynamics and implications for counseling. *Journal of Counseling and Development, 63*, 612–615.

Fulero, S. M. (1988). Tarasoff: Ten years later. *Professional Psychology: Research and Practice, 19*(2), 184–190.

Gallagher, R. P. (1992). *Gallagher's national survey of counseling center directors.* (1992). Unpublished monograph; printed at University of Pittsburgh.

Ganje-Fling, M. A., & McCarthy, P. (1996). Impact of child sexual abuse on client spiritual development: Counseling implications. *Journal of Counseling and Development, 74*, 253–257.

Garbarino, J., & Vondra, J. (1987). Psychological maltreatment: Issues and perspectives. In M. R. Brassard, R. Germain, & S. N. Hart (Eds.), *Psychological maltreatment of children and youth* (pp. 24–44). New York: Pergamon.

Gargiulo, R. (1990). Child abuse and neglect: An overview. In R. Goldman & R. Gargiulo (Eds.), *Children at risk: An interdisciplinary approach to child abuse and neglect* (pp. 1–36). Austin, TX: Pro-Ed.

General Accounting Office. (1991). *Child abuse prevention: Status of the challenge grant program* (GAO/HRD 91–95). Washington, DC: Author.

Getz, H., & Protinsky, H. (1994). Training marriage and family counselors: A family-of-origin approach. *Counselor Education and Supervision, 33*, 183–190.

Gilchrist, R. (1992). The need for holistic counseling. *American Counselor, 1*, 10–13.

Gilligan, C. (1979). Woman's place in man's life cycle. *Harvard Educational Review, 49*(4), 431–434, 616.

Gilliland, B. E., James, R. K., & Bowman, J. T. (1989). *Theories and strategies in counseling and psychotherapy.* Englewood Cliffs, NJ: Prentice-Hall.

Glantz, T. M., & Hunt, B. (1996). What rehabilitation counselors need to know about adult survivors of child sexual abuse. *Journal of Applied Rehabilitation Counseling, 27*(3), 17–22.

Glaser, R. D., & Thorpe, J. S. (1986). Unethical intimacy: A survey of sexual contact and advances between psychology educators and female graduate students. *American Psychology, 41*, 43–51.

Goldberg, I., & Goldberg, H. (1985). *Family therapy: An overview* (2nd ed.). Pacific Grove, CA: Brooks/Cole.

Goldman, R. (1993). Sexual abuse of children with special needs: Are they safe in day care? *Day Care and Early Education, 20*(4), 37–38.

Goodman, R. W., & Carpenter-White, A. (1996). The family autobiography assignment: Some ethical considerations. *Counselor Education and Supervision, 35*, 230–238.

Goodwin, D. W., & Warnock, J. K. (1991). Alcoholism: A family disease. In R. J. Frances & S. I. Miller (Eds.), *Clinical textbook of addictive disorders* (pp. 485–500). New York: Guilford.

Gray, E. A., & Harding, A. K. (1988). Confidentiality limits with clients who have the AIDS virus. *Journal of Counseling and Development, 66*(5), 219–223.

Green, R. J., & Saeger, K. E. (1982). Learning to "think systems": Five writing assignments. *Journal of Marital and Family Therapy, 8*, 285–294.

Grieger, I., & Ponterotto, J. W. (1988). Students' knowledge of AIDS and their attitudes toward gay men and lesbian women. *Journal of College Student Development, 29*, 415–422.

Grob, M. C., Klein, A. A., & Eisen, S. V. (1982). The role of the high school professional in identifying and managing adolescent suicide behavior. *Journal of Youth Suicide, 12*, 163–173.

Gross v. Prudential Health Care Plan, No. CJ–947 4267 (Okla. City, Ct. October 1, 1996).

Groth, A. N. (1979). Sexual trauma in the life histories of rapists and child molesters. *Victimology, 4*, 10–16.

Guest, P. D., & Beutler, L. E. (1988). Impact of psychotherapy supervision on therapist orientation and values. *Journal of Counseling and Clinical Psychology, 56*(55), 653–658.

Hall. (1988). Protection in supervision. *Register Report, 4,* 3–4.

Hamilton-Usher, C., & Borders, I. D. (1993). Practicing counselors' preferences for supervisory style and supervisory emphases. *Counselor Educational Supervision, 33,* 66–79.

Handelsman, M. M., & Galvin, M. D. (1988). Facilitation informed consent for outpatient psychotherapy: A suggested written format. *Professional Psychology: Research and Practice, 19*(2), 223–225.

Harding, A. K., Gray, L. A., & Neal, M. (1993). Confidentiality limits with clients who have HIV: A review of ethical and legal guidelines and professional policies. *Journal of Counseling and Development, 71,* 297–305.

Hardy, K. V., & Laszloffy, T. A. (1995). The cultural genogram: Key to training culturally competent family therapists. *Journal of Marital and Family Therapy, 21*(3), 227–237.

Hare-Mustin, R. (1980). Family therapy may be dangerous for your health. *Professional Psychology, 11,* 935–938.

Harrar, W. R., VandeCreek, L., & Knapp, S. (1990). Ethical and legal aspects of clinical supervision. *Professional Psychology: Research and Practice, 21*(1), 37–41.

Harris, S. M. (1995). Ethics, legalities, professionalism, and the professor: A document analysis. *American Journal of Family Therapy, 23*(1), 38–47.

Hass, L. J., & Malouf, J. L. (1989). *Keeping up the good work: A practitioner's guide to mental health ethics.* Sarasota, FL: Professional Resource Exchange.

Hauerwas, S. (1981). *A community of character.* South Bend, IN: University of Notre Dame Press.

Haugaard, J. J., & Emery, R. E. (1989). Methodological issues in child sexual abuse research. *Child Abuse and Neglect, 13,* 89–100.

Hedlund v. Superior Court of Orange County, 669 P.2d 41, 191 Cal. Rptr. 805 (1983).

Heiden, J. M. (1993). Preview-prevent: A training strategy to prevent counselor-client sexual relationships. *Counselor Education and Supervision, 33,* 53–60.

Heppner, M. J., & O'Brien, K. M. (1994). Multicultural counselor training: Students' perceptions of helpful and hindering events. *Counselor Education and Supervision, 34,* 4–18.

Herek, G. M. (1991). Stigma, prejudice, and violence against lesbians and gay men. In J. C. Consiorek & J. D. Weinrich (Eds.), *Homosexuality: Research implications for public policy* (pp. 60–80). Thousand Oaks, CA: Sage.

Herlihy, B., & Golden, L. B. (1990). *Ethical standards casebook.* Alexandria, VA: American Association of Counseling and Development.

Hetherington, C., & Orzek, A. (1989). Career counseling and life planning with lesbian women. *Journal of Counseling and Development, 68,* 52–57.

Hillman, D., & Solek-Tefft, J. (1988). *Spiders and flies: Help for parents and teachers of sexually abused children.* Lexington, MA: Lexington Books.

Hinterkopf, E. (1994). Integrating spiritual experience in counseling. *Counseling and Values, 38,* 165–175.

Hirsch, H., & White, E. (1982). The pathological anatomy of medical malpractice claims: Legal aspects of medical malpractice. *Journal of Legal Medicine, 6*(1), 25–26.

Hoffman, M. A. (1991). Counseling the HIV-infected client: A psychosocial model for assessment and intervention. *Counseling Psychologist, 19*(4), 167–542.

Hogan, D. B. (1979). *The regulation of psychotherapists: A handbook of state licensure laws* (4 vols.). Cambridge, MA: Ballinger.

Holroyd, J. (1983). Erotic contact as an instance of sex-biased therapy. In J. Murray & P. Abramson (Eds.), *Bias in psychology.* New York: Praeger.

Holroyd, J., & Brodsky, A. (1977). Psychologists' attitudes and practices regarding erotic and non-erotic physical contact with patients. *American Psychologist, 32*(10), 843–849.

Holroyd, J. C., & Brodsky, A. (1980). Does touching patients lead to sexual intercourse? *Professional Psychology, 11*(5), 807–811.

Hood, G. (1994). The statute of limitation barrier in civil suits brought against adult survivors of child sexual abuse: A simple solution. *University of Illinois Law Review, 2,* 417–442.

Horowitz, I. A., & Willging, T. E. (1984). *The psychology of law: Applications.* Boston: Little, Brown.

Hrabowy, I. (1987). *Self-reported correlates of adult-child sexual relations.* Unpublished master's thesis, Bowling Green State University, Bowling Green, Ohio.

Huber, C. H., & Baruth, L. G. (1987). *Ethical, legal, and professional issues in the practice of marriage and family therapy.* Columbus, OH: Merrill.

Humpreys, H. C. (1987, October). Cross-examining the expert. *Trial, 75–78.*

Ibrahim, F. A. (1986). *Cultural encapsulation of the APA ethical principles.* Unpublished manuscript, University of Connecticut, Storrs.

Ibrahim, F. A., & Arredondo, P. M. (1986). Ethical standards for cross-cultural counseling: Counselor preparation, practice, assessment, and research. *Journal of Counseling and Development, 64(5),* 349–352.

Illingworth, P.M.L. (1995). Patient-therapist sex: Criminalization and its discontents. *Journal of Contemporary Health Law and Policy, 11,* 389–416.

Ingersoll, R. E. (1994). Spirituality, religion, and counseling: Dimensions and relationships. *Counseling and Values, 38,* 98–111.

Institute of Medicine. (1989). *Controlling costs and changing patient care: The role of utilization management.* Washington, DC: National Academy Press.

Ivey, A. E. (1986). *Ethics and multicultural therapy: An unrealized dream.* Unpublished manuscript, University of Massachusetts, Amherst.

Ivey, A. E. (1988). *International interviewing and counseling* (2nd ed.). Pacific Grove, CA: Brooks/Cole.

Ivey, A. E., Ivey, M. B., & Simek-Morgan, L. (1993). *Counseling and psychotherapy: A multicultural perspective.* Boston: Allyn & Bacon.

Jablonski v. United States, 712 E.2d 391 (9th cir. 1983)

Jacobson, N. S., & Margolin, G. (1979). *Marital therapy: Strategies based on social learning and behavior exchange principles.* New York: Brunner/Mazel.

Jordan, A. E., & Meara, M. (1990). Ethics and the professional practice of psychologists: The role of virtues and principles. *Professional Psychology: Practice and Research, 21*(2), 107–115.

Josephson, G. S., & Fong-Beyette, M. L. (1987). Factors assisting female clients' disclosure of incest during counseling. *Journal of Counseling and Development, 65,* 475–478.

Jung, C. G. (1958). *The undiscovered self.* Boston: Little, Brown.

Kagan, N. (1977). Presidential address, division 17. *Counseling Psychologist, 7,* 2–4.

Kahn-Edrington, M. (1981). Abortion counseling. In E. Howell & M. Bayes (Eds.), *Women and mental health* (pp. 395–399). New York: Basic Books.

Kane, S., & Keeton, R. (1985, October/November). Informed consent. *Campus Voice,* 52–54.

Kaufman, J., & Zigler, E. (1987). Do abused children become abusive parents? *American Journal of Orthopsychiatry, 57,* 186–192.

Kazdin, A. E. (1989). Developmental psychology: Current research, implications, and directions. *American Psychologist, 44*(2), 180–187.

Keene, K. M., & Stewart, N. R. (1989). Evaluation: RX for counseling program growth. *The School Counselor, 37,* 62–66.

Keith-Spiegel, P., & Koocher, G. P. (1985). *Ethics in psychology: Professional standards and cases.* New York: Random House.

Kelly, J. B. (1992). Who should be the family mediator? *Family Advocate, 14*(4), 19–21.

Kelly, K. (1987). AIDS and ethics: An overview. *General Hospital Psychiatry, 9,* 331–340.

Kelson v. City of Springfield, 767 F.2d 651 (9th Cir. 1985).

Kempe, R. S., & Kempe, C. H. (1978). *Child abuse.* Cambridge, MA: Harvard University Press.

Kermani, E. J., & Weiss, B. A. (1989). AIDS and confidentiality: Legal concept and its application in psychotherapy. *American Journal of Psychotherapy, 43*(1), 25–31.

Kilburg, R., Nathan, P., & Thoreson, R. (Eds.). (1986). *Professionals in distress.* Washington, DC: American Psychological Association.

Kilpatrick, A. C. (1986). Some correlates of women's childhood sexual experiences: A retrospective study. *Journal of Sex Research, 22,* 221–242.

Kirkorian v. Barry, 242 Cal. Rptr. 312 (Cal. Ct. App. 1987).

Kitchener, K. S. (1984). Intuition, critical evaluation, and ethical principles: The foundation for ethical decisions in counseling psychology. *Counseling Psychologist, 12*(3), 43–55.

Kitchener, K. S. (1996). There is more to ethics than principles. *Counseling Psychologist, 24*(1), 92–97.

Klein, C. (1986). *Counseling our own.* Reston, VA: Publication Service.

Kluckhohn, C.K.M., & Murray, A. (Eds.). (1953). *Personality in nature, society, and culture.* New York: Alfred A. Knopf.

Knapp, S., & Tepper, A. (1995, May). Risk management issues in the false memory debate. *Pennsylvania Psychologist, 55*(3), 26–27.

Knapp, S., & VandeCreek, L. (1993). What psychologists need to know about AIDS. *Journal of Training and Practice in Professional Psychology. 3*(2), 3–16.

Knapp, S., & VandeCreek, L. (1995). *Risk management for psychologists treating patients who recover lost memories of childhood abuse.* Manuscript in development.

Kohlberg, L. (1984). *Essays in moral development. Vol. 2: The psychology of moral development.* New York: Harper & Row.

Kohn, A. (1987). Shattered innocence. *Psychology Today 21*(2), 54–58.

Koop, C. E., & Lundberg, G. D. (1992). Violence in America: A public health emergency. *JAMA, 267,* 3075–3076.

Korn, J. H., Davis, R., & Davis, S. F. (1991). Historians' and chairpersons' judgments of eminence among psychologists. *American Psychologist, 46,* 789–792.

Kraepelin, E. (1923). *Textbook of psychiatry.* New York: Macmillan.

Kramer, J. (1985). *Family interfaces: Transgenerational patterns.* New York: Brunner/Mazel.

Krug, R. S. (1989). Adult male reports of childhood sexual abuse by mothers: Case descriptions, motivations, and long-term consequences. *Child Abuse and Neglect, 13,* 111–119.

Kuehnel, F. M., & Liberman, R. P., (1986). Behavior modification. In I. L. Kutash & A. Wolf (Eds.), *Psychotherapist's case book* (pp. 240–262). San Francisco: Jossey-Bass.

Kurpius, D., Fuqua, K., & Rozecki, T. (1993, July/August). The consulting process: A multidimensional approach. *Journal of Counseling and Development, 71,* 601–606.

Kush, F. R. (1990). *A descriptive study of school-based adolescent suicide prevention/intervention programs: Program components and the role of the school counselor.* Unpublished doctoral dissertation, University of Pittsburgh.

Ladnay, N., Hill, C. E., Corbett, M. M., & Nutt, E. A. (1996). Nature, extent, and importance of what psychotherapy trainees do not disclose to their supervisors. *Journal of Counseling and Development, 43*(1), 10–24.

Lamson, A. (1995). Evaluating child sexual abuse allegations. *Research and Treatment Issues, 11*(3–4), 24–27.

Landesman, S. H. (1987). AIDS and a duty to protect: Commentary. *Hastings Center Report, 17,* 23.

Larry P. v. Riles, 343 F. Supp. 1306 (N.D. Cal., 1972), aff'd 502 F.2d 963 (9th Cir., 1974), No. C–71–2270 R.F.P. (N.D. Cal., 1979), appeal docketed, No. 80–4027 (9th Cir., 1980).

Lasko, C. A. (1986). Childhood depression questions and answers. *Journal of School Guidance and Counseling, 4,* 283–287.

Lawson, C. (1991). Mother-son sexual abuse: Rare or under-reported? A critique of the research. *Child Abuse and Neglect, 17*, 261–269.

Leigh, G. (1985). Psychosocial factors in the etiology of substance abuse. In T. E. Bratter & G. G. Forrest (Eds.), *Alcoholism and substance abuse* (pp. 3–48). New York: Free Press.

Leigh, G., Loewen, I., & Lester, M. (1986). Caveat emptor: Values and ethic in family life education and enrichment. *Family Relations, 35*, 573–580.

Levy, R. (1987). Custody investigations as evidenced in divorce cases. *Family Law Quarterly, 21*(2), 149–167.

Lindsay, R. T. (1985, August). *Moral sensitivity: The relationship between training and experience.* Paper presented at the annual meeting of the American Psychological Association, Los Angeles.

Lipari v. Sears Roebuck, 497 F. Supp. 185 (D. Neb. 1980).

Lloyd, A. P. (1987). Multicultural counseling: Does it belong in a counselor education program? *Counselor Education and Supervision, 26*, 164–167.

Loftus, E. F. (1993). The reality of repressed memories. *American Psychologist, 48*(5), 518–537.

Loftus, E. F. (1994). The repressed memory controversy. *American Psychologist, 49*, 409–420.

Loiacano, D. K. (1989). Gay identity issues among Black Americans: Racism, homophobia, and the need for validation. *Journal of Counseling and Development, 68*, 21–25.

Lum, D. (1986). *Social work practice and people of color: A process-stage approach.* New York: Macmillan.

Lyman, B. J., Storm, C. L., & York, C. D. (1995). Rethinking assumptions about trainees' life experience. *Journal of Marital and Family Therapy, 21*(2), 193–203.

Malley, P. B., Kush, F., & Bogo, R. J. (1994). School-based adolescent suicide prevention and intervention programs: A survey. *The School Counselor, 42*(2), 130–136.

Marecek, J. (1987). Counseling adolescents with problem pregnancies. *American Psychologist, 42*(1), 89–93.

Margolin, G. (1982). Ethical and legal considerations in marital and family therapy. *American Psychologist, 37*, 788–801.

Markus, H. R., & Kitayama, S. (1991). Culture and the self: Implications for cognition, emotion, and motivation. *Psychological Review, 98*, 224–253.

Marlatt, A. (1985a). Cognitive factors in the relapse process. In G. A. Marlatt & J. R. Gordon (eds.), *Relapse prevention* (pp. 128–193). New York: Guilford.

Marlatt, A. (1985b). Relapse prevention: Theoretical rational and overview of the model. In G. A. Marlatt & J. R. Gordon (eds.), *Relapse prevention* (pp. 3–67). New York: Guilford.

Marlatt, G. A., Baer, J. S., & Larimer, M. (1995). Preventing alcohol abuse in college students: A harm-reduction approach. In G. M. Boyd, J. Howard, & R. A. Zucker (Eds.), *Alcohol problems among adolescents: Current directions in prevention research* (pp. 147–172). Hillsdale, NJ: Lawrence Erlbaum.

Marsiglio, W. (1993). Attitudes toward homosexual activity and gays as friends: A national survey of heterosexual 15- to 19-year-old males. *Journal of Sex Research, 30*, 12–17.

Martin, A. D., & Hetrick, E. S. (1988). The stigmatization of the gay and lesbian adolescent. *Journal of Homosexuality, 15*, 163–183.

Mathiasen, R. (1988). Evaluating suicidal risk in the college student. *NASPA Journal, 25*, 257–261.

May, R. (1967). *Psychology and the human dilemma*. Princeton, NJ: Van Nostrand.

McCarthy, P., Julakowski, D., & Kenfield, J. (1994). Clinical supervision practices of licensed psychologists. *Professional Psychology: Research and Practice, 25*, 177–181.

McCarthy, P., Sugden, S., Koker, M., Lamendola, F., Maurer, S., & Renninger, S. C. (1995). A practical guide to informed consent in clinical supervision. *Counselor Education and Supervision 35*, 134–138.

McClellan, A. T. (1986). "Psychiatric severity" as a predictor of outcome from substance abuse treatments. In R. E. Meyer (Ed.), *Psychopathology and addictive disorders* (pp. 97–135). New York: Guilford.

McClellan, A. T., Luborsky, L., & Cacciola, M. A. (1985). New data from the *Addiction Severity Index*: Reliability and validity in three centers. *Journal of Nervous and Mental Disease, 173*(7), 36–47.

McCormick, R. A. (1989). *The critical calling: Reflections on moral dilemmas since Vatican II*. Washington, DC: Georgetown University Press.

McDermott, D., Tyndall, L., & Lichtenberg, J. W. (1989). Factors related to counselor preference among gays and lesbians. *Journal of Counseling and Development, 68,* 31–35.

McDonald v. State of Oregon, Children's Services Division, 694 P.2d 569 (Ore. Ct. App. 1985).

McNeill, B. W., Hom, K. L., & Perez, J. A. (1995). The training and supervisory needs of racial and minority students. *Journal of Multicultural Counseling, 23,* 246–258.

McRoy, R. G., Freeman, E. G., Logan, S. L., & Blackmon, B. (1986). Cross-cultural field supervision: Implications for social work education. *Journal of Social Work Education, 22,* 50–56.

Meara, N. M., Schmidt, L. D., & Day, J. D. (1996). Principles and virtues: A foundation for ethical decisions, policies, and character. *Counseling Psychologist, 24*(1), 4–77.

Mears, F., & Gatchel, R. J. (1979). *Fundamentals of abnormal psychology*. New York: Rand McNally.

Meissner, W. W., Mack, J. E., & Semrad, E. V. (1975). Theories of personality and psychopathy: I. Freudian school. In A. M. Fredman, H. I. Kaplan, & B. J. Sadock (Eds.), *Comprehensive textbook of psychiatry/II* (Vol. 1). Baltimore, MD: Williams & Wilkins.

Melton, G. B. (1987). Legal regulation of adolescent abortion: Unintended effects. *American Psychologist, 42*(1), 79–82.

Melton, G. B. (1991). Ethical judgments amid uncertainty: Dilemmas in the AIDS epidemic. *Counseling Psychologist, 19*(4), 561–565.

Menola, M. (1980). *The Menola report: A new look at gay couples*. New York: Crown.

Milkovich v. Lorain Journal Inc., 497 U.S. 1 (1990).

Mitchell, J., & Morse, J. (1997). *From victim to survivor: Women survivors of female perpetrators*. Muncie, IN: Accelerated Development.

Monahan, J. (1993, March). Limiting therapist exposure to *Tarasoff* liability: Guidelines for risk containment. *American Psychologist, 48,* 242–250.

Moore, T. (1992). *Care of the soul*. New York: HarperCollins.

Moore, T. (1994). *Soul mates*. New York: HarperCollins.

Moreno, J. L. (1962). Common ground for all group psychotherapists: What is a group psychotherapist? *Group Psychotherapy, 15,* 263–264.

Morra v. State Board of Examiners, 212 Kan. 103, 510 P.2d 614 (Kan., 1973).

Morrison, C. F. (1989). AIDS: Ethical implications for psychological intervention. *Professional Psychology: Research and Practice, 20*(3), 166–171.

Morrissey, M. (Ed.). (1997, March). Client bill of rights unveiled: ACA joins eight other professional organizations in joint health initiative. *Counseling Today, 1,* 1–2.

Morrow, S. L., & Hawthurst, D. M. (1989). Lesbian partner abuse: Implications for therapists. *Journal of Counseling and Development, 68,* 59–62.

Murphy, W., Rau, T., & Worley, P. (1994). Offender treatment: The perils and pitfalls of profiling child sex abusers. *APSAC Advisor, 7*(1) 3–4, 28–29.

Myers, F. B. (1991). When the parents are at war. How to get the child's side of the story. *Family Advocate, 14,* 36–48.

Myers, J.E.B. (1982). Legal issues surrounding psychotherapy with minors. *Clinical Social Work Journal. 10,* 303–314.

National Association of Social Workers. (1990). *Policy statement on HIV and AIDS clients*. East Lansing, MI: Author.

National Association of Social Workers. (1997). *Code of ethics*. East Lansing, MI: Author.

National Board for Certified Counselors. (1997). *Code of ethics.* Alexandria, VA: Author.

Nelson, E., & Crawford, B. L. (1990). Suicide among elementary school-aged children. *Elementary School Guidance and Counseling, 25*, 123–127.

Newman, J. L. (1993). Ethical issues in consultation. *Journal of Counseling and Development, 72*, 148–156.

Ney, P. G. (1987). Does verbal abuse leave deeper scars? A study of children and parents. *Canadian Journal of Psychiatry, 32*, 371–378.

Niles, F. S. (1993). Issues in multicultural education. *Journal of Multicultural Counseling, 21*, 14–21.

Norris, T. L. (1986, October). Victim therapy with adult survivors of child sexual abuse (Report No.CG020400). Paper presented at the annual conference of the American Association for Marriage and Family Therapy, Orlando, FL. (Eric Document Reproduction Service No. ED 289 133)

NOW Legal Defense and Education Fund Legal Resource Kit. (1994). *Issues Quarterly: An Intelligent Resource for Research, Policy, and Action Affecting the Lives of Women and Girls, 1*(1), p. 8. National Council for Research on Women.

O'Connor-Slimp, P. A., & Burian, B. K. (1994). Multiple role relationships and recommendations. *Professional Psychology Research and Practice, 25*(1), 39–45.

Olson, T. D., & Doherty, W. J. (1996). Soul searching: Why psychotherapy must promote moral responsibilities. *Journal of Marital and Family Therapy, 22*(3), 411–412.

Orlinsky, D. E., & Howard, K. I. (1986). Process and outcome in psychotherapy. In S. L. Garfield & A. E. Bergin (Eds.)., *Handbook of psychotherapy and behavior change* (pp. 311–381). New York: Wiley.

Orpinas, P., Kedler, S., Murray, N., Tourney, A., Conroy, F., McReynolds, L., & Peters, R., Jr. (1990). Critical issues in implementing a comprehensive violence prevention program for middle schools: Translating theory into practice. *Education and Urban Society, 24*(4), 456–472.

Orvaschel, H. (1993). *Social functioning and social supports: A review of measurers suitable for use with substance abusers.* Washington, DC: National Institute on Drug Abuse, U.S. Department of Health and Human Services.

Paridies v. Benedictine Hospital, 431 N.Y.S.2d 175 (APP.Div. 1980).

Pate, R. H., Jr., & Bondi, A. M. (1992). Religious beliefs and practice: An integral aspect of multicultural awareness. *Counselor Education and Supervision, 32,* 108–115.

Pate, R. H. (1992, Summer). Are you liable? *American Counselor, 10,* 23.

Patrick, K. (1989). Unique ethical dilemmas in counselor training. *Counselor Education and Supervision, 28,* 337–341.

Peach, L., & Reddick, T. L. (1991). Counselors can make a difference in preventing adolescent suicide. *The School Counselor, 39,* 207–217.

Pearson, Q. M. (1994). Treatment techniques for adult survivors of childhood sexual abuse. *Journal of Counseling and Development, 73,* 32–37.

Peck v. the Counseling Service of Addison County, 499 A.2d 422 (1985).

Pedersen, P. B. (1986). *Are the APA ethical principles culturally encapsulated?* Unpublished manuscript, Syracuse University, NY.

Pedersen, P. B. (1991). Multiculturalism as a generic approach to counseling. *Journal of Counseling and Development, 70,* 6–12.

Pedersen, P. B., & Marsella, A. J. (1982). The ethical crisis for cross-cultural counseling and therapy. *Professional Psychology, 13*(4), 492–500.

Pesce v. J. Sterling Morton High School District, 830 F.2d 789 (7th Cir. 1987).

Philips, I. (1983). Childhood depression: Interpersonal interactions and depressive phenomena. *American Journal of Psychiatry, 136,* 511–515.

Piaget, J. (1926). *The language and thoughts of the child.* London: Kegan Paul.

Pines, A., & Aronson, E., with Katry, D. (1981). *Burnout: From tedium to personal growth.* New York: Free Press.

Poland, S. (1990). *Suicide intervention in the schools*. New York: Guilford.

Ponterotto, J. G., Alexander, C. M., & Grieger, I. (1995). A multicultural competency checklist for counseling training programs. *Journal of Multicultural Counseling, 23*, 11–20.

Pope, K. S. (1985). Dual relationships: A violation of ethical, legal, and clinical standards. *California State Psychologist, 20*(3), 1–4.

Pope, K. S. (1989). Malpractice suits, licensing, disciplinary actions, and ethic cases: Frequencies, causes, and costs. *Independent Practitioner, 9*(1), 22–26.

Pope, K. S., & Bouhoutsos, J. C. (1985). *Sexual intimacy between therapists and patients*. New York: Praeger.

Pope, K. S., Keith-Spiegel, P., & Tabachnick, B. G. (1986). Sexual attraction to clients: The human therapist and the sometimes inhuman training system. *American Psychologist, 41*(2), 147–158.

Preli, R., & Bernard, J. M. (1993). Making multiculture relevant for majority culture graduate students. *Journal of Marital and Family Therapy, 19*(1), 5–16.

Prest, L., & Keller, J. (1993). Spirituality and family therapy: Spiritual beliefs, myths, and metaphors. *Journal of Marital and Family Therapy, 19*, 137–148.

Pulvino, C. J., & Sanborn, M. P. (1972). Feedback and accountability. *Personnel and Guidance Journal, 51*(1), 15–20.

Ratzinger, J. (1986). *Letter to the bishops of the Catholic church on the pastoral care of homosexual persons*. Rome: Vatican Congregation for the Doctrine of the Faith.

Ray, O., & Ksir, C. (1990). *Drugs, society, and human behavior*. Newport Beach, CA: Times Mirror/Mosby.

Rencken, R. H. (1989). Intervention strategies for sexual abuse (Report No. CG022806). Alexandria, VA: American Association for Counseling and Development (ERIC Document Reproduction Service No. ED 323 483).

Repressed memory claims expected to soar. (1995, May). *National Psychologist, 4*(3), 3.

Rest, J. R. (1983). Morality. In J. F. Flavel & E. M. Markham (Eds.), *Handbook of child psychology: Vol. 3. Cognitive development* (pp. 556–620). New York: Wiley.

Rich, K. (1988). *A duty to take reasonable care: An analysis of health care professionals' responses to selected case studies.* Unpublished doctoral dissertation, University of Pittsburgh.

Ridgeway, I. R., & Sharpley, C. F. (1990). Empathic interactional sequences and counselor trainee effectiveness. *Counseling Psychology Quarterly, 3*(3), 257–265.

Ritter, K. Y., & O'Neil, C. W. (1989). Moving through loose: The spiritual journey of gay men and lesbian woman. *Journal of Counseling and Development, 68*, 9–14.

Robbins, R. H. (1959) *The encyclopedia of witchcraft and demonology.* New York: Crown.

Rogers, C. R. (1961). *On becoming a person.* Boston: Houghton Mifflin.

Rogers, C. R. (1980). *A way of being.* Boston: Houghton Mifflin.

Rosario, M., Rotheram-Borus, M. J., & Reid, H. (1992). *Personal resources, gay-related stress, and multiple problem behaviors among gay and bisexual male adolescents.* Unpublished manuscript, Columbia University, NY.

Rosenberg, M. L., Smith, J. C., Davidson, L. E., & Conn, J. M. (1987). The emergence of youth suicide: An epidemiological analysis and public health perspective. *Annual Review of Public Health, 8*, 417–440.

Rotheram-Borus, M. J., Rosario, M., & Koopman, C. (1991). Minority youths at high risk: Gay males and runaways. In M. E. Colten & S. Gore (Eds.), *Adolescent stress: Causes and consequences.* (pp. 181–200). New York: Alsine.

Rowell, L. L., McBride, M. C., & Leaf, J. N. (1996). The role of the school counselor in confronting peer sexual harassment. *The School Counselor, 43*, 196–205.

Roy, A. (1982). Risk factors for suicide in psychiatric patients. *Archives of General Psychiatry, 39*, 1089–1095.

Rutter, P. (1989). Sex in the forbidden zone. *Psychology Today, 23*(10), 34–38.

Sandoval, J. (1985). Crisis counseling: Conceptualization and general principles. *School Psychology Review, 14,* 257–265.

Sanford, L. T. (1980). *The silent children: A parent's guide to the prevention of child sexual abuse.* Garden City, NY: Doubleday.

Savin-Williams, R. C. (1994). Verbal and physical abuse as stressors in the lives of lesbian, gay male, and bisexual youths: Associations with school problems, running away, substance abuse, prostitution, and suicide. *Journal of Consulting and Clinical Psychology, 62,* 261–269.

Schlossberger, E., & Heckler, L. (1996). HIV and the family therapist's duty to warn: A legal and ethical analysis. *Journal of Marital and Family Therapy, 22*(1), 27–40.

Schroeder, L. O. (1979). Legal liability: A professional concern. *Clinical Social Work Journal, 7*(3), 194–199.

Schwitzgebel, R. L., & Schwitzgebel, R. K. (1980). *Law and psychological practice.* New York: Wiley.

Scott, K. (1995). Seventy-five years later: Gender-based harassment in the schools. *Social Education, 50*(5), 293–297.

Seigel, D. L., Hallgarth, S. A., & Capek, M. E. (1992). *Sexual harassment: Research and resources.* New York: National Council for Research on Women.

Seppa, N. (1996, April). Fear of malpractice curbs some psychologists' practice. *American Psychological Monitor, 2,* 129–137.

Sheeley, V. L., & Herlihy, B. (1989). Counseling suicidal teens: A duty to warn and protect. *The School Counselor, 37,* 89–101.

Shertzer, B., & Stone, S. C. (1980). *Fundamentals of counseling.* Boston: Houghton Mifflin.

Shibutani, T., & Kwan, K. M. (1965). *Ethnic stratification.* New York: Macmillan.

Shields, C. G., Wynne, L. C., McDaniel, S. H., & Gawinski, B. A. (1994). The marginalization of family therapy: A historical and continuing problem. *Journal of Marital and Family Therapy, 20,* 117–138.

Simon, J. M. (1996). Pathways to prejudice: Predicting students' heterosexist attitudes with demographics, self-esteem, and contact with lesbians and gay men. *Journal of College Student Development, 37*, 68–78.

Skinner, H. A. (1982). *The drug abuse screening test–20 (DAST–20): Guidelines for administering and scoring.* Toronto: Addiction Research Foundation.

Sloan, I. J. (1983). *Child abuse: Governing law and legislation.* Dobbs Ferry, NY: Oceana.

Smith, D. (1982). Trends in counseling and psychotherapy. *American Psychologist, 37*(7), 802–809.

Smith, S. R. (1994). Liability and mental health services. *American Journal of Orthopsychiatry, 64*(2), 235–251.

Sowers v. Bradford Area School District, 694 F. Supp. 125 (W.D. Pa 1988).

Spiller, N. (1988). Bad vibrations. *Los Angeles Times Magazine, 4*(25), 8–15.

Stanton, M. D. (1991). Strategic approaches to family therapy. In A. Gurman & D. Kniskern (Eds.), *Handbook of family therapy* (pp. 361–402). New York: Brunner/Mazel.

State v. Freitag (1986). (unreported, Dist. Ct., Wake County, N.C., 1986). *School Law Bulletin, 17*(2), 46–47.

Stone, L. (1980). *A study of the relationship among female patients' vulnerability to sexual involvement with their male therapists.* Unpublished doctoral dissertation, California School of Professional Psychology, Los Angles.

Strother, D. B. (1986). Suicide among the very young. *Phi Delta Kappan, 67*, 756–759.

Sue, D. W. (1991). A conceptual model for cultural diversity training. *Journal of Counseling and Development, 70*, 99–105.

Sue, D. W., Arredondo, P., & McDavis, R. J. (1992). Multicultural counseling competencies and standards: A call to the profession. *Journal of Multicultural Counseling and Development, 20*, 64–88.

Swenson, L. C. (1997). *Psychology and law for the helping professions.* Pacific Grove, CA: Brooks/Cole.

Tarasoff v. Regents of the University of California, 113 Cal. Rptr. 14, 551 P.2d. 334 (Cal. 1976).

Tarasoff v. Regents of the University of California, 13 Cal.3d 177, 529 P.2d 533 (1974), vacated, 17 Cal.3d 425, 551 P.2d 334 (1976).

Tarvydas, V. M. (1995). Ethics and the practice of rehabilitation counselor supervision. *Rehabilitation Counseling Bulletin, 38*, 294–306.

Thompson v. County of Alameda, 614 P.2d 728 (1980).

Tranel, D. (1994). The release of psychological data to non-experts: Ethical and legal considerations. *Professional Psychology: Research and Practice, 25*, 33–37.

Trimble, J. (1981). Value differences and their importance in counseling American Indians. In P. Pedersen et al. (Eds.), *Counseling across cultures* (pp. 203–226). Honolulu: University of Hawaii Press.

Tueting, P., Koslow, S. H., & Hirschfield, R.M.A. (1983). *National Institute of Mental Health: Special report on depression research* (DHHS Publication No. ADM 83–1085). Washington, DC: Government Printing Office.

Tuma, J. M. (1989). Mental health services for children: The state of the art. *American Psychologist, 44*(2), 188–189.

U.S. Department of Health and Human Services. (1990). *Healthy people 2000: National health promotion and disease prevention objectives* (DHHS Publication No. PHS 91–50213). Washington, DC: Government Printing Office.

United States Bureau of the Census. (1992). *Population projections for the United States by age, sex, race, and Hispanic origin: 1992 to 2050.* Washington, DC: CENDATA.

VandeCreek, L., & Knapp, S. (1993). *Tarasoff and beyond: Legal considerations in the treatment of life-endangering patients* (revised ed.). Sarasota, FL: Professional Resource Press.

VandenBos, G. R. (1993). U.S. mental health policy: Proactive evolution in the midst of health care reform. *American Psychologist, 48*, 283–290.

Vasquez, M.J.T. (1996). Will virtue ethics improve ethical conduct in multicultural settings and interactions. *Counseling Psychologist, 24*(1), 98–104.

Vasquez, M. J., & McKinley, D. (1982). Supervision: A conceptual model— reactions and extension. *Counseling Psychologist, 10*(1), 59–63.

Waldo, S., & Malley, P. B. (1992). *Tarasoff* and its progeny: Implications for school counselors. *The School Counselor, 40*, 56–63.

Wallace, B. (1991). *Crack cocaine.* New York: Brunner/ Mazel.

Walters, K. L., & Simon, J. M. (1993). Lesbian and gay male group identity attitudes and self-esteem: implications for counseling. *Journal of Counseling Psychology, 40*, 94–99.

Water, Barbara v. Bourhis, *R., et al.,* 40 Cal. 3d 424, 220 Cal. Rptr. 666 (Cal. Supreme Ct., 1986).

Weikel, W. J. (1986). The expanding role of the counselor as a vocational expert witness. *Journal of Counseling and Development, 64*, 523–524.

Weinstock, R., & Weinstock, D. (1989). Clinical flexibility and confidentiality: Effects of reporting laws. *Psychiatric Quarterly, 60*(3), 195–214.

Weisman v. Blue Shield of California, 163 CAL. App. 3d61, 209 CAL. Rptr. 169 (CAL., ct. app., 1985).

Weissman, N. H. (1984). Psychological assessment and psycho–legal formulations in psychiatric traumatology. *Psychiatric Annals, 14*(7), 517–529.

Welch, B. L. (1996). *Holding managed care accountable: The irony of malpractice.* Webmaster Marian Benjamin. Copyright 1995–1996. CME Incorporated.

Welfel, E. (1992). Psychologist as ethics educator: Successes, failures, and unanswered questions. *Professional Psychology: Research and Practice, 23*, 182–189.

West, C. E. (1996). Spiritual wellness and depression. *Journal of Counseling and Development, 75*, 26–35.

Westefeld, J. S., Whitchard, K. A., & Range, L. M. (1990). College and university student suicide: Trends and implications. *Counseling Psychologist, 18*(3), 464–476.

Westgate, C. E, (1996). Spiritual wellness and depression. *Journal of Counseling and Development, 75,* 26–35.

Whitaker, C. A., & Miller, M. H. (1969). A reevaluation of psychiatric help when divorce impends. *American Journal of Psychiatry, 126,* 56–64.

White, M. B., & Russell, C. S. (1995) The essential elements of supervision: A modified delphi study. *Journal of Marital and Family Therapy, 21*(1), 33–53.

White, R. W. (1964) *The abnormal personality.* The Ronald Press Company. USA.

Whiteside, R. G. (1993). Making a referral for family therapy: The school counselor's role. *Elementary School Guidance and Counseling, 27,* 273–279.

Whitfield, D. (1994). Toward an integrated approach to improving multicultural education. *Journal of Multicultural Education 22,* 239–252.

Whiting, R. A. (1995). Natural law and the right to die. *Omega, 1*(32), 11–26.

Wickline v State, 228 Cal. Rptr. 661 (Cal. App. 2Dist., 1986).

Wiggins, J. D. (1985) Six steps toward counseling program accountability. *NASSP Bulletin, 69*(485), 28–31.

Wiggins-Frame, M., & Stevens-Smith, P. (1995). Out of harm's way: Enhancing monitoring and dismissal processes in counselor education. *Counselor Education and Supervision, 35,* 118–129.

Wilson, B. G., & Masson, R. L. (1986). The role of touch in therapy: An adjunct to communication. *Journal of Counseling and Development, 64*(8). 497–500.

Wilson, C. (1991). *The occult.* New York: Random House.

Wise, P. S., Smead, V. S., & Huebner, E. S. (1987). Crisis intervention: Involvement and training needs of school psychology personnel. *Journal of School Psychology, 25,* 185–187.

Wood, G. J., Marks, R., & Dilley, J. (1990). *AIDS law for mental health professionals.* San Francisco: University of California AIDS Health Project.

Worthington, E. L. (1984). Empirical investigation of supervision of counselors as they gain experience. *Journal of Counseling Psychology, 31*, 63–75.

Yarmey, A. D., & Jones, H.P.T. (1983). Is the psychology of eye witness testimony a matter of common sense? In S. M. Lloyd-Bostock & B. R. Clifford (Eds.), *Evaluating witness evidence* (pp. 323–339). New York: Wiley.

Zehlen, S. L., Sonne, J., Meyer, C., Borys, D., & Marshall, V. (1985, April). Clients' reaction to sexual intimacy in therapy. *American Journal of Orthopsychiatry, 4,* 183–188.

Zerbe Enns, C. (1996). Counselors and the backlash: "Rape hype" and "false memory syndrome." *Journal of Counseling and Development, 74*, 358–366.

Zipkin v. Freeman. 436 S.W. 2d 753 (Missouri, 1968).

INDEX

A

Abortion, 204–205
Addiction Severity Index, 214
Addiction: see Substance abuse
Adler, A., 7, 239–240
Adlerian therapy, 8, 239–240
Advertising, 70–71
Agency for Health Care Policy &
  Research, 208
AIDS, 16, 146–153
  legal & ethical issues, 147–150
  learning facilitation, 152–153
Alcalay, R., 178
Alexander, C. M., 107
Alexander, P. C., 160
Allen, D. L., 83
Allsopp, A., 160, 229
Alpert, J. L., 191
Amer. Assn. for Marriage & Family
  Therapy, 210, 239, 261, 266, 267
  on advertising, 71
  on dual relationships, 169, 170, 270
  on suicide, 115
American Civil Liberties Union, 204

Amer. Counseling Assn., 210, 248,
  271
  on advertising, 71
  on assessment, 78, 196–197
  on clients with AIDS, 146
  on confidentiality, 246
  on counselor competence, 244
  on dual relationships, 169, 170
  on referrals, 72
  on releasing raw data, 199
  on research with humans, 284
  on setting fees, 73
  on suicide, 116
  on test scores, 200
Amer. Family Therapy Assn., 210
Amer. Group Psychotherapy Assn.,
  210
Amer. Medical Assn., 147, 207, 290
Amer. Nurses' Assn., 210
Amer. Psychiatric Assn., 6
  on clients with AIDS, 148
Amer. Psychiatric Nurses' Assn.,
  210

Amer. Psychoanalytic Assn., 210
Amer. Psychological Assn., 5, 45,
    100, 210, 290, 277, 278
  on advertising, 70
  on assessment, 196, 198
  on clients with AIDS, 148
  on consulting, 196
  on counselor competence, 245
  on dual relationships, 169, 170–
    171
  on referrals, 72
  on releasing raw data, 199
  on setting fees, 73
  on suicide, 115
  on test scores, 200
  Task Force on Sex Bias and Sex-
    Role Stereotyping, 263–264
Amer. School Counselor Assn., 122,
    225, 226–227
  on suicide, 115
Anderson, D. A., 187, 190
Annell, A. L., 120
Aponte, H. J., 269
Aponte, J. F., 98
Applebaum, P. S., 134, 135–136,
    138–139, 210
Aristotle, 27
Aronson, E., 79
Arredondo, P. M., 95, 200
Assessment
  dangerous clients, 135–138
  in consulting, 196–198
  substance abuse, 214
  suicide, 117
  validity, 197
Assn. for Counselor Education &
    Supervision, 278
Assn. for Specialists in Group Work,
    291
  Ethical Guidelines, 247–258
Atcherson, E., 77
Ausdale, D. V., 105–106

Austin, K. M., 195
Autonomy, 26, 30–44
Axelson, J. A., 96

B

Baer, J. S., 213
Banning, A., 161
Barlow, D., 208
Barrett, T., 121
Barron, F., 114
Barth, F., 96
Baruth, L. G., 25, 261, 265, 266
Bauer, G. B., 114
Baxter, A., 160, 162
Beauchamp, T. L., 25, 26, 27, 113
Beck, A., 213
Bednar, R. L., 69, 80, 116, 282, 283
Bednar, S. C., 69, 80, 116, 282, 283
Behavioral therapy, 8, 14, 166, 189,
    241–242
Being sued, 73, 85
Belote, B., 173
Beneficence, 27, 30–44
Benner, D. G., 187
Berenson, D., 187, 192
Bergin, A. E., 188
Berman, A. L., 114
Bernard, J., 96, 102–103, 277, 279,
    281
Bersoff, D. H., 46
Besharov, D. J., 155, 156, 228
Beutler, L. E., 278, 280
Bickhard, M. H., 189
Blackmon, B., 103
Bogo, R. J., 310
Bondi, A. M., 187
Bongar, B., 114
Bonilla, L., 176
Borders, I. D., 278, 280
Borenstein, D. B., 208
Borys, D. S., 75, 170, 173
Boszormenyi-Nagy, I., 262

Bouhoutsos, J. C., 169, 172, 173, 174, 175, 281
Bowman, J. T., 9
Boylan, J. C., 193, 205
Bradley, D. F., 229
Bradley, R., 269
Brainer, C. J., 164
Brammer, L. M., 14–15
Brandse, E., 164
Brandt, L. M., 229
Brassard, M. R., 158
Bray, J. H., 265
Briere, J., 166
Brodsky, A., 172
Bromberg, W., 5
Bross, A., 161
Bross, D. C., 159
Brown, D., 194–195, 196
Brown, J. H., 266
Buckley, J., 157
Buckner, S., 295
Bukstein, O. G., 215
Burck, H. D., 227
Burian, B. K., 278
Burnout, 79–80
Butler, S., 160, 173

C
Cacciola, M. A., 214
Callahan, T., 128
Callanan, P., 15, 79
Cannon, G., 121
Capek, M. E., 230
Caplan, G., 193–194
Capuzzi, D., 121
Carballo-Dieguez, A., 182
Carmen, S. J., 277
Carpenter-White, A., 270–271
Caudill, B., 167
Celotta, B., 121
Chaffin, M., 157
Chan, C. S., 179–180, 181, 183

Chandler, C. K., 188
Chauvin, J. C., 172–173
Cheatham, H. E., 101
Chemtob, C. M., 114
Cherniss, C., 281
Child abuse, 155–164
  adult survivors, 165–168
  and spirituality, 190–191
  interviewing children, 162–164
  reporting, 83, 84, 155, 156–157
  school counselors, 228–229
Child Protective Services Law Act of 1975, 296
Childress, J. F. , 25, 26, 27
Christensen, D. N., 266
Christopher, J. C., 188, 189–190, 200
Claims-made insurance policies, 79
Client records, 75–77
Client-centered therapy, 7, 189
Closen, M. L., 152
Cochran, F. R., 118
Cognitive behavioral therapy, 8, 166, 189
Cohen, E. D., 149
Cohen-Sandler, R., 114
Cole, K. M., 229–230
Cole, S. S., 165
Coleman, E., 171, 175
Colucci, N. D., 158
Computers, 77–78
Confidentiality, 14, 82, 88, 211
  child abuse, 156
  clients with AIDS, 146–151
  dangerous clients, 138–146
  in family counseling, 264–265
  in groups, 246–247, 250–251
  in schools, 226–227
Conn, J. M., 121
Connell, H. M., 120
Conroy, F., 231
Conroy, M., 188

Consulting, 193–202, 256–257
ethical issues, 195–196
Cook, D. A., 105
Cooksey, D. R., 302
Cooper, C. L., 177
Corbett, M. M., 280
Corey, G., 15, 79, 242–243, 246, 280
Corey, M. S., 15, 79
Cormier, L. S., 14
Cottingham, H. F., 283
Council of University Directors of
Clinical Psychology, 114
Council on Ethical and Judicial
Affairs, Amer. Medical Assn., 297
Counselor competence, 243–246
multicultural skills, 101–107
Cox, M., 209
Crabbs, M. A., 297
Crawford, B. L., 114
Credentials, 282–283
Culture, 96
and spirituality, 188–190
and virtue, 44–45
influence on test scores, 199–200

D
D'Augelli, A. R., 178, 179
Dangerous clients, 133–145
assessing risk, 135–138
learning facilitation, 139–145
Tarasoff case, 133–135
Darton, N., 166
Davidson, L. E., 121
Davis, A., 283
Davis, J. M., 121
Davis, R., 7, 309
Davis, S. F., 7, 309
Davis, T., 226, 227
Day, J. D., 45
Defamation of character, 69
Delarosa, R., 150
Depression, 7, 120 , 191–192

DeStefano, A. M., 178
Deutsch, C. J., 79, 114
Deutsch, P. M., 83
*Diagnostic and Statistical Manual of
Mental Disorders*, 6, 178
Diamond, A. L., 266
Dickens, B. M., 147
DiGiuseppe R., 213
Dilley, J., 149
Dixon, W. A., 117
Doherty, W. J., 259, 260
Dorland, D., 75
Dorn, F., 84
Dorwart, R. A., 208
Dreukers, R., 240
Drug Abuse Screening Test–20, 214
Dual relationships, 74–75, 168–177,
270, 281
in groups, 255–256
Duncan, J., 270
Durkheim, E., 7
Duty to warn, 82, 133–145, 146–153
Duty-to-report statutes, 84, 156–157,
228–229

E
Eddy, W. B., 238
Edel, A., 45
Egnatios, E., 281
Ehrenwald, J., 3, 4–5
Eisen, S. V., 121
Eisenberg, L., 121
Ellenberger, H. F., 4
Ellis., A., 213
Elwork, A. E., 203
Emery, G. D., 213
Emery, R. E., 160, 266
Erickson, E. L., 7, 158
Erickson, L., 229
Ernst, P. A., 178
Essandoh, P. K., 97, 98, 101
Etherington, K., 161

Ethical codes, 25–26, 225
  criticisms, 99–100
  on advertising, 70–71
  on assessment, 78, 196–197
  on clients with AIDS, 148–149
  on consulting, 196
  on dual relationships, 169-171
  on fees, 73
  on referrals, 72
  on releasing raw data, 199
  on suicide, 115–116
  on test scores, 200–201
Ethical issues, 25–62
  clients with AIDS, 147–150
  consulting, 195–196
  dilemmas, 30–44
  genograms, 270–271
  guidelines for groups, 247–258
  learning facilitation, 30–44, 47–62
  managed care, 207–208
  research with humans, 283–285
  suicidal clients, 115–116
  training, 277–278, 279
*Ethical Standards for School
  Counselors* (ASCA), 225
Ethnicity, 96
  and homosexuality, 179–181
Evaluation, 257–258
Evans, S., 166
Existential therapy, 8, 14, 190, 240–241
Expert witnesses, 84

F
Fairchild, T., 227
Falik, M., 208
False Memory Syndrome, 166–168
  Foundation, 167
Family counseling, 8, 189, 261–273
  biases, 263–264
  confidentiality, 264–265
  informed consent, 265

  learning facilitation, 272–273
  privileged information, 264
  training issues, 265–271
Family Educational Rights and
  Privacy Act, 228
Fannibanda, D. K., 196
Farber, B. A., 79
Feagin, J. R., 105–106
Federal Child Abuse Prevention and
  Treatment Act, 156
Fee-splitting, 72–73, 86–87
Fees, 72–73, 89
Fidelity, 27, 29, 30–44
Fieldsteel. N., 263
Finkelhor, D., 160
Fitzgerald, K., 280
Flower, E., 45
Fong-Beyette, M. L., 166
Forer, B. R., 169
Forester-Miller, H., 270
Forge, J. L., 83
Forrest, G. G., 213
Frances, R. J., 213
Francis, R. A., 178
Frankl, V., 187
Freed, D. L., 202, 265
Freeman, E. G., 103
Freeman, L., 74
Fremouw, W., 128
Freud, S., 7, 8, 10, 161, 239, 241
Friedman, J. T., 84
Fritz, B. R., 283
Frome, M. W., 262
Fromm, E., 7
Fromuth, M. E., 160
Fujimura, L. E., 118
Fulero, S. M., 150
Fuqua, K., 195

G
*Gallagher's National Survey of
  Counseling Center Directors*, 128

Galvin, M. D., 80
Ganje–Fling, M. A., 187, 188, 190
Garbarino, J., 158
Gargiulo, R., 155
Gatchel R. J., 4
Gawinski, B. A., 239, 261
General Accounting Office, 155
Genograms, 268–271
Germain, R., 158
Gersick, K. E., 196
Gestalt therapy, 8, 166, 189, 242
Getz, H., 269
Gilchrist, R., 187
Gilligan, C., 28, 29
Gilliland, B. E., 9
Girardi, J. A., 302
Glantz, T. M., 165
Glaser, R. D., 281
Gold, S., 133
Goldberg, H., 263
Goldberg, I., 263
Golden, L., 123, 171
Goldman, R., 155
Goodman, R. W., 270, 271
Goodwin, D. W., 213
Goodyear, R. K., 279, 281
Gray, E. A., 149
Gray, L. A., 147
Green, R. J., 269
Greenberg, M., 169
Grieger, I., 107, 178
Griffin, R., 178
Grob, M. C., 121
Groth, A. N., 161
Group counseling, 235–259
  confidentiality, 245–246
  ethical guidelines, 246–257
  leading, 241–245
  learning facilitation, 258–259
  privileged information, 246
  theories, 237–240
Guest, P. D., 278, 280

H

Hackney, H. C., 14
Hall, G. S., 6, 245
Hall, R., 83
Hallgarth, S. A., 230
Hamada, R. S., 114
Hamilton-Usher, C., 280
Handelsman, M. M., 80
Harding, A. K., 147, 149–150
Hardy, K. V., 269
Hare-Mustin, R., 264, 265
Harmatz, M., 114
Harrar, W. R., 278, 279
Harris, S. M., 277, 288
Hart, S. N., 157
Hass, L. J., 70, 82
Hauerwas, S., 30, 46
Haugaard, J. J., 159
Hawthurst, D. M., 178
Hays, J. R., 265
Heckler, L., 151, 151, 152
Heiden, J. M., 174–175
Helms, J. E., 105
Henderson, P., 83
Heppner, M. J., 104–105
Heppner, P. P., 117
Hepworth, 261
Herek, G. M., 178
Herlihy, B., 121, 170
Hetherington, C., 182–183
Hetrick, E. S., 178
Hill, C. E., 280
Hillman, D., 160, 229
Hinterkopf, E., 187
Hippocrates, 4–5, 10
Hippocratic Oath, 27, 75
Hirsch, H., 69
Hirschfield, R.M.A., 120
Hoffman, M. A., 152
Hogan, D. B., 283
Holroyd, J., 169, 171, 172
Hom, K. L., 103

Homosexual clients, 96, 178–185
  ethnic minorities, 178, 179–181
  learning facilitation, 184–185
Hood, G., 166
Horowitz, I. A., 64
Howard, K. I., 280
Hrabowy, I., 159
Huber, C. H., 265
Huber, H. H., 25, 261, 265, 266
Huebner, E. S., 121
Humanistic therapy, 238–239
Humpreys, H. C., 84
Hunt, B., 165
Hypnotherapy, 166, 168

I

Ibrahim, F. A., 100, 200
Illingworth, P.M.L., 169, 177
Incest, 160–164, 165–168
Information release, 81–82
Informed consent, 80–81, 283–284
  forms, 84–85, 90–91, 227
  marriage/family counseling, 265
Ingersoll, R. E., 187
Institute of Medicine, 208
Interpreting test scores, 199–201
  cultural influences, 200–201
Interrupted therapy, 75
Isaacman, S. H., 151
Ivey, A. E., 16, 98, 99
Ivey, M. B., 98

J

Jacobson, N. S., 262
James, R. K., 9
James, W., 6, 7
Jones, H.P.T., 162
Jordan, A. E., 45, 46
Josephson, G. S., 166
Julakowski, D., 278
Jung, C. G., 187
Justice, 27, 28–29, 30–44

K

Kagan, N., 8
Kahn-Edrington, M., 205
Kane, S., 83, 125
Kashden, J., 128
Katry, D., 315
Kaufman, J., 157
Kazdin, A. E., 203
Kedler, S., 301
Keene, K. M., 227
Keene-Osborn, S., 166
Keese, R. M., 302
Keeton, R., 83, 125
Keith-Spiegel, P., 73, 74, 172, 226
Keller, J., 188
Kelly, J. B., 266
Kelly, K., 147, 149
Kempe, C. H., 160, 229
Kempe, R. S., 159, 229
Kenfield, J., 278
Kermani, E. J., 149
Keys, S. S., 121
Kilburg, R., 246
Kilpatrick, A. C., 160
Kinney, B., 114
Kitayama, S., 200
Kitchener, K. S., 26, 47
Klein, A. A., 121
Klein, C., 178
Kluckhohn, C.K.M., 97, 108
Knapp, S., 134–135, 147, 168, 278
Kohlberg, L., 28–29
Kohn, A., 158–159
Koker, M., 279
Kolander, C. A., 188
Koocher, G. P., 73, 74, 226
Koop, C. E., 231
Koopman, C., 317
Korn, J. H., 7
Koslow, S. H., 120
Kraepelin, E., 6
Kramer, J., 269

Krug, R. S., 161
Ksir, C., 316
Kuehnel, F. M., 242
Kurpius, D., 195
Kush, F. R., 121
Kwan, K. M., 96

L

Ladnay, N., 280
Lambert, M. J., 69
Lamendola, F., 279
Lamson, A., 309
Landesman, S. H., 149
Larimer, M., 213
Lasko, C. A., 120
Laszloffy, T. A., 269
Laws, 63–66, 80, 280–281
Lawson, C., 161–162
Lawsuits; see also Malpractice
  Bellotti v. Baird, 203
  Boynton v. Burglass, 135
  Carlino v. State, 117
  Comiskey v. State of New York, 117
  Commissioner of Corp. of Califor-
    nia v. TakeCare Health Plan, 209
  Dalton v. State, 117, 298
  Eisel v. Board of Education, 226
  Farrow v. Health Service Corp., 68,
    116–117
  Gault v. U.S. Supreme Court, 199
  Gross v. Prudential Health Care
    Plan, 209
  Hedlund v. Superior Court of
    Orange County, 135
  Huges v. Blue Cross of Northern
    California, 210
  Jablonski v. United States, 135
  Kelson v. City of Springfield, 226
  Kirkorian v. Barry, 228
  Larry P. v. Riles, 199–200
  Lipari v. Sears Roebuck, 135
  McDonald v. State of Oregon, 228
  Milkovich v. Lorain Journal, 69
  Morra v. State Board of Examiners,
    171
  Paridies v. Benedictine Hospital,
    117
  Peck v. the Counseling Service of
    Addison County, 135
  Pesce v. J. Sterling Morton High
    School District, 229
  Roe v. Wade, 204
  Sowers v. Bradford Area School
    District, 229
  State v. Freitag, 229
  Tarasoff v. Regents of the University
    of California, 117, 133–135, 151,
    153
  Thompson v. County of Alameda,
    135
  Walter, Barbara v. Bourhis, 171
  Weisman v. Blue Shield of Califor-
    nia, 73
  Wickline v. State, 208–209
  Zipkin v. Freeman, 281
Leaf, J. N., 230
Learning facilitation and focus
  abortion, 206–207
  child abuse, 164–165
  clients with AIDS, 153–154
  consulting, 200–202
  dual relationships, 177
  ethical dilemmas, 30–44
  group counseling, 259–260
  helping context, 19–21
  historical, 10–11
  homosexual clients, 184–185
  incest survivors, 168
  legal issues, 86–91
  managed care, 212–213
  marriage/family therapy, 272–273
  multicultural counseling, 110–111
  school counseling, 233–245
  spirituality, 193

substance abuse, 219–221
suicidal clients, 131–135
training, 286–288
virtue ethics scale, 47–62
Leaving a group, 252–253
Liberman, R. P., 242
Leddick, G. R., 278
Legal issues, 63–91, 279
  clients with AIDS, 151–152
  learning facilitation, 86–91
  malpractice, 68–69
  marriage/family counseling, 266
  sexual intimacy with clients, 171
  special relationship, 66–68, 70–85
  suicidal clients, 116–117
Leigh, G., 213, 264
Lemeh, C. A., 178
Lerman, H., 169
Lester M., 264
Levy, R., 266
Liability insurance, 78–79
Lichtenberg, J. W., 181
Lindsay, R. T., 277
Lloyd, A. P., 97
Loewen, I., 264
Loftus, E. F., 165, 167
Logan, S. L., 103
Loiacano, D. K., 180–181, 182
Lubin, B., 238
Luborsky, L., 214
Lum, D., 96
Lundberg, G. D., 231
Lupfer, S. L., 160
Lyman, B. J., 266–267

M
MacDonald, G., 14–15
Mack, J. E., 7
Malley, P. B., 134, 193
Malouf, J. L., 70, 82
Malpractice, 66, 68–69
  suicide, 116

Managed care, 207–213
  ethical issues, 207–208
  learning facilitation, 212–213
Mandated reporters, 155
Marecek, J., 205
Margolin, G., 262, 263, 265
Marks, R., 149
Markus, H. R., 200
Marlatt, A., 213, 217
Marriage counseling, 261–273
  biases, 263–264
  confidentiality, 264–265
  informed consent, 265
  learning facilitation, 272–273
  privileged information, 265
  training issues, 266–271
Marsella, A. J., 100
Marshall, V., 173
Marsiglio, W., 178
Martin, A. D., 178
Masson, R. L., 173
Mathiasen, R., 128
Maurer, S., 279
May, R., 46, 188
McBride, M. C., 230
McCarthy, P., 187, 188, 190, 278, 279
McClellan, A. T., 214
McCormick, R. A., S.J., 147
McDaniel, S. H., 239, 261
McDavis, R. J., 95
McDermott, D., 181
McEnvoy, A., 158
McInerney, J., 213
McKinley, D., 107
McNeill, B. W., 103, 106
McReynolds, L., 231
McRoy, R. G., 103
Meara, M., 45, 46
Meara, N. M., 45
Mears, F., 4
Meisel, M. A., 138–139
Meissner, W. W., 7

Melton, G. B., 149, 204
Menola, M., 178
Meyer, C., 173
Meyers, J., 157, 193
Miller, M. H., 262
Miller, S. I., 213
Mills, D. H., 283
Milner, J., 157
Mims, G., 269
Miner-Holden, J., 188
Minors, 202–207
  learning facilitation, 206–207
  pregnant, 204–205
  sexual harassment, 230–231
  student records, 228
  student referral, 232–233
  substance abuse, 230–231
  suicide, 121–128, 236
  violence, 231–232
Mitchell, J., 162, 178
Moline, M. E., 195
Monahan, J., 135, 137
Moore, L., 134
Moore, T., 187
Moreno, J. L., 237
Morrison, C. F., 149
Morrissey, M., 211
Morrow, S. L., 178
Morse, J., 162
Multicultural issues, 16, 95–109
  counseling skills, 101–107
  learning facilitation, 108–109
Murphy, W., 157
Murray, A., 97, 108
Murray, N., 231
Myers, F. B., 247
Myers, J.E.B., 203

N
Nathan, P., 246
Natl. Assn. of Drug and Alcohol
  Abuse Counselors, 210

Natl. Assn. of Social Workers, 210
  on advertising, 71
  on clients with AIDS, 148–149
  on confidentiality, 246–247
  on counselor competence, 244–245
  on dual relationships, 169, 170
  on suicide, 116
  on referrals, 72
Natl. Board of Certified Counselors,
  225
  on assessment, 78
  on interpreting test scores, 200–201
Natl. Council for Research on
  Women, 230
National Counselor Exam, 225
Natl. Federation of Societies for
  Clinical Social Work, 210
Natl. Mental Health Assn., 210
Neal, M., 148
Negligence, 69
  suicide, 117
Nelson, E., 114
Nevels, H., 178
New York Times, 187, 230
Newman, I. M., 229
Newman, J. L., 195
Ney, P. G., 158
Niles, F. S., 97
Nonmaleficence, 27, 30–44
Norris, T. L., 165, 166
NOW Legal Defense Fund, 314
Nutt, E. A., 280

O
O'Brien, K. M., 104–105
O'Connor, F. W., 45
O'Connor-Slimp, P. A., 278
O'Leary, E., 280
O'Neil, C. W., 179
Occurrence-based insurance, 78
Olson, T. D., 262, 314
Orlinsky, D. E., 280

Orpinas, P., 231
Orvaschel, H., 214
Orzek, A., 182–183

P

Parker, E. C., 83
Pate, R. H., 125, 187
Patrick, K., 270
Payne, R., 177
Peach, L., 121
Pearson, Q. M., 166
Pedersen, P. B., 96, 100, 101
Perez, J. A., 103
Person-centered therapy, 8, 14
Peters, R., 231
Peterson, G. W., 227
Philips, I., 120, 128
Piaget, J., 105
Pinel, P., 5
Pines, A., 79
Poddar, P., 133–134
Poland, S., 121
Ponterotto, J. G., 178
Ponterotto, J. W., 107
Pope, K. S., 74–75, 169, 170, 172, 173, 174, 281
Porter, J., 178
Preli, R., 96, 102–103
Prest, L., 188
Pretrial hearings, 66
Principles for the Provision of Mental Health and Substance Abuse Treatment, 210–211
Privileged communication, 82–83, 89–90
  child abuse, 156
  in groups, 247
  in marriage/family counseling, 265
  in schools, 226–227
Prosen, S., 160, 229
Protinsky, H., 269
Pryzwansky, W. B., 194–195, 196

Psychogenic hypothesis, 6–9
Psychological screening/school, 124
Pulvino, C. J., 316

R

Range, L. M., 128
Rational-emotive therapy, 8, 14
Ratzinger, J., 179
Rau, T., 157
Ray, O., 316
Reality therapy, 8, 14, 189, 242
Reddick, T. L., 121
Referrals, 72, 232–233, 258
Reid, H., 178
Releasing raw data, 198–199
Religion; see also Spirituality
  and child abuse, 158
  and homosexuality, 179
Remley, T. P., 176–177
Rencken, R. H., 166
Renninger, S. C., 279
Reporting
  AIDS cases, 147
  child abuse, 155
  past criminal acts, 138–139
  unethical conduct, 176
Repressed memories, 164–168
Rest, J. R., 317
Reyna, C. F., 164
Rich, K., 139
Richie, M., 226, 227
Ridgeway, I. R., 280
Ritter, K. Y., 179
Rivers, R. Y., 98
Robbins, R. H., 5
Rogers, C. R., 7, 13, 240, 283
Rosario, M., 178
Rose, M. L., 178
Rosenberg, M. L., 121
Rotheram-Borus, M. J., 178
Rowell, L. L., 230
Roy, A., 117–118

Roy, J., 74
Rozecki, T., 195
Rudd, H. D., 117
Russell, C. S., 268
Rutter, P., 75

S

Saeger, K. E., 269
Sanborn, M. P., 316
Sandoval, J., 121
Sanford, L. T., 160
Sartre, J. P., 18
Savin-Williams, R. C., 178–179
Schaefer, S., 166, 171, 175
Schlossberger, E., 150, 151, 152
Schmidt, L. D., 45
School counseling, 225–236
  child abuse, 228–229
  confidentiality, 226–227, 235
  learning facilitation, 233–236
  preventing violence, 231–232
  psychological screening, 124
  sexual harassment, 230–231
  student records, 228
  student referral, 232–233
  substance abuse, 229–230
  suicide interventions, 121–131, 236
Schroeder, L. O., 156
Schulte, A. C., 194–195, 196
Schwitzgebel, R. K., 69, 70, 247, 282
Schwitzgebel, R. L., 69, 70, 247, 282
Scott, J., 193
Scott, K., 230–231
Seigel, D. L., 230
Self-disclosure, 14, 21, 280
Semrad, E. V., 7
Seppa, N., 167
Sexual abuse, 155–177
  interviewing children, 162–164
  learning facilitation, 164–165, 168, 177

therapist-abused clients, 168–177
Sexual intimacy with clients, 75, 168–177, 256; see also Duel relationships
  accused of, 176–177
  learning facilitation, 177
  reporting, 176
  training strategy, 174–175
Sharpley, C. F., 280
Sheeley, V. L., 121
Shepherd, J. N., 265
Shertzer, B., 13
Shibutani, T., 96
Shields, C., 239, 262, 267–268
Simbovg, M., 266
Simek-Morgan, L., 98
Simon, J. M., 178, 179
Skinner, H. A., 214
Slander, 69
Sloan, I. J., 156
Smead, V. S., 121
Smith, D., 8
Smith, J. C., 121
Smith, S. R., 171
Sniderman, P. M., 178
Snow, D. L., 196
Solek-Tefft, J., 160, 229
Somatogenic hypothesis, 5–6
Sonne, J., 173
Special relationship, 66–68, 86
  implementing, 80–85
  negligence in, 67–68
  preparing for, 70–80
Spiller, N., 169
Spirituality, 187–193
  and child abuse, 190–191
  and culture, 188–190
  and depression, 191–192
  learning facilitation, 193
Springer, K., 166
Standard of care, 66–67, 68
Stanton, M. D., 319

Stevens-Smith, P., 280, 281–282
Stewart, N. R., 227
Stone, L., 173
Stone, S. C., 13
Storm, C. L., 266–267
Stress, 79–80, 113–114
Strother, D. B., 319
Subpoenas, 82, 84–85, 89
Substance abuse, 215–223
  assessment instruments, 214
  counseling recommendations, 215–217
  in schools, 229–230
  learning facilitation, 219–221
  preventing relapse, 217–218
Sue, D. W., 95, 97, 99, 101, 102
Sugden, S., 279
Suicidal clients, 113–133
  characteristics, 117–119
  college students, 128
  interventions, 119–120, 121–127, 128
  learning facilitation, 129–133
  legal issues, 116–117
Suicide, 7
  assessing danger, 117
  ethical mandates, 115–116
  factor in lawsuits, 69
  intervention, 119–120
  school programs checklist, 129–131
  training regarding, 113–115
Sweeney, J., 169
Swenson, L. C., xi, 9, 63–64, 65, 66, 68, 69, 75, 84, 157, 203–204, 262, 266
Systems theory, 261, 271

T

Tabachnick, B. G., 172
Tail-coverage insurance, 79
Tarasoff, T., 133–135
Tarasoff v. Regents of the University of California, 117, 133–135, 151, 153
Tarvydas, V. M., 270
Tepper, A., 168
Testifying in court, 83–84
Theory of contracts, 68
Therapist-abused clients
  characteristics, 173–174
  counseling, 175–176
Third-party payments, 73
Third-party rule, 247
Thoreson, R., 246
Thorpe, J. S., 281
Torigoe, R. Y., 114
Touching in therapy, 21, 171, 173
Tourney, A., 231
Training issues, 277–288
  counseling suicidal clients, 113–115
  credentials, 282–283
  dismissal processes, 281–282
  dual relationships, 175–177
  ethics, 277–278
  genograms, 268–271
  learning facilitation, 285–288
  marriage/family therapy, 266–271
  multicultural issues, 101–107
  research with humans, 283–285
  suicide prevention in schools, 121–122
  supervision, 268, 278–281
Tranel, D., 198, 199
Transactional analysis, 7, 8, 166, 241
Traver, L. B., 302
Trial court, 64–65
Trimble, J., 97
Tueting, P., 120
Tuma, J. M., 203
Tyndall, L., 181

U ~ V

U.S. Bureau of the Census, 95
U.S. Department of Health and Human Services, 231

Ugarte, T., 230
Ulrich, D. N., 262
Unethical conduct
  accused of, 176–177
  reporting, 176
Utilitarianism, 28, 189
Values
  counselor-imposed, 253–254
  multiculturalism, 98–101
VandeCreek, L., 134–135, 146, 168, 278
VandenBos, G. R., 208
Vasquez, M.J.T., 99, 103, 107
Victims of Child Abuse Laws, 167
Violence in schools, 231–232
Virtue ethics, 44–62
Vondra, J., 158

W

Waite, D. R., 69
Waldo, S., 134
Walker, T. B., 202, 265
Wallace, B., 213
Walters, K. L., 179
Warnock, J. K., 213
Weikel, W. J., 84
Weinstock, D., 157
Weinstock, R., 157
Weis, D. M., 120
Weiss, B. A., 150
Weissman, N. H., 83
Welch, B. L., 210
Welfel, E., 277
West, C. E., 188
Westefeld, J. S., 128

Westgate, C. E., 188, 191–192
Whitaker, C. A., 262
Whitchard, K. A., 130
White, E., 69
White, M. B., 268
White, R. W., 5, 6
Whiteside, R. G., 230
Whitfield, D., 98, 103
Whiting, R. A., 322
Wiggins, J. D., 227, 282
Wiggins-Frame, M., 280–282
Willging, T. E., 64
Williams, G. T., 195
Wilson, B. G., 173
Wilson, C., 4
Wise, P. S., 121
Wohl, T., 98
Wood, G. J., 148, 152
Worley, P., 157
Worthen, D., 187, 190
Worthington, E. L., 280
Wright, L., 166
Wundt, W., 6, 7
Wyer, M. M., 266
Wynne, L. C., 239, 261

Y ~ Z

Yarmey, A. D., 162
Yeager, R., 213
York, C. D., 266–267
Yzak, D., 283
Zehlen, S. L., 173
Zerbe Enns, C., 166
Zigler, E., 158
Zins, J. E., 227

ABOUT THE AUTHORS

Patrick Brendan Malley, a licensed psychologist, is associate chairperson of the Graduate Department of Psychology in Education at the University of Pittsburgh, where he teaches a required course in ethical and legal issues for mental health professionals. In addition, he has served as a consultant on ethical and legal issues to counseling centers, corporations, and various government agencies.

Dr. Malley has authored a number of journal articles on ethical and legal issues, including these:

- "Tarasoff and Its Progeny: Implications for School Counselors"

- "Comprehensive and Systematic Suicide Prevention Programs for Schools"

- "Ethical and Legal Dilemmas in University and College Counseling Centers"

- "Evaluating a School's Suicide Prevention Program"

Dr. Malley also has written on the ethical and legal dimensions of counseling in *Practicum Internship Textbook for Counseling and Psychotherapy* (Accelerated Development, 1995), and *Practicum and Internship Textbook for Counseling and Psychotherapy,* 2nd edition (Accelerated Development, 1995).

Eileen Petty Reilly, a school counselor, received her B.A. in psychology from Carnegie-Mellon University, and an M.Ed. from the University of Pittsburgh.